PILE

of

MASKS

Exposing Christian Hypocrisy

DUSTIN RENZ

PILE
of
MASKS

Exposing Christian Hypocrisy

DUSTIN RENZ

MAKE WAY MINISTRIES

For more information, please contact MAKE WAY MINISTRIES online at:
www.makewayministries.com

Library of Congress Control Number: 2016914886
Renz, Dustin 1983-
Pile of Masks: Exposing Christian Hypocrisy
First Edition: October 2016
Make Way Ministries

ISBN: 978-0-9979060-0-4

Printed in the United States of America.
10 9 8 7 6 5 4 3 2 1

OTHER TRANSLATIONS AND PARAPHRASES USED
(in order of appearance)

ACKNOWLEDGMENTS

I was recently introduced at a speaking engagement as "Dustin Renz—a graduate of Teen Challenge, Southeastern University and Pure Life Ministries." Both Teen Challenge and Pure Life Ministries are residential Christian programs that assist in setting people free from addictions and bondage. So, as you can see, most of my credentials come from time living in the wilderness. The seasons I spent in these two programs serve as book-ends for nearly ten years of running from God, much like the biblical prophet, Jonah. However, my running was done internally, and the fish that swallowed me was called hypocrisy. But like Jonah, I too realized the desperate situation I was in and cried out to God for mercy.[1]

There are two men who have impacted my life in ways that only Heaven truly knows. The first is the late Reverend David Wilkerson. Had he not obeyed the prompting of the Lord to work in the streets of New York City, Teen Challenge would never have existed. Consequently, the place I first met Jesus in 2002 would not have been available for me to run to in my time of need.

The second is Reverend Steve Gallagher. His obedience to the Lord made a place for me to turn to when I was steeped in hypocrisy and could find no way out. Pure Life Ministries is where the Lord restored me and poured unspeakable mercy into my life. To both of these men I owe a great debt. Thank you for your service to the Lord.

I also want to thank those who have helped to edit this book, namely Terri Eiffert, Cinthia Stephens, Dan Ford and Nate Danser. Your input on this project has been invaluable to me.

DEDICATION

I dedicate this book to Brittany, my wife of ten years. No one else knows this story like you do. You have stood by me when many would have turned their backs. May the Lord use our story to rescue others who are in the same difficult place we found ourselves in years ago. I love you dearly.

TABLE OF CONTENTS

A divided heart loses both worlds.

-A.B. Simpson[1]

PREFACE: MY STORY

THE EARLY YEARS: 1983-1994

I F THERE IS ONE CONSTANT THEME I have noticed throughout my life, it is the great spiritual contest over my soul. Looking back over the last thirty years, I can see clearly how Jesus has been consistently calling me to Himself, and how Satan has also been at work to drag my soul into Hell.

I grew up in a middle-class home. I had parents who loved me and we lived a comfortable life. The greatest attacks came not from inside my home, but outside. We moved to Florida from New York when I was in the second grade. It was that year—at age seven—I was first exposed to pornography. All throughout my childhood, pornography continued to be readily available to me, which became a deeply-rooted stronghold in my life.

I became friends with another young boy and frequently spent time at his house. It was there I was first exposed to satanic music, Ouija boards, horror movies, violent video games, hypnotism and even sexual experimentation. Satan had a plan.

I went to church as a kid. I claimed to be a Christian, but I had not been born again. I remember a boy in middle school who was into the Goth rock band Marilyn Manson. He would pressure me to listen to their music, but I continually resisted him. I told him I could not participate in it because I was a Christian. He would call me after school to try to force me to listen to the music through the phone, but at that point there was nothing in the music that interested me.

THE DARKNESS INCREASES: 1994-1997

When I was eleven years old, my parents announced to my siblings and I that they had decided to get a divorce. Like any young child, I was shocked by the news and felt betrayed. I remember crying once that day, then shoving the pain down deep inside. I told myself that it did not matter. I was not willing to deal with the internal turmoil I felt and just hardened my heart.

A day came shortly after that I will never forget. I was at a friend's house and he turned on some music; I was instantly captivated by it. I asked him what album it was and he told me it was Marilyn Manson's *Antichrist Superstar.* I immediately plunged myself headfirst into this dark genre of music, consuming my life with bands like Nine Inch Nails, Korn and Tool. I listened to their albums thousands of times, never going anywhere without my headphones. My parents would find my CD collection and confiscate it because of its content, but I always found a way to steal more. The music had an inexplicable power over me; I became obsessed with it. I began to feed on the music for strength. The anger, hatred and depression it produced inside me became an addiction.

As a freshman in high school, I sank deeper into the Gothic lifestyle. I studied black magic and Satanism. To emulate my favorite bands, I began to cross-dress in school. I had never fit the typical, masculine, male stereotype. I had always been a deeply emotional person and most of my friends were females. I came to the conclusion that I was supposed to be a girl and began to live more like one. The humiliation I suffered only made me hate the world and myself more. I cut satanic symbols into my body. I still attended church, but I despised Christians and hated God. I learned how to completely disengage mentally from my surroundings. I could be sitting in one place, yet be a thousand miles away inside; it helped me disconnect from my reality.

I also started fantasizing about homicide. It was an escape route for me. I wrote dark poetry and imagined what it would be like to kill the people I hated. Something inside made me believe that I had the power to get revenge on the world. I know now it was a demonic lie. I even confessed to a friend that I believed I was "some kind of god." They laughed at me and I never mentioned it to anyone again.

One night, when I was fourteen years old, I announced to my mother that I wanted to go to my girlfriend's house, but she refused to let me go. I walked into our bathroom—as if in a trance—and swallowed a bottle of pain relievers. I then proceeded to tear a Bible apart page-by-page until the sheets of paper covered my room. I ended up in a hospital for a week. I was diagnosed bi-polar, put on anti-psychotic medication and assigned a mental health counselor.

CLEANING THE OUTSIDE OF THE CUP: 1997-2002

There was talk from government authorities about forcing me to go into a program for troubled teens. In fear of that happening, I began to make outward changes. I cut my hair, started dressing normally and expanded my musical tastes to include hip-hop. I got hooked on Eminem's albums the first time I heard them. His music had the same evil spirit behind it that the Goth rock bands had in theirs, but it was dressed in a different outfit. My high school was packed with drugs, so when I started using them, I was quickly accepted into the popular crowd that had previously mocked and rejected me. I discovered that I had the talent to rap and began rapping at parties and writing songs.

It was not long before I began using a variety of drugs. I thought I had finally found the escape I had been searching for. Marijuana quickly became a daily habit. I progressed to acid, ecstasy, narcotic meds and alcohol. I spent all weekend partying and all week getting high or drunk before and after school. When these things lost their newness, I took the leap to cocaine. This became the greatest struggle with addiction I would ever know.

I graduated high school, left home and began living with friends so that I could do as I pleased. I moved from place to place and severed many friendships because I would steal from those who tried to help me. My conscience was completely seared. Soon, I became a driver for a drug dealer in town, just so I could get high for free. It became necessary to live in my car after having burned all bridges with family and friends.

My father allowed me to stay with him for a couple of weeks to try to help me get straightened out. After a near overdose, I realized I was out of control, and agreed to go to a program called Teen Challenge.

TEEN CHALLENGE: 2002-2003

In July of 2002, I found myself in the intake office of Teen Challenge in Tarpon Springs, Florida. I had told my dad on the way to the program that I was not going to let them "brainwash me with all of that Jesus stuff." My plan was to get sober enough that I could go back out on the streets, sell drugs and actually make money. It soon became evident that God had a different plan!

My first month there was miserable. I attempted to leave, but friends in the program dissuaded me from it. I started experiencing intense demonic attacks on my mind, but was unable to escape them with drugs. I returned to my homicidal poetry and fantasies of murder. In spite of the fact that I uttered the sinner's prayer dozens of times, nothing changed. I was on the brink of giving up.

One day, one of the students shared with me, "There is a spiritual battle going on for your soul." I felt like I was at a breaking point. In the evening, I entered the chapel, crying out to Jesus from my heart for the first time. I do not remember exactly what I said. My prayer was basically, "God, if you are real, prove yourself to me. Otherwise, I'm out of here!" From that night on, my life radically changed.

I experienced what Scripture promises to those who surrender their lives to the Lord: "Therefore, if anyone is in Christ, the new creation has come: The old has gone, the new is here!"[1] The depression lifted and the demonic attacks immediately ceased. I fell in love with Jesus. For the next year, I could not get enough of the Bible. I spent hours in prayer and worship. Everyone was astounded at the change that took place in my life. I learned the fundamentals of Christianity and even felt called into the ministry. The blessing of the Lord was on my life in a real way. There was no doubt I had a real encounter with Jesus Christ!

If my story ended here—and I could say I went on to live a good, holy life for Jesus—I would have no grounds for writing this book. Until this point in my life, I had no firsthand knowledge of Christian hypocrisy; this was about to change.

FALLING BACK INTO SIN: 2002-2008

After graduating from Teen Challenge, I once again enjoyed freedom to do as I pleased—something I soon discovered I was not prepared for. I was on the internet one day when I impulsively typed a sexual term into a search engine. Before I knew it, an addiction to pornography had once again taken control of my life. It was then that I met a girl named Brittany at the Christian college I was attending, and we fell in love. However, when I confessed to her about the pornography, she made it clear that unless I got victory over that area, there was no future for us. I went through counseling, but still did not manage to find freedom. I did not want to lose Brittany, so I simply told her that I had quit looking at pornography.

We got married in May 2005. I justified my secret life. "I know I'll find freedom eventually, so there's no sense in telling her about it now," I declared to myself. I cried out to God over and over again: repenting, apologizing and promising to do better. It was always supposed to be the last time. Clearly, I was only giving the Lord lip service and empty promises.

Over the coming months, I fell further from God. Soon, I was drinking liquor and abusing prescription pills whenever I had the chance. I was constantly trying to clean up my act, but always doing it in secret. While all of this was going on, I was still a student in Bible college. I cried out to the Lord for deliverance countless times at the altar, but I was not really serious about ridding my life of the idols. When I was stressed, angry or depressed, I ran to the computer, alcohol and drugs for comfort—rather than my heavenly Father.

In spite of the inner turmoil, I began a hip-hop music ministry. The Lord blessed me with many opportunities to perform in concerts all over the state of Florida. I even recorded two albums. I rapped in ghettos, schools, youth groups, street corners, conferences and music festivals. God used my testimony to lead many young people into salvation—despite my hypocrisy. This only deepened my pride. The ministry began with a sincere desire to glorify Jesus with my talent, but I did not have the humility to handle even the smallest amount of the limelight.

I began to visualize becoming famous in the music industry and I was confident my career would soon take off. I convinced myself that since it was Christ-centered, my dream had to be from God. Looking back, I truly believe that it was the Lord's leading for that season in my life, but I turned it into something He never intended it to become.

Brittany and I got involved in youth ministry, and I became the Assistant Student Pastor at our church. I felt like my sin was manageable, but there was a growing unrest in me. I consistently felt the conviction of the Holy Spirit. I frequently sensed an urgency to come clean to my wife, but I resisted the thought. My devotional life was dry and lifeless. Lust grew in my heart, and whenever I was depressed, I would still go back to satanic music in my head for comfort. I listened to secular music when no one was around and watched things on TV that should have caused me to cringe. I bought into the lie that God's grace covered all my sins, so it did not really matter how I lived. I ignored all the clear warnings in Scripture about continuing in sin as a believer.

HYPOCRISY TAKES ITS GRIP: 2008-2010

When we were accepted to go overseas to assist missionaries for two years, everything escalated. We began the process of raising the necessary funds to go. I had definite fears about relocating to a foreign country, but instead of taking those concerns to God, I returned with great fervor to the old empty cisterns of this world. I grew bored with the over-the-counter drugs I had been abusing. Having more freedom and less accountability, I became willing to take incredible risks to find street drugs.

I clearly remember the tragic day I succeeded. I was angry with God because I felt like He was standing between me and what I truly wanted. I drove into the ghetto that day and approached the first person I saw. When I asked about drugs, he got into my car with a bag of cocaine. It was as if Jesus was saying, "Fine. If that is what you want, I will not protect you from it any longer." Even as I drove home that day, I felt the Holy Spirit nearly begging me to change my mind. But my heart was set, and over the next few weeks, I indulged myself with drugs that I had not touched since entering Teen Challenge six years prior. All the while, I was going to churches, preaching and raising money, always sharing my testimony about how God had "set me free" from drugs and alcohol. I had become a complete hypocrite and a liar.

I persuaded myself that when we got overseas, the struggle would end. I assumed that if I was on the other side of the world and away from the familiar, I would be able to find freedom and get my life right with the Lord. When we finally arrived, I really cried out to Him, but it seemed as though the 'heavens were brass' above me. I could not understand why He did not seem to respond. I know now that I had to bring everything into the light through confession—something I was unwilling to do. I just wanted to deal with it between the Lord and myself, but He was not going to let repentance happen on my terms.

Once again, I started looking at pornography and abusing over-the-counter meds, but these things lost their luster after a while. I waited until I learned the country's language well enough to purchase narcotics from the pharmacies. I grew increasingly bitter at God. I felt like He was standing in the way of a successful music career. My self-ambition was so strong within me that I even considered recording the trashy secular music I wrote before I was saved.

Our ministry involved establishing youth groups throughout the country. Amazingly, the Holy Spirit really used us at times. This only served to deepen my delusion that I was still walking with God. I minimized my sin; convincing myself that I just had some little issues from my past—just like everyone else. I was unwilling to acknowledge to myself that my true character was what existed when no one else was around. Instead, I believed that the *real me* was the image I presented to other people. I had worn the mask so long I believed the mask was genuine. Looking back, I can see that the Lord only used me because of His great love for those people to whom I was ministering. Yet, I was filled with spiritual pride at the anointing that was on my life.

Throughout this entire period, my addiction to drugs grew worse. There were times I felt as though I was going insane. Every night I went to sleep telling myself I would stay sober the next day. But by 10 o'clock the next morning, I was on a mission to get high again. Every day I told myself it would be "one last time."

Our first daughter, Abigail, was born in May of 2010. This drastic change in our lives caused me to panic. I knew I was not ready to be a father, and the weight of that responsibility was more than I could take. Once again, I turned to drugs rather than to the Lord. I was so desperate to get high one day that I drove into a shady part of town. I approached the first person I met and he took me to a drug dealer. I entered a dark and shabby alley to find a gang sitting around a table with their guns in front of them. I bought my cocaine and left, realizing I could easily have been hurt, robbed or even killed.

I wrestled once again with the idea of coming clean, but came to the conclusion that the cost of confession was just too great. I knew it would break my wife's heart and possibly destroy our marriage. So I made the conscious decision to continue in my hypocrisy. I consoled myself that I just needed to be more careful in the future.

CONFESSION, BUT NOT REPENTANCE: 2010-2011

Brittany began sensing that something was not right in my life. One morning, about a week after the cocaine incident, she asked me what was going on. Without any intention of admitting anything, I found myself confessing everything to her. The words just seemed to fall out of my mouth. I told her that I had been lying and carrying on a secret life during the entire seven years of our relationship. She was devastated and immediately told our superiors. We were flown back to the U.S. and asked to resign.

You would think this would have been enough to bring me to repentance, but instead I grew bitter. Suddenly, I had no religious mask to hide behind. My wife took control of our finances and watched my every movement. And yet, I occasionally managed to get my hands on enough money to get high or drunk. I reached out to a psychiatrist who diagnosed me with "double-depression" and wrote me a prescription for antidepressants. I counseled with a Christian psychologist, who dug through my past, but never challenged me to repent. He basically informed me that it was not my fault; that it was because of the difficult things I had dealt with in my life. I even attended a Christian twelve-step program. However, confessing my sin in group discussions and continuing to live in it caused no change in my life. I was trying to find breakthrough in my own strength and nothing worked. I was prepared to do anything but truly repent before God.

I despaired of ever being able to change. As the darkness grew, I once again began listening to satanic music. This ushered back the old suicidal and homicidal thoughts into my mind. I even began to cut myself again. In my anguish, I told my wife that I wished I had never become a Christian. I wanted to walk away from God completely, but I felt trapped in a Christian life. I had surrounded myself with believers and was even married to one. I told her if I died, I wanted to go to Hell because that is where I belonged. It really looked like the devil was winning a total victory over my life.

I began to notice an interesting phenomenon. When I would visit my pastor's office for counseling, I could not concentrate. Yet, I had no problem thinking clearly when I would go to an appointment with the psychologist.

As my pastor would share Scripture with me and encourage me to repent, I could hear voices in my head saying, "Don't listen to him! He's lying to you." I even had to strain to be able to make out the words he was saying. At first, I was open and honest about my struggles with my pastor. Yet desperation drove me to retreat to the secret life of sin, and it was not long before I began lying to him as well.

My addiction had developed to the point that I had to steal to support it. I could not break free from my lust for drugs and alcohol. We had been living in the U.S. for eight months and things had escalated from bad to worse. One day, I finally confessed my continued hypocrisy to my wife in tears—I was ready to get help.

PURE LIFE MINISTRIES: 2011

When I arrived at Pure Life Ministries in April of 2011, one of the counselors said I looked like a dead man. I had no hope that God could do anything for me. I only agreed to enter the program in the hopes of saving my marriage, which at that point was almost certainly going to end in divorce. If this program did not work, I figured I would just overdose on drugs in a hotel room somewhere.

I entered the program very skeptical. I doubted whether another Christian program could teach me anything I had not already learned. The schedule was structured in such a way that we were constantly encouraged to seek Jesus. *Repentance* and *the cross* were words I heard every day. I thought I knew their meanings, but I came to realize that all I had was a head knowledge of these truths.

The staff members at Pure Life were unlike most Christians I had met. I noticed that their lives were incredibly separated from the things of this world. There was no network television in any of their homes. They were not consumed with the latest technologies like smart phones and video games. They were required to spend over an hour each day in prayer. At first, because of their lifestyles, I thought they were all crazy.

And yet they were the clearest examples of Jesus I had seen. This was in spite of the fact that all of them had come out of gross sexual immorality and sin—just like me. There was a power behind what they said because it was true in their hearts. They had genuine discernment. Often, my counselor left me shocked at what the Holy Spirit revealed to him about me. I knew there was something different about what they had and I began to cry out to the Lord for it.

It was in the program that the Lord brought me on a journey that transformed my life. It began with a breaking down of my self-life. Every time I turned around, He was exposing the arrogance and spiritual pride in my life. I was faced with my complete selfishness. I had a covetous heart, filled with lust and perversion. I had a critical spirit and was quick to judge others over the small issues in their lives, while completely ignoring the massive issues in my own. As I began to see what my heart was really like, it caused me to cry out to God for His mercy. I saw what I was…a complete hypocrite; a liar; a deceiver; a rebel against God. Week after week, new experiences only emphasized the fact that my heart was desperately wicked and that I had used religion as a spiritual mask to deceive others. For the first time in my life I recognized what an utter spiritual fraud I had become.

I became so weighed down, I felt like I could not stand the pressure. I saw the hurt I had inflicted on the innocent people in my life. I realized that my life centered only on my desires and that I manipulated others to get what I wanted from them. I thought the weight of these revelations was going to crush me. But just when I thought I could not take anymore, something happened.

THE TURNING POINT

It began with a phone call from my wife. In spite of the fact that our regular phone calls were very important to her, she told me that she felt as though we should not talk together for a week so I could focus on seeking God. I took her message as from the Lord, so I began using that time to go into the chapel every evening to seek Him. There is no way to explain in words what my Father did that week. It was as if He lavished me with His love. Through it, He was saying, "Now that you see what you are…now that you see your sin and all you have done against Me, you need to see that I love you more than you could ever know." The revelation came to me that God knew all about my rebellion in advance; I had hidden nothing from Him. And although He knew what He was getting, He still chose to save me. A love like that is almost unimaginable, but it is real.

This was the turning point and the Lord began to restore me. He taught me that I could trust Him. He showed me that I did not have to live with a backup plan. I was still on antidepressants, even though I had been at Pure Life Ministries for eight months. I finally decided I was ready to rid my life of that last crutch, but it was not without a battle. For a week I wept uncontrollably. I cried myself to sleep every night and I could barely get through a day of work. I would come back to the campus and tell my counselor, "I can't do this! I need to get back on the meds." He assured me that he believed that God wanted me off the medication, and things slowly got better. As of this writing, I have been off the medication now for over four years and the depression and anxiety no longer control me!

Another great victory that the Lord accomplished in my life was the destruction of my ambition to make it big in the music world. Over time He helped me to destroy this idol I had built in my heart. Even after being restored to Him, I was still holding onto the dream. But glory to God, He enabled me to finally let go and commit myself to His purposes rather than my own. I cannot describe how liberating that has been!

The Lord achieved something else that I had believed to be impossible. For years, my mind was constantly plagued with music from my past. No matter how much I tried to fight it, those songs were always replaying. My mind was like a jukebox—playing secular music constantly—and I could never seem to get the victory over it. Just about a month after I graduated the program, I suddenly realized it was not there anymore! Yes, the enemy will occasionally bring memories of that music back into my mind, but the power of it has been broken. When the attacks do come, I can quickly shift to worshiping God. What an amazing God we serve!

My life is not perfect. There are still issues the Lord is helping me work through. But my relationship with Jesus is radically different today. He truly is the center of my life. I now have an abundant life in Christ and He has truly made me an overcomer. I do not have to live in bondage to sin, addiction or lust. The grace of God empowers me to live free from chains. I used to believe that I had to live as a struggling believer the rest of my days, hoping to somehow manage to limp my way to Heaven. But the Lord has opened my eyes to the reality that there is freedom for the addict, purity for the lustful, and righteousness for the wicked. It comes through the power of God and the blood of Jesus Christ!

The remainder of this book will give you an in-depth insight into my journey out of hypocrisy. Unfortunately, I am not the only person in the church today who has lived a double-life. In fact, there are many who remain trapped in that state. My goal is to share principles that can help others find the same freedom I have found in Christ.

It was drug addiction that brought me to the place where God saved me: Teen Challenge. It was sexual sin that got me to the place that He restored me: Pure Life Ministries. But what about those who are living a double-life who are not involved in these types of sin? Or what about those who are in sin but are not able to get into a program? I believe the Lord has taught me valuable lessons about entering into a genuine life in God that can be a help to every reader, even those who just desire to grow closer to the Lord. My prayer is that you will be blessed as we embark on this journey into the unified life.

SECTION ONE:

DEFINING HYPOCRISY

This first section will give us a better understanding of Christian hypocrisy. It is difficult to overcome what we do not fully comprehend. In the following chapters, we will define hypocrisy and show how this enemy of God's people has been active on the Earth from the beginning of time—and still thrives today.

Masquerade:

1. **noun.** a ball or party at which masks and fancy costumes or disguises are worn

2. **verb.** to live or act under false pretenses[1]

*   *   *

Luke 12:1-3 (MSG)- …He [Jesus] said to them, "Watch yourselves carefully so you don't get contaminated with Pharisee yeast, Pharisee phoniness. You can't keep your true self hidden forever; before long you'll be exposed. You can't hide behind a religious mask forever; sooner or later the mask will slip and your true face will be known. You can't whisper one thing in private and preach the opposite in public; the day's coming when those whispers will be repeated all over town."

*   *   *

"I've seen firsthand the horrors of a man of God who allowed his heart to grow hard. He was a minister friend of mine who pastored a large church…I was there the night he was exposed again. Five women came forward and confessed to having an affair with him. Some said they even had sexual relations with him just moments before he stepped into the pulpit to preach.

"A friend of mine later asked this pastor, 'How could your conscience allow you to do that? How could you conduct an affair with a woman and then purport to preach from God's Holy Word?' The pastor answered with a laugh, 'You have to be a good actor.'"

-David Wilkerson[2]

1

WELCOME TO THE MASQUERADE

I AM AN EX-PRISONER WHO HAS BEEN liberated from the cold, dark cell of hypocrisy by the merciful love of God. It was not an easy journey. I had to walk through a great deal of pain to escape. But nothing I have been through for Jesus compares to even a fraction of what He gave so that I could be brought into wholeness from a life of duplicity.

I am just at the beginning of my journey on this narrow road. The primary credentials that I hold in order to speak on this subject are those from spending years living a double-life. Now that I have been rescued and made whole by Jesus, I have been given a story to tell.

What I can offer to you—the reader—is simply my experience of how God took back this wicked, double-minded backslider and brought him into an authentic and vibrant Christian life I never believed could exist. This book is an attempt to put into writing not only the dreadful life that God rescued me from, but also the amazing life He has brought me into.

Unfortunately, my life is not the only one in the church touched by hypocrisy. Hypocrisy is an issue that is prevalent among leadership and laypeople alike. Yet it is an area that is often swept under the rug rather than dealt with. If you can come away with a single thought from this book, my hope is that it would be: "Jesus is willing and able to rescue the hypocrite."

If there is any area of dividedness in your life, I pray that you would allow the principles described here—along with the help of the Holy Spirit—to bring you into an undivided devotion to Him.

PILE OF MASKS

The title for this book came out of an experience I had during a worship service. It happened during the season of restoration I went through when my preaching license was suspended due to my sin. I was thinking about the first time I would step back into the pulpit and preach. As I pictured that moment, it was as if I could actually hear myself sharing a message in front of a congregation. I heard myself saying that many people in churches today have designed elaborate masks of spirituality. I imagined that as I was speaking those words, men and women began to get up out of their seats. They came up front, took off their masks and discarded them into a pile. A pile of masks formed on the floor by the altar. A prayer rose up in my spirit: "Lord, let there be a pile of masks laid down on altars throughout my ministry." That is my heart's cry for the church and my prayer for this book.

Right at the onset, let me warn you. Many who are reading these words are wearing religious masks and they *do not even know it*. Some are wearing masks, but no one has ever shown them that there is more to Christianity than participating in a religious masquerade. Others have spent so much time making their masks look convincing, they mistake them for the real thing. Some have hidden behind their masks so long, they simply do not know if it is possible to remove it. I once lived in that place, but by the grace of God, I found the way out.

I wrote a song about the spiritual masquerade years ago during a very broken place in my walk with the Lord. At that time, I had enough discernment to realize that my Christianity was a farce. Yet my stubborn refusal to let Jesus lead me into the light prevented the freedom I was crying out for. True liberty would not come into my life until years after I had penned these lyrics:

Welcome to my life, it's a masquerade
Please, tell me do you like this mask I've made?
It took so many years to make it perfect
Through the sorrow and the tears I hope it's worth it—is it worth it?

Come inside and let me pour you some tea
As you talk to a person that's not even me
It's so comfortable now, that I forget it's on at all
And the person who's deep down inside has grown so small

Jesus, if I let you take this mask off, I'm scared of what you'll see
I'm ugly and weak, and I'm not the strong person I think I should be
I'm sick of pretending, this is the ending, take all of me, I ask
I give you my mask

Without my mask, I'm broken—
Torn apart and these words that I've spoken
Are really just a desperate cry for help; will you rescue me from myself?
I'm hiding because I'm afraid you won't really love this creature you made
Yet my every attempt to hide is in vain;
You knew the real me before I even had a name

Jesus, if I let you take this mask off, I'm scared of what you'll see
I'm ugly and weak, and I'm not the strong person I think I should be
I'm sick of pretending, this is the ending, take all of me, I ask
I give you my mask

THE YEAST OF HYPOCRISY

Some might say, "Maybe I do have hypocrisy in some areas of my life, but I just make little compromises. Overall, I try to be a good Christian." Well, that is a dangerous and deceptive train of thought. Jesus gave us valuable insight in Luke 12:1. He said, "Be on your guard against the yeast of the Pharisees, which is hypocrisy." Yeast is a single-celled fungus that by nature reproduces itself. This is why Paul writes, "Don't you know that a little yeast works through the whole batch of dough?"[3] Active yeast can do nothing but reproduce. That is its nature.

Hypocrisy is just like that yeast cell. If you allow it to have a tiny area of your heart, by nature it will grow. You might think you have a little area of compromise neatly tucked away in your heart. But, unknowingly, it will reproduce, and it has the potential to take over every area of your life unless it is dealt with.

Another passage referring to yeast is found in Exodus 12:15. Jehovah gave instructions for Israel to prepare for the Passover. He specifically commanded:

> For seven days you are to eat bread made without yeast. On the first day remove the yeast from your houses, for whoever eats anything with yeast in it…must be cut off from Israel.

Israel was commanded to rid their houses of yeast during the Passover celebration. I hear the Spirit of God saying the same thing to His church today. "Remove the yeast of hypocrisy from your lives completely. Do not even let it into the house of your spirit because it will multiply!"

That is how it happened in my life. I let a little of hypocrisy's yeast into the house of my spirit. What began as a small compromise, eventually led to full-scale rebellion. The only way to prevent it from gaining more access into your soul is to get it out of your house now.

THE HISTORY OF HYPOCRISY:
FROM GENESIS TO REVELATION

Hypocrisy is a problem that goes back to the beginning of time. It is interesting to note that out of the thirty-seven times a derivative of the word *hypocrisy* is used in the Bible, nineteen times were out of Jesus' mouth.[4] But even though the specific term is not used in the Bible frequently, the concept is carried throughout the Scriptures. Wherever you find sin, you will find men and women who are faced with a decision. They can do one of three things:

1. Repent of that sin before God
2. Outwardly rebel against God
3. Choose not to repent in their hearts, but outwardly portray obedience

Like Adam and Eve covering their nakedness with fig leaves, the Christian hypocrite chooses to hide behind an intricate mask. It may fool others, but it is a foolish attempt to hide from the all-seeing God. He knew Adam and Eve were still naked; He was not fooled by the façade. Likewise, the hypocrite cannot pull the wool over the Lord's eyes today.

THE HYPOCRISY OF CAIN

Adam and Eve's oldest son provides for us the earliest example of hypocrisy. The life of Cain—whose story is found in Genesis 4—is a picture of a man whose heart did not line up with his actions. We know that Cain becomes the first murderer in mankind's history. But if we rewind the story, we can learn how it all took place. The Bible records the story in a very simple manner. There are two brothers and two sacrifices. Abel's is acceptable; Cain's is not—and Cain gets angry.

There are different beliefs about why Cain's sacrifice was not acceptable to God. Some suggest it should have been a blood sacrifice. Whether or not that factor played a part is not important for our purposes here. Based on the whole of Scripture, we can make a couple of assumptions. First, the Lord's *primary* objection to Cain was not the type of sacrifice but the heart behind it. God always sees the heart, not just the outward obedience. Regardless of the reason his sacrifice was unacceptable, God still held Cain accountable and expected him to make it right. Cain could not plead ignorance of his responsibility in the situation. Second, even though Cain's heart was not right, he was *still* carrying on the outward appearances. He still gathered the crops and brought them before the Lord.

From the outside, everything seemed fine. Adam may have looked over at his two boys that day and thought, "Lord, thank you for my two godly sons. Look at them obeying you and offering sacrifices." He and Eve might have been proud of Cain for setting the example for his little brother.

But something was seriously wrong…and God saw it. The Lord initiated an interesting conversation with Cain. He offered him mercy by giving him a chance to repent when He called him on the carpet about his anger and poor attitude. God asked him:

> Why are you angry? Why is your face downcast? If you do what is right, will you not be accepted? But if you do not do what is right, sin is crouching at your door; it desires to have you, but you must rule over it. (Genesis 4:6-7)

There was a distinct moment in time when the Lord offered Cain a chance to repent. The choice was to either do the right thing or harden his heart toward God. This is the same offer the Lord gives to every person whose heart and actions do not line up. We can either repent and get right with Him, or refuse and harden our hearts. The choice is ours. What was Cain's decision? The next sentence reveals:

> Now Cain said to his brother Abel, "Let's go out to the field." While they were in the field, Cain attacked his brother Abel and killed him. (v. 8)

Sin and death are always the by-products of a hypocritical life.

THE HYPOCRISY OF KING DAVID

David—called a man after God's own heart[5]—fell into hypocrisy after his adulterous affair with Bathsheba and the subsequent murder of her husband, Uriah. Since Bathsheba gives birth to David's baby before his confrontation with Nathan the prophet, we know there is at least a nine-month period when David continued to live a lie. The day that Nathan came to David and he repented, the baby was struck ill.[6] We are not told how old the baby was when this occurred, but David had been given plenty of time to come clean long before the prophetic word was given.

Although we are not given many details about this time in David's life, we can assume that David continued to present himself in a favorable light. He wanted to cover up the whole scandal. He would have continued to fulfill the role of a godly king, which included worshiping the Lord, reading the Scriptures and offering sacrifices. At this time in his life, he lived in blatant hypocrisy.

OTHER BIBLICAL EXAMPLES OF HYPOCRISY

Other characters that give us clear descriptions of hypocrisy in the Bible are:

- Saul, who was rejected as the first king of Israel due to his track record of disobedience. Yet when confronted by Samuel, his one request was: "Please honor me before the elders of my people and before Israel." (I Samuel 15:30) Saul's greatest concern was wearing a spiritual mask before the people rather than pleasing God.

- Ananias and Sapphira brought the apostles an offering to the Lord, but had sin in their hearts.[7] They gave the appearance that they had given all their earnings from the land they sold, but kept a portion for themselves.

- Peter slipped into hypocrisy when he separated himself from the Gentile believers because of his fear of what the Jewish Christians would think of him. Paul called him to account in front of everyone for not practicing what he preached. Paul wrote, "The other Jews joined him in his hypocrisy, so that by their hypocrisy even Barnabas was led astray." (Galatians 2:13)

As we can see from these examples, hypocrisy is not a new phenomenon. And none of us are exempt from the possibility of it forming in our lives. Even Peter—the powerful man of God who walked closely with Jesus—got tripped up by it. None of us should think that we are above temptation in this area.

THE WIDE RANGE OF CHRISTIAN HYPOCRISY

When we talk about hypocrisy, many will immediately plead innocent of it because of the picture that pops into their minds when they hear the word *hypocrite*. Most people in the church world will automatically think of past scandals when famous ministers were exposed for immorality. This is what I would consider extreme hypocrisy, and this is where hypocrisy can lead. But one never ends up in a place like that without little compromises along the way.

The range of hypocrisy in spiritual matters is a broad one. Hypocrisy can be boiled down to any area in a believer's life where their actions do not line up with what they say they believe. It occurs when they choose to project a different image to others than what is truly inside their hearts. Like Jesus said of the Pharisees, "They do not practice what they preach."[8]

Take for instance the faithful churchgoer who is a habitual gossip. If you were to ask them what they believe about gossip, they would tell you it is a sin. However, if you are around them for any length of time, you will discover they are always talking about other people. Of course, it is either in the disguise of "just venting my frustrations" or "please pray about this…" Yet the bottom line is that they run their mouths about others (gossip) but dress it up differently to make it seem like it is not sin. That person has hypocrisy in that area of their life.

Here is another way to look at it. Imagine someone hired a private investigator to follow you around and find inconsistencies about how you live in contrast to what you say you believe. What evidence would he find against you? When you begin to define hypocrisy in this way, you get the picture that this issue is much bigger and more widespread in today's church than you may have thought before picking up this book.

However, I do want to add that all of us who are sincere believers have areas that God is working on. We are justified at salvation, but sanctification is a life-long process. The Holy Spirit will continually use whatever means necessary to form our lives into the image of Jesus. If someone is sincerely struggling in an area—and they are allowing the Lord to help them—that would not be the same as blatant hypocrisy.

Hypocrisy is found in the lives of those who continue in unrepentant sin, yet still go through the religious motions. Hypocrisy always starts off small. Even those popular preachers who have fallen in the last thirty years did not dive head-first into sin; it started with a little yeast. Because they continued on without repentance, the hypocrisy grew until it had full control of their lives. They are examples of where all hypocrisy eventually leads. We cannot forget that some of them have truly repented and been restored. God is willing to forgive anyone and is very patient with us, but we have to be willing to repent and get right with Him.

The intent of this book is to reach all Christians wearing masks of any size and for any length of time. A mask is a mask no matter how brilliant it may appear. From the person in the very first steps of hiding to the one in the darkest spiritual place, my desire is to give hope to all readers that Jesus is passionate about saving hypocrites and setting them free.

DOUBLE-MINDEDNESS

Double-mindedness is a term that the Bible uses to describe hypocrisy. James uses this term when he talks about a man who prays for something, but does not believe that anything will happen.[9] The Greek word for double-minded is *di* (twice) *psychos* (mind/ soul). It means to be "inclined toward antithetical ideologies, having conflicting disposition."[10] One lexical aid explains it this way:

It is not merely weak in faith, but being disposed to embrace the way of righteousness in faith (believing God's commands and ethical dictates to be good and following them, and believing His promises to be true and relying upon them) while being equally disposed to embrace the way of unrighteousness (disbelieving God's commands and ethical dictates to be good and disbelieving His promises and relying upon one's own means). Such a person is spiritually unstable and prone to duplicity.[11]

At the very root of hypocrisy is a desire to have two lifestyles that are diametrically opposed to each other. Like a child trying to fit a square peg into a round hole, the hypocrite tries to force two lives to fit together that simply cannot and will not co-exist. This can be seen when we try to live for both God and ourselves. If we do this, we will begin to resent Him for standing in between us and what we want.

The Christian life is one that demands self-denial and self-sacrifice. If you live to please yourself—to fulfill *your* desires, to do things *your* way, and to accomplish *your* dreams—then a life of following Christ cannot be joined to the life you are living. You may call it a 'Christian' life, but that does not make it so.

I saw this principle at work in my own life. In the beginning of my walk with Christ, I wanted only to serve Him. I was more concerned about other people's needs than myself. But as I began to live more and more for my own selfish desires, the Lord became an obstacle between me and what I truly desired. At the onset, I was so grateful for the freedom I had in Christ. But soon I grew to despise the freedom and longed to go back to my old lifestyle. I resented God for 'holding out on me.' By living more for myself rather than Him, I became double-minded.

LOVING GOD AND THE WORLD

James talks about another form of double-mindedness. He tells us that a friend of the world is an enemy of God.[12] The Christian who lives a carnal life will find this to be true if they are honest with themselves. They might say, "I don't really love the world *that* much," but their actions prove otherwise. They might swear to themselves that they do love the Lord, but the presence of the love of the world in their heart *proves* they are God's enemy. Just because someone does not believe they hate the Lord or love the world does not change the truth of God's Word.

I know this from my own personal experience. I was greatly self-deceived. I read through this Scripture and shrugged it off as if it simply did not apply to me. I built a protective wall around my heart to keep the Holy Spirit out because His presence brought conviction—and I did all of this subconsciously. Living like this was misery, yet in spite of that, I still attempted to love Him and the world at the same time.

SERVING TWO MASTERS

Jesus makes a very strong statement regarding people with divided hearts. He advises us that we cannot "serve two masters."[13] The reason for this is because we will always end up hating one and loving the other. Jesus—the One who created the human heart—is explaining that it is *impossible* to whole-heartedly serve more than one master. He does not say it is difficult—He says it is not possible.

Paul uses different language to describe the same principle in I Corinthians 10:21:

> You cannot drink from the cup at the Lord's Table and at Satan's table, too. You cannot eat bread both at the Lord's Table and at Satan's table. (TLB)

Both of these passages clearly illustrate that we are either on one side or the other. There is no in-between Christian walk.

So what about the person who 'serves' the Lord, but is not fully devoted because he is actually living for himself? The answer may be tough to swallow, but it is simple: that person is not serving God at all. They cannot be. The proof is that they are not serving Him *alone*. As Hudson Taylor once said, "Christ is either Lord of all, or is not Lord at all."[14]

In discussing Christ's lordship, we are talking about the overall picture of a person's life. I realize that we are all in the process of becoming less selfish and more like Jesus. What is important is the driving force in our hearts. I am not advocating that a sincere believer, who at times lives for themselves, is not saved. However, a true believer will allow Christ to be Lord and his life will reflect that decision.

In our church culture, it seems like this cannot really be true. So many professing believers are very active in ministry, and yet seem to live for themselves the rest of the week. Can so many people in the church really not be serving God? Is a Christian who lives some of the time for the Lord and other times for themselves really not serving Him? According to the Scriptures, the mark of a true believer is that Christ is the Lord over all of his life.

WHY THE LUKEWARM PATH IS CHOSEN

If hypocrisy is such an age-old problem within the church, it leads us to ask the question: "If a double-life is such a terrible thing, why do people choose the lukewarm path?" There are many answers to that question, but here are a few general characteristics of hypocrites that deserve attention. Each of these will be discussed in more depth later in this book.

1. *Hypocrites do not want to give up their sin.*

It is true that not everyone living a watered-down version of Christianity has blatant outward sins like I had in my life. However, it is common that people in hypocrisy have areas of sin that they are trying to cover up and are unwilling to fully surrender to the Lord.

2. *Hypocrites do not want to give up control of their lives.*

While they will outwardly conform to religious expectations, hypocrites have a death grip on their internal lives. They think Jesus can be Savior without making Him Lord. Walking with the Lord requires a complete surrender of personal rights and control over our lives. Anything less is not true Christianity.

3. Hypocrites do not want to do the hard thing.

Many start out in the faith, but do not expect to face the pressures of walking with Jesus. When it gets hard, they choose comfort in order to protect themselves from suffering, persecution and hardship. Like the people following Jesus in John 6, hypocrites will only follow Him to a point. Then, if His sayings get too difficult, they turn away. (v. 66) Yet Jesus promises these things to all true believers. He tells us to expect persecution (John 15:20); trouble (John 16:33); and that we will be hated (John 15:18-19).

4. Hypocrites fear men more than God.

In order to avoid the guaranteed rejection, suffering and confrontation of truly following Christ, people often become hypocrites. They hate the idea of being labeled as radical or extreme, so they choose to conform. They think they can have enough Christianity to 'stay saved,' but enough of this world to stay accepted.

5. Hypocrites are deceived.

Deception is a major component of hypocrisy. All hypocrites have areas in their lives in which delusion plays a part. There are many who just flat-out refuse to see it; they are blinded. They think they can just go through the motions and everything will be alright.

THE DECEPTIVE NATURE OF HYPOCRISY

If hypocrisy is such a rampant issue in the church, then why is it so hard to identify? Why does it only seem obvious when a scandal occurs, but often goes unnoticed in the lives of the people sitting next to us in church? Well, by the very nature of hypocrisy, the goal is to make oneself look spiritual. When someone puts on a disguise, they try to make it look as realistic as possible.

For example, imagine that I want to impersonate a wealthy man so that I can walk into a bank and withdraw a fortune from their account. It would be of utmost importance that I looked, acted, dressed, wrote and spoke exactly like that person. Why all the attention to detail? Because I would not want to pay the price of being found out to be a fraud. I know the consequences of this type of activity would be arrest, huge fines and imprisonment.

This is the same for the hypocritical Christian. They have to make every effort to act, talk and look like a truly spiritual person. The religious mask they wear cannot be a makeshift mask they have thrown together, otherwise people will easily see through it. The reason they do this is because of the price they would have to pay if they were found out. Albert Barnes said of hypocrites:

> Strongly resembling Christians in their experience, and, in some respects, their lives, it is impossible to distinguish them from genuine Christians.[15]

Spotting the true from the false is not easy—or even possible at times—because of the deception that is involved.

THE ENEMY'S LOVE FOR HYPOCRISY

One of the most sobering aspects of hypocrisy is that when we choose to live with one foot in the church and the other in the world, we make ourselves accomplices with the enemy. The devil loves disguises. The Bible says, "Satan himself masquerades as an angel of light."[16] He makes himself look like something different than what is truly in his heart. This is so different from Jesus, who had the same character on Earth as He has had from eternity. God "does not change like shifting shadows."[17] He is "the same yesterday and today and forever."[18] Who do we really want to imitate with our lives, Jesus or Satan?

The enemy loves hypocrisy. Certainly he has used it effectively in innumerable lives for centuries. You might think, "But I go to church, sing in the choir and teach Sunday school. I'm a decent Christian compared to others I know." That type of thinking comes from a faulty perception of what the enemy cares about. He *wants* the church to be filled with hypocrites. He loves it when the lives of Christians are exposed to be frauds. Just think of how much damage has been done to the church in the past from ministers in the public eye revealing secret lives full of sin. The enemy loves to use hypocrisy to bring shame to the Christian community.

HOW THE ENEMY STRIKES

When a public figure is running for a prestigious government office, they will always meet opposition. Their opponents will often take drastic measures to 'dig up dirt' in their lives to defame their character. We have seen this play out countless times in American politics.

Sometimes a private investigator will be hired to follow the candidate around in secret. Often, because these people are very careful to cover their tracks, it is difficult to catch someone in the act itself. What the investigator will do is observe that person's life in detail. They look for clues—little inconsistencies—to build a case for what they might expect. They look at their phone call history, watch to see where they go and how often they go there. They examine what they spend their time and money on. Inevitably, if you observe someone's life long enough, even the most careful person will tell on himself. Either he will prove to be innocent, or his behavior will make it obvious that he is not.

The enemy uses the same tactics against us. He cannot see our hearts the way the Lord does. He does not know our thoughts like God does either. But all he has to do is observe us.

He listens to the words you speak and the spirit behind them.
- Are you talking about the Lord?
- If you do, are your words authentic or superficial?
- Are they full of passion for Him or cold, dead formalism?

- Are your spiritual conversations merely revolving around church and church activities?

He watches how you spend your time.
- Is God a part of your life outside of the church?
- How much quality time do you spend with the Lord?
- Are there idols in your life that you are chasing after?
- How is your time spent when no one is around?

He examines your relationships.
- How do you treat your spouse and children?
- What kind of people do you hang out with?
- Are you crossing moral boundaries with a classmate or co-worker?

He looks for Christian charity in your life.
- Do you have any concern for the less fortunate around you?
- Are you generous to others?

The investigation would not have to go much further than that to get a good idea of where a person really is in their faith. It does not take long for the devil to detect signs of inconsistency in what people say they believe and what they show they believe by their lives. The enemy can spot hypocrisy in the life of a believer a mile away. When he finds it, he will attack them at the point of their weakness to cause the yeast to grow.

In my years in hypocrisy, the enemy could hear the sermons I preached and the counsel I gave. He could see me lifting my hands in worship to God. He even saw how the Lord used our ministry to bless others. He could also see what my life was like when no one was around. Unlike the people around me, he was not deceived by my false sincerity. He easily sees when a Christian life is nothing more than an act…and he *loves* it. He recognizes how easy it is to get sucked into the status quo and he knows how few find their way out once the mask has been put on.

THE SUBTLE FADE INTO HYPOCRISY

Regardless of the underlying reasons someone ends up living a double-life, it always happens slowly over time. It is almost never an intentional, conscious decision to pretend to be a Christian. Much more frequently, an erosion takes place, like a sink hole that begins to cave in. The Christian's spiritual life slowly degrades over time, until it eventually collapses.

There was not a day I just decided, "I am going to see if I can live two lives." It happened gradually, with little choices in my heart. Our lives occur one choice at a time. Where we are today is a direct result of a myriad of decisions we have made along the way. Today's decisions determine where we will be tomorrow. This is especially true of our relationship with the Lord. Long before I fell into blatant sin, I was making small decisions in my heart that led me down the hypocrite's path.

When I first accepted Jesus as Savior at the age of eighteen, the change in my life was drastic. My life in God became my whole life. I experienced what the Scriptures say about becoming a new creation. The old man was dead and I was a new man in Christ.[19] No one could argue that I had radically changed at conversion.

Do not misunderstand me, the tug of the world and the enemy were still forces I had to contend with. I still had my flesh to put to death, but I was no longer a slave to it. I was able to see that the world, the devil and my flesh were merely forces trying to pull me back into a life I was no longer a part of.

Getting from that point to the place I ended up nearly nine years later is a challenge to explain. Casting Crowns wrote a song called *Slow Fade*. The chorus says:

It's a slow fade, when you give yourself away,
It's a slow fade, when black and white are turned to gray,
And thoughts invade, choices are made,
A price will be paid when you give yourself away,
People never crumble in a day,
It's a slow fade.[20]

These lyrics perfectly describe my own experience. It was a gradual, almost unnoticeable change of heart. This tends to be the case for hypocrites. Due to small, seemingly unimportant decisions they make in their hearts, they begin to slip into a double-life. They often do not even realize it is happening. They do not think to themselves one day, "I am going to live my life the way I want, while outwardly portraying to others I am a spiritual person." They just go on living their lives their own way until one day, they stop and think, "How did I end up here?"

THE HARD ROAD OUT OF HYPOCRISY

Once a hardening has taken place in a hypocrite's heart, repentance becomes an extremely undesirable option. Because of the intricate web of lies they have had to create to protect their image, coming clean could result in drastic consequences. Many times, a marriage could be put in jeopardy. Often, revealing the truth could cost a career, ministry position or their reputation. This is especially true when the hypocrite's life involves some secret outward sin.

Early on in the process, repenting of hypocrisy would have been relatively easy. But depending on the length of time and the depth to which a hypocrite has hidden behind a mask of spirituality, repentance eventually presents a legitimate crisis.

It is no wonder we hear so few testimonies of pretenders coming back to the Lord. For some, the cost is just too great. They think God is asking them to do the impossible. They have been deceived into thinking this is just their lot in life. "After all," they will tell themselves, "I'm not that bad. I might not be Mother Teresa, but everyone has their demons, right?"

What they fail to realize is that the 'spirituality' they are trying so hard to protect is not even genuine. Like the backdrop of a theatre set, their walk with the Lord appears to be sincere when taken at face value. Upon closer examination, you will find that the beautiful scenery is really just a thin piece of decorated cardboard, easily pushed over with the slightest touch. When this is the case, exposure could be extremely painful and relationships may be greatly affected. Confession might even cause irreversible damage. However, doing so could be the only way to save their souls.

The good news is that the Lord does not leave us guessing; wishing we could figure out what to do. The Bible is full of clear pictures of what a true, unified life in Him looks like. Throughout this book, we will look in-depth at hypocrisy as a spiritual issue in the lives of God's people from the Israelites until today. Then, we will learn how to examine our lives for spiritual life and be taught basic principles in overcoming hypocrisy.

Our journey starts at the very place where hypocrisy is born, which is the same place it must be put to death. It is also the most important area of our lives, because what we do with it determines our destiny. We will begin by examining what Scripture teaches about the heart. I urge you to ask the Lord to reveal what is *truly* in yours. I believe the sincere reader will have the help of the Holy Spirit, who desires to give you true life in Christ. God will always give the grace to accomplish the work needed in the willing heart.

He is willing…are you?

Heart:
1. **noun.** a hollow muscular organ maintaining the circulation of blood by rhythmic contraction and dilation
2. the heart regarded as the center of thought, feeling and emotion (esp. love)[1]

*　　　*　　　*

I Samuel 16:7 (MSG)- God judges persons differently than humans do. Men and women look at the face; God looks into the heart.

Psalm 86:11 (NIV)- Teach me your way, Lord, that I may rely on your faithfulness; give me an undivided heart, that I may fear your name.

*　　　*　　　*

"The heart may be compared to a reservoir which supplies a large town with its hundreds of streets and thousands of houses. The water is conveyed by some thousands of pipes. If the water be pure in the reservoir it will be conveyed in its purity through the pipes to the inhabitants; but if turbid there, it will be impure at its destination. The heart is the reservoir from which life flows. The mouth, hands, feet, looks, actions, etc., are the pipes. If the heart is pure, purity will be manifested in life."

-J Harries[2]

2

THE HEART OF THE ISSUE

I F YOU OPEN A CONCORDANCE AND search for the word *heart*, you will see that it is a significant theme throughout the Bible; the references are extensive. Here are just a few examples:

- God alone knows the hearts of all men (I Kings 8:39; Acts 1:24; Acts 15:8)
- The Lord looks at the heart (I Samuel 16:7)
- We should walk before the Lord in "integrity of heart" (I Kings 9:4)
- The Lord searches every heart and exposes its motives (I Chronicles 28:9; I Corinthians 4:5)
- We should have a pure heart (Psalm 24:4; James 4:8)
- God "knows the secrets of the heart" (Psalm 44:21)
- The pure in heart will see God (Matthew 5:8)
- Sin is committed in the heart (Matthew 5:28)
- Our heart is found where our treasure is (Matthew 6:21)
- We are to love one another from the heart (I Peter 1:22)

- We should remain true to the Lord with all of our hearts (**Acts 11:23**)

The obvious point being made by Scripture is that our hearts are a big deal to God. We are judged by our hearts, and our relationship with the Lord is dependent upon the purity of them. Before you think, "I already know this," let us dive a little deeper into God's concern for the hearts of men.

THE GREATEST COMMANDMENT

In Mark 12, a teacher of the Law came to Jesus while He was debating with the Sadducees. He approached Jesus with a loaded question: "Of all the commandments, which is the most important?" (v. 28) For the teachers of the Law, keeping the commandments was the main focus of their spiritual lives. At this point in Jewish history, there were many rules and traditions in written form such as the Talmud. These were added to the already meticulous rules given by Jehovah in the Torah. The religious leaders of the day put all of their energy into trying to obey every little command and tradition perfectly. This included the Sabbath laws, hand-washing rituals, sacrificial practices and festivals. For a teacher of the Law, this man was essentially asking Jesus, "Out of *all* of these laws we obey, which is the most important?" His intent was to set Jesus up to fail, but it was not going to work.

Jesus did not beat around the bush. He did not ask for a minute to confer with His disciples. In fact, the Bible does not even record a moment to reflect. To the Jews, this was a question that could not be answered fairly—hence the reason for asking. To them, every law was important and to be fully obeyed. To Jesus, the answer was simple. He quotes from Deuteronomy:

Love the Lord your God with all your heart and with all your soul and with all your mind and with all your strength. (**Mark 12:30**)

To most believers who have heard this verse countless times, the concept of what is being said is mostly void of any impact. If you were to ask a Christian if they love the Lord with all their heart, soul, mind and strength, most professing believers would say, "Of course!" Every Christian would at least admit that they try to. However, if Jesus said this is *the* most important command of God (and there are a lot of them), maybe it is worth getting past our shallow 'Sunday school' understanding of this passage and really ask ourselves, "What is Jesus telling us here?" Like Paul Washer said:

> Such a seemingly despised verse. You know, there's a problem when you almost make verses into Sunday school verses for Sunday school children, and you relegate them to, "I understand that." And when you do that, it's like taking a book you've once read and sticking it up in your library, never to pull it out again. The fact of the matter is, if there is anything in the Bible you don't understand, it's this.[3]

This verse about loving the Lord with our entire being is found in both the Old and New Testaments. The Spirit of God is repeating Himself to make sure that we catch it. This verse should make the lukewarm Christian squirm. Instead, many will not feel convicted because they have been deceived into believing they are already obeying this command.

A quick look into the Hebrew and Greek will give us more insight into what is being expressed here:

- The words for *heart* (Hebrew- *lebab*; Greek- *kardia*) mean a lot more than just the physical organ pumping blood throughout the human body. These terms include a person's feelings, conscience, will, understanding and intellect.[4] They basically describe the very center of a person's life.

- The words for *soul* (Hebrew- *nepes*; Greek- *psyche*) mean life, self, person and spirit. The Hebrew concept of man was that he consisted of an inner self and an outer self. This word for soul was the term they used to describe the inner self of a person.

The soul means the very life of a person. To love with all one's soul means with one's entire affection.[5]

- The word *mind* is only used in the New Testament rendition of this verse. It is the Greek word *dianoia*. It includes a person's imagination, mind, intellect and understanding. It implies deep thought, not just surface-level knowledge.[6]

These terms describe everything that encompasses who a person is. When God says to love Him with *all* of these things, you get the idea He is talking about a love that goes much deeper than just surface-level Christianity. He is not merely looking for a portion of our hearts, nor is He looking to be on the top of our list, as if anything else could compete with Him. He is looking for it all and He will accept no less.

The first three words (heart, soul and mind) describe the things with which we are to love God. The last word used in this verse is translated as *might* or *strength* (Hebrew- *me'od*; Greek- *ischyo*). These terms are used to explain the *way* we should love Him. They include adverbs like vehemently, diligently, exceedingly, greatly, mightily or utterly. These words describe a very strong love for Him.[7]

Take an honest evaluation of your love for God right now. Can all of these adverbs describe your love and devotion to Him? Do you love Him vehemently? What about utterly? Exceedingly? If not, how can we so easily claim to love God with all of our strength?

DOES ALL REALLY MEAN ALL?

God's goal is to win the hearts of men. We tend to get this confused. We think that He is merely concerned with our actions, so we focus on the things that we do. The Lord sees past each action (whether righteous or unrighteous) and evaluates the motives of the heart behind it.

I Samuel 16:7 says, "The Lord does not look at the things people look at. People look at the outward appearance, but the Lord looks at the heart." Since we so often focus on the outward—and because we are unable to see into a person's heart—we tend to think that God is the same way. One day every person on Earth will stand before a holy God, who will judge whether or not that man or woman's heart was *wholly* devoted to Jesus.

When we read Scripture, it is easy for most of us to accept the verses about God's judgment against obvious sins like murder, adultery or theft. We might grow a little more uncomfortable when it discusses more hidden sins that are harder to spot, such as lust, jealousy or gossip. But what about the people who faithfully attend church? What about the ones who are doing everything right? What about the ones who abstain from those outward sins? Is it really that big of a deal if they are not one hundred percent sold-out and in love with Jesus? Should Christians be expected to stay constantly in love with Him? Does a Christian really need to spend time alone with the Lord every day? Isn't going to church three or four times a week enough?

If you ask the average believer, you will hear something different than what God's Word is telling us. When He said to love the Lord with all of our heart, soul, mind and strength, did He misspeak when He said *all*? Did He mean most of your heart? If this is what a relationship with Jesus is supposed to look like, is it wrong to wonder if many professing believers in our churches are even saved? This issue of hypocrisy spreads a lot further and deeper in the church than we might want to admit.

ABSOLUTE DESTRUCTION

When God brought the Israelites into the land of Canaan, they had to fight to gain control of the land. Part of Hebrew warfare involved the term *haram*. This verb is literally defined as "to destroy totally,"[8] and is used in Deuteronomy 20:16-17, where God commands the Israelites:

However, in the cities of the nations the Lord your God is giving you as an inheritance, do not leave alive anything that breathes. Completely destroy (*haram*) them...as the Lord your God has commanded you.

As one source explains, "*Haram* is used in signifying that Canaanite cities were to be treated like contraband, removing the lure toward idolatry by destroying the sources."[9] When Jehovah sent Israel into battle, He wanted no trace of the idolatrous paganism from the surrounding nations left intact. This is because He knew it would prove to be a stumbling block to them. *Haram* was "intended to remove permanently the pagan influence from the Israelite vicinity."[10] *Haram* was total destruction declared by God and executed by men. He gave the command, but the Israelites were expected to do the work.

We can take this concept of totally destroying every trace of idolatry and apply it to our hearts. This is what the Lord is declaring over your heart. He is saying: "In order for you to come into the promised wholeness I desire for you, you have to *totally* destroy every stronghold and idol in your heart." Through the process of sanctification, the Holy Spirit will keep vying for control of our hearts. It is only our own stubborn refusal that can keep Him from having it all.

Haram was to be a permanent destruction. The Lord is playing for keeps when it comes to our hearts. The Christian who will not cooperate with God in *haram* will end up with a divided heart—it is just a matter of time. Sanctification is the process of cooperating with the Holy Spirit to rid our lives of every hint of worldliness, sin and control of the flesh. This is not to say that we will ever reach perfection on the Earth, but this is the direction every genuine Christian life should be taking.

A DIVIDED HEART

In Psalm 119:113, King David makes a strong statement: "I hate double-minded people, but I love your law." That Hebrew word for *hate* (*sane*) means "to be an enemy."[11] The word for double-minded is *se'ep,* which means "divided in heart."[12] What David is saying is, "I am an enemy of those with divided hearts." Why would King David write these words under the inspiration of the Holy Spirit? It is because a divided heart is a big deal to God.

A person with a divided heart is someone who is not able to make up his mind—he is constantly going back and forth. When Elijah had his big showdown with the prophets of Baal on Mount Carmel, he asked the Israelites an important question: "How long will you waver between two opinions?"[13] This question revealed the hearts of the people. They could not decide whether to follow Jehovah or Baal, so Elijah had to bring them to a crossroad.

That same challenge is being made to every Christian who is holding back a portion of their heart from God. How long will it be until you fully give your heart to Jesus? How long will you waver between the sold-out life and the world? Make up your mind!

A SALEM HEART

During the service in which Solomon's temple was dedicated, Jehovah gave a clear command to Israel through Solomon. In his speech in I Kings 8:61, the king announces to the whole assembly: "But your hearts must be fully committed to the Lord our God, to live by his decrees and obey his commands, as at this time." Solomon declared that God's will was that the people's hearts should be fully committed to Him. The word used in Hebrew to describe that commitment is *salem*. It is defined, "complete, whole, perfect."[14] Here are some other Scripture references that include *salem*:

Isaiah 38:3- Hezekiah prayed: "Remember, Lord, how I have walked before you faithfully and with wholehearted devotion (*salem*) and have done what is good in your eyes."

I Chronicles 29:19- David prayed: "And give my son Solomon the wholehearted devotion (*salem*) to keep your commands…"

I Kings 11:4- As Solomon grew old, his wives turned his heart after other gods, and his heart was not fully devoted (*salem*) to the Lord his God, as the heart of David his father had been.

God wanted his people to have *salem* hearts. His will for the Israelites was the same as for believers today. He desires a simple, undivided devotion to Him. The Lord will do whatever it takes to capture our attention, but He demands a response from us.

If the Lord were to look down from Heaven at your life right now, what would He say about the condition of your heart? Could He say that it is fully devoted to Him? Or would He say that it is divided and distracted by other things? It is comforting to know what His will is, because when we pray according to His will, we can be sure it will be accomplished. I encourage you to pray right now that God will give you a *salem* heart—one that is fully devoted to Him in every way.

PLAN B CHRISTIANITY

My heart was completely divided when I was living a hypocritical life. In a conversation with a friend, I remember confessing that I felt like I always had a 'Plan B' in my life, in addition to Jesus. I must have had some understanding that my life was not fully devoted to the Lord because I said, "I feel like I have to have something to fall back on in case God does not work out." The fallbacks were the idols I had allowed in my heart and, occasionally, pulled off the shelf when I felt like I needed them.

While I was being restored at Pure Life Ministries, I kept hearing the staff teach about really giving our all to Christ. They told us there was a place we could get to in our spiritual lives where Jesus really was our heart's desire. I confided in my counselor, "I want to give God my all, but I'm afraid. If I really give Him everything—without any fallback—what if He doesn't come through? What if He fails me?"

His response was, "The Lord has *never* let you down. You are the one who let Him down." It was a simple answer, but one that I needed to hear. The lie that God had somehow failed me had to be replaced with the truth.

I realized at that moment that I had developed a belief about God that He was not trustworthy. I understood He was faithful theologically, but it was not real in my heart. I had read about the abundant life in Christ in the Bible. Yet, since I was not seeing it operating in my own life, I concluded that He was the one to blame. I believed that if I really sold-out to Jesus, my walk with Him would inevitably fall apart at some point. So my conclusion was that it was not worth the risk. I had grown content with living outside of God's will, using the "one day I will really pursue the Lord but not today" excuse.

The problem is that one *cannot* live a sincere, devoted Christian life unless they are completely sold-out to Jesus. I believed there was an in-between Christianity where I did not really have to commit my whole heart and life to Him. What I understand now is that there was never even an opportunity for me to have a rich walk with Christ until I was willing to surrender all to Him—and that is what I did.

My testimony is that Jesus came through! He responded to my cry and has done so much to prove His love and faithfulness to me in immeasurable ways. I can see clearly how different my life has been since I totally surrendered to Christ. I was waiting for God to magically force me to become a true believer. All along, He was waiting for me to give Him everything.

HEAD KNOWLEDGE VS. HEART KNOWLEDGE

When it comes to spiritual truth, there is a huge difference between knowing something in your head and knowing it in your heart. A person can read through the Bible and let it affect their mind without allowing the truth to truly penetrate their inner man.

I experienced this first-hand. It was during Bible college that my sincere passion for the Lord began to wane. As I became increasingly interested in my own ambitions and grew less sincere in my pursuit of God, sin went from an occasional occurrence to a habitual practice. Throughout my three and a half years in school, I sat under some of the most profound teaching. I studied the Word constantly, meditated on deep theology and had my mind often on the things of God. Yet inside, I was backsliding and falling into the grips of hypocrisy.

I took my first ministry position during my senior year of college. The next few years, I spent much of my time preparing sermons. I had to read the Bible and I often studied various passages in-depth. Yet the divide between the love for God in my heart and my love for this world only grew larger; my heart continued to harden.

How could this be? Are we not taught that reading Scripture is a necessary discipline in the life of a believer? Yes, this is a very important part of our lives, but we have to be on guard. If we are not careful, we can turn an essential spiritual discipline (the study of God's Word) into nothing more than mental exercise.

In I Corinthians 8:1, Paul says, "knowledge puffs up." Some of the most spiritually proud people are experts in the Bible. They can quote Scriptures, discuss deep theological issues and sound really impressive...to men. But the true litmus test to determine how much of God's Word is getting into your heart is *how much you are living it.* If you are not applying the truth personally, then it is not a reality in your life. You can tell yourself, "I know all the right answers and can discuss really important truths," but until it affects the way you live, it is simply head knowledge.

There are a lot of professing Christians in the church who are full of knowledge about Scriptural truths and the things of God. However, when carefully examined, their lives are no different than their unsaved neighbors and co-workers. Other than the fact that they attend church and are involved in Christian activities, the truth of the Bible in their minds is not translating into a change in their lives. Therefore they have only head knowledge. Charles Finney once wrote:

> What is growing in grace? Is it hearing sermons and getting some new ideas about religion? No, not at all. The Christian who does this, and nothing else, will grow worse and worse, more and more hardened. Finally it will be nearly impossible to rouse him.[15]

If someone's walk with the Lord is based more on what they know— rather than who they know—they need to beware. Head knowledge can be very deceiving. We need to make sure that our knowledge of God and His Word runs deep into our hearts.

ARE YOU OBEYING THE LORD?

There are many Christians who enjoy reading the Bible and listening to sermons, but God is clear that obedience *must* follow. In Ezekiel 33:31, the Lord tells the prophet:

> My people come to you, as they usually do, and sit before you to hear your words, but they do not put them into practice. Their mouths speak of love, but their hearts are greedy for unjust gain.

The Israelites heard the message being spoken to them and even acknowledged it as the Word of the Lord, but they did not obey it. There was no follow-through.

We must not fool ourselves to believe that merely hearing, reading or even enjoying the Word equates with putting it into practice in God's eyes. Jesus said it this way:

> You study the Scriptures diligently because you think that in them you have eternal life. These are the very Scriptures that testify about me, yet you refuse to come to me to have life.[16]

Jesus was speaking to people who made reading, memorizing and teaching the Scriptures a way of life, yet they were not really allowing the truth to pierce their hearts.

John Bevere gives some insight into the importance of allowing God's Word to impact us:

> We deceive ourselves when we just listen to the Word of God instead of allowing it to penetrate deep into our heart to judge our thought processes, attitudes, perceptions, intentions, and so forth—thus changing the way we behave. If the Word doesn't penetrate our inner being, then we will have the mental knowledge of God and His ways but only in the moment (when we are looking in the mirror). However, when we aren't consciously aware of our faith

(once we've stepped away from the mirror), we'll act in a manner totally contrary to what we profess.[17]

I am growing more and more convinced that God would rather us get back to the very simple truths of His Word—and *obey* them—than to be able to discuss doctrine and have all the right answers to every popular argument. When we meet a brother or sister in Christ, our immediate questions should not be, "What denomination are you from? What are your views about such and such pet theology?" Rather, they should be, "Tell me what the Lord has been showing you lately. How is your faith affecting the way you live? What passage of Scripture has recently come alive to you?"

Often, the people who quickly revert to theological discussions and controversial issues are more interested in showing off how much they 'know' (head knowledge) than hearing the other person's point of view. This know-it-all attitude is a great indicator of spiritual pride and reveals a self-centered character and immature walk with the Lord. Yet, they disguise it with enough Scripture and "Christianese" to look like genuine Christianity.

KNOWING GOD

A Bible degree does not guarantee a true heart knowledge of the Lord. In Jeremiah 9:24, God says, "but let the one who boasts boast about this: that they have the understanding to know me." The Hebrew word used for *know* in that passage (*yada*) is the same word used for sexual relations because it involves intimacy.[18] Rather than a casual acquaintance, *yada* describes knowing someone on a much deeper level.

In Matthew 7:21-23, a group of people who 'know' a lot of spiritual things appear before Christ, looking to enter the Kingdom of Heaven. These are not casual Christians. The Scripture says they prophesied, cast out demons and worked miracles. They must have had a foundation of spiritual knowledge to perform such works. They tried to use these works as evidence that they had a relationship with Jesus. They tell Him, "Did we not *do* all these things?" In other words, "Can't you see all that we did? That must count for something!" Jesus does not deny that they operated in the supernatural, but simply says, "I never *knew* you." He gives us a sober warning that "many" will come to Him in this condition on that day.

Judgment day will be a horrifying moment for many who will appear before Christ and list their spiritual achievements and all their head knowledge about the things of God. "Didn't I attend church every Sunday and Wednesday? Didn't I go to Bible school? Didn't I memorize Scripture? Didn't I sing on the worship team? Didn't I go to the mission field?" But they will hear the same heartbreaking words from the Savior's lips: "Depart from me, I never knew you." Those words will echo through the caverns of their minds for eternity.

Knowing God is a heart issue. Reading the Bible, praying and being involved in spiritual activities mean *nothing* to God if our hearts are not in them. They will only serve to make us feel more spiritual and self-righteous, and push us further away from the Lord. This is a crucial point for the hypocrite to consider if they have any desire to experience a true Christian life. Stop focusing your attention on the outside and start looking at your inner life. That is where God is focusing already.

AN UNDIVIDED HEART

Now that we have examined several biblical teachings about the heart, let us look at the condition God desires our hearts to be in. *Anypokritos* is an amazing Greek word. This term is the exact opposite of the word for hypocrisy. Its original meaning is "inexperienced in the art of acting."[19] Basically, *anypokritos* describes a bad actor.

Have you ever been to a school play before? It seems like there is always one kid who gets on stage and you can quickly discern that acting is not his strong suit. You cannot wait until his part is over because you feel so bad for him. That is what this word is describing. In the New Testament, it came to mean "unfeigned, genuine."[20] This is precisely what the Lord is after in the heart of every person who claims to belong to Him. In a church culture where most are really good at playing the part, God is looking for some bad actors. Hypocrites are known for award-winning performances and their ability to fool everyone. The Father wants to do exactly the opposite in our hearts. Here are some examples of *anypokritos* from Scripture:

Romans 12:9 (NKJV)- Let love be without hypocrisy (*anypokritos*). Abhor what is evil. Cling to what is good.

II Corinthians 6:6- Paul says we should commend ourselves, "in the Holy Spirit and in sincere (*anypokritos*) love."

I Timothy 1:5- The goal of this command is love, which comes from a pure heart and a good conscience and a sincere (*anypokritos*) faith.

Anypokritos is the idea of wholeness. If hypocrisy is a divided heart, *anypokritos* is a heart that is put back together. This is part of the New Covenant promise given to us through the prophets. The Lord says in Ezekiel 11:19:

I will give them an *undivided heart* and put a new spirit in them; I will remove from them their heart of stone and give them a heart of flesh. *(emphasis added)*

In another Old Testament prophecy about the New Covenant, God promises through the prophet Jeremiah to give His people *singleness of heart* and action.[21] When we come into a living relationship with Jesus and are born again, we are given a heart that is whole—it is undivided. That is the promise God made. If you are not born again, you have not received this new heart. However, for those who have been born again of the Spirit, but find themselves with a divided heart, that is evidence that they have strayed from the Lord. We must cry out with King David, "Give me an undivided heart, that I may fear your name."[22]

Think about it. If walking with the Lord requires a sincere heart (without hypocrisy) and single-mindedness, unless those characteristics line up with who we truly are inside, *we are not walking with God!* We may have walked with Him in the past. We may have religiosity. We may have the respect and approval of others, but we cannot say that we are in right relationship with God. It is simply not true.

When Jesus first met Nathanael in John 1, he makes a bold statement. He says, "Here truly is an Israelite in whom there is no deceit." (v. 47) The word being used for the term *deceit* is *dolos* and it means "slyness, trickery."[23] Jesus looks right into the heart of this man without *dolos* and sees someone who is not playing games. Can Jesus look into your heart and say the same about you? If not, keep reading. This book is designed to help you allow God to accomplish that very thing. The Lord is looking for men and women with nothing false in them like Nathanael; He has a plan to help us get there.

GOD LONGS FOR YOUR HEART

There is a Greek word, *kardiognostes*, which is found in Acts 1:24 when the apostles prayed, "Lord, you know everyone's heart." This comes from combining the word for *heart* and *to know*.[24] It is literally translated as *heart-knower*. No one knows our heart like God does—nor does anyone long for it the way He does.

In worship not long ago, the Lord showed me something in the spiritual realm. As we were worshiping, I could see the Lord trying to draw each person unto Himself. He was above them, tugging on their hearts to get them to surrender their whole lives to Him. I could see that there were many who were down on the other end, struggling to hold onto their lives. It was like a spiritual tug-of-war for control.

I could tell there was desperation in the Lord's heart. He was pulling firmly, trying to get control of people's lives. He was hoping to get them to surrender their hearts once and for all. He wanted their lives because He knew that was the only way they could be free. It reminded me of a father trying to wrestle a loaded gun out of the hands of a suicidal teenaged son. Some think of God like a dictator—trying to take over—but I saw a loving Father wanting what is best for His children. I began to weep, "Lord, please let them give it all to you." He could not force anyone to let go. I heard Him speak to my heart, "Many of them will win."

The truth is that the Lord is trying to draw all men unto Himself, including professing believers who are not really living sold-out lives for Him. The sad fact is that many will win the tug-of-war against God. Many will not let go and let Him have everything, no matter what He does. God—in His great love—lets people have what their hearts truly desire. That can be a life completely filled with His presence, or a life with a 'form of godliness,' but one without His power.[25]

God is the heart-knower. He knows where you really are. As we progress through this book, the goal is to allow the Lord to reveal to us our hearts' condition so that we can surrender them completely to Him.

The next three chapters will provide an overview of how hypocrisy has affected God's people from ancient Israel until today.

Idolatry:

1. **noun.** worship of idols
2. excessive devotion to or reverence for some person or thing[1]

*   *   *

Psalm 106:34-43 (NIV)- They did not destroy the peoples as the Lord had commanded them, but they mingled with the nations and adopted their customs. They worshiped their idols, which became a snare to them. They sacrificed their sons and their daughters to false gods. They shed innocent blood, the blood of their sons and daughters, whom they sacrificed to the idols of Canaan, and the land was desecrated by their blood. They defiled themselves by what they did; by their deeds they prostituted themselves. Therefore the Lord was angry with his people and abhorred his inheritance. He gave them into the hands of the nations, and their foes ruled over them. Their enemies oppressed them and subjected them to their power. Many times he delivered them, but they were bent on rebellion and they wasted away in their sin.

*   *   *

"Have you ever read through the Old Testament and wondered how the people of God could walk into the Temple of God, could offer sacrifices to God, could praise God and then turn right around and find the biggest tree on the highest hill and worship every number of idols and not be able to tell the difference and not be able to recognize the wrong in a multiplicity of gods?"

-Paul Washer[2]

3

THE HYPOCRISY OF ISRAEL

L ONG BEFORE OUR DAY—AND EVEN BEFORE the time of Christ—hypocrisy was an issue for God's people. A lifestyle of hypocrisy was at the root of the downfall of Jehovah's chosen nation, Israel. This can be seen throughout the Old Testament, from the time Moses led Israel out of Egypt, to the time of the Babylonian and Assyrian captivities. It was the people's unwillingness to be fully devoted to the Lord that resulted in countless trials and judgments. In this chapter, we will discuss how hypocrisy affected Israel, and apply the lessons they learned to our lives today.

CHOOSE THIS DAY

Hypocrisy is the reason that the Israelites were called to make a decision throughout the Old Testament. Perhaps the most popular Scripture where a line is drawn in the sand occurs in the book of Joshua. At this point in history, the Israelites were just setting foot into the Promised Land, but they had already shown their divided hearts on several occasions. They had complained against Moses and Aaron several times (and therefore against Jehovah).[3] They had absolutely no faith to believe that the God who rescued them from Egypt could provide for their needs. The nation gave themselves over to worshiping idols, as in the incident with the golden calf.[4] To top it all off, they believed the bad report from the spies rather than the Word of God and had to wander forty years aimlessly for it.[5]

In his final words to the Israelites, Joshua paints a very clear picture. His speech begins by rehearsing what the Lord had done through their deliverance from slavery in Egypt and how He had brought them into the Promised Land. Joshua reminds them of the Lord's track record. Jehovah had been good to them and provided for them the whole way. Then Joshua calls the nation to a distinct decision. In Joshua 24:15, he says:

> But if serving the Lord seems undesirable to you, then choose for yourselves this day whom you will serve, whether the gods of your ancestors served beyond the Euphrates, or the gods of the Amorites, in whose land you are living. But as for me and my household, we will serve the Lord.

The Israelites have the choice to either serve the Lord or to worship other gods. There is no middle ground. In spite of this, the rest of the Old Testament shows that the Israelites as a whole tried to pave a middle way between the two options. The history from Judges through Kings is a spiritual roller coaster of indecision. The Lord grows tired of it and He says, "Enough is enough." After countless attempts to win their hearts back to Himself, all that is left is judgment. They pay an incredibly high price: they lose their homes, families, country and even their lives because they just *would not* choose God. Following the Lord has always been left up to the decision of mankind. He has never forced anyone to obey Him.

ISRAEL: A SYNCRETIZED NATION

The first and second commandments did not have any gray areas. God made His expectations of the nation extremely clear. Exodus 20:1-5 records:

> And God spoke all these words: "I am the Lord your God, who brought you out of Egypt, out of the land of slavery. You shall have no other gods before me. You shall not make for yourself an image in the form of anything in heaven above or on the earth beneath or in the waters below. You shall not bow down to them or worship them; for I, the Lord your God, am a jealous God..."

In spite of these clear commandments, the picture we get of the Israelites is not one of an obedient people. In fact, the habitual sin that plagued the Israelite culture and eventually brought judgment upon the nation was *syncretism*. Syncretism is defined by one source as:

> a combination, reconciliation, or coalescence of varying, often mutually opposed beliefs, principles, or practices, esp. those of various religions, into a new conglomerate whole typically marked by internal inconsistencies.[6]

Basically, syncretism is a blending of spiritual things. The Israelites maintained their identity as Jehovah-worshipers, but borrowed from the religions of the surrounding nations in an attempt to form some kind of hybrid Judaism. However, in the first commandment, God clearly condemned worship to anyone but Himself.

If the Lord clearly forbade the worship of other gods, why did the nation continue to partake in idol worship? The answer to that question can be found in the benefits that syncretism offered. For example, the common belief of the surrounding cultures was that each god had his or her own unique powers. By worshiping them, the people believed they could coerce them to cause it to rain, bring a bountiful harvest and pour down blessings upon the land. Jehovah's desire was for Israel to depend on Him alone. The

Israelites were bombarded with the folklore of the neighboring nations and their gods. In a time of drought, it was easier to cry out to these specialty gods than to submit to the Lord, because He held them accountable for the way they lived their lives.

THE FERTILITY CULTS

When the Israelites came into the Promised Land, they found themselves surrounded by nations who were steeped in some of the most perverse practices you could imagine. These foreign religious systems were centered on sexual rites, and are classified as fertility cults. The Canaanites had a group of gods they worshiped. Two of the most common gods they believed in—Baal and Asherah—are names found frequently throughout the Old Testament.

The nations believed that there were certain things they could do to please their gods. One of those practices involved temple prostitutes. The fertility cults taught that by committing certain acts on Earth, the people could incite the gods to do the same activities. As one source explains:

> Sacred or cultic prostitution was practiced in order to ensure the fertility of the land. Fertility of the field, flock, and family was thought to depend upon the sexual relations between Baal and Anath (or Asherah). According to a pattern of sympathetic magic, the worshipers of Baal imitated the actions they desired Baal to perform. Thus male and female worshipers engaged in sacred sexual acts in the temple in order to assure for themselves the blessings of nature.[7]

Fertility cults maintained the belief that if the gods had sexual relations, it would bring blessings on the land, such as rain and agricultural success. In order to incite the gods to have sex, people had to have it themselves. So men and women of all ages were stationed at the temples to sleep with any 'worshiper' who wanted to make the gods imitate their behavior.

Though the practices of Canaan were expressively forbidden throughout the Torah, they certainly appealed to the flesh of the Israelites. The gods of Canaan became a fallback. If Jehovah did not seem to be responding, rather than searching their hearts and turning to Him in fasting and prayer (which would have cost them something), they could take a trip to the temple prostitutes and try to make things happen in their own strength and please their flesh at the same time.

Outwardly, Israel did not completely abandon their religious activities for Jehovah, but they simply kept all options available. This prevented them from having to live completely by faith and provided a way to get what they wanted by trying to side-step obedience.

THE BLENDING OF RELIGIONS

Two examples of syncretism in the Old Testament are found in the following passages. Here, you can see the blending of Judaism with the worship of other gods:

I Kings 12:28-30- After seeking advice, the king made two golden calves. He said to the people, "It is too much for you to go up to Jerusalem. *Here are your gods, O Israel, who brought you up out of Egypt.*" One he set up in Bethel, and the other in Dan. And this thing became a sin; the people came to worship the one at Bethel and went as far as Dan to worship the other. *(emphasis added)*

Zephaniah 1:4-6- I will destroy every remnant of Baal worship in this place, the names of the idolatrous priests—those who bow down on the roofs to worship the starry host, those who bow down and *swear by the Lord and who also swear by Molech*, those who turn back from following the Lord and neither seek the Lord nor inquire of him. *(emphasis added)*

These actions are an outward manifestation of what was occurring in the Israelites' hearts. Remember, God is always concerned with our hearts, and our motives will inevitably show through our actions. The Israelites wanted the spiritual blessings without the spiritual disciplines. They wanted to indulge their fleshly desires but still convince themselves that they were spiritual.

Syncretism is a hypocrisy issue. The Israelites stubbornly sought to make two contradictory lifestyles co-exist, and eventually they reached a point where they could not see the conflict, or at least refused to. They still maintained the outward appearances of serving Jehovah. The Archaeological Bible says:

> Although Baal worship, viewed from a distance, was obviously horrendous, those who were involved in it were so influenced by the dominant culture that they remained convinced that they were devout and orthodox followers of the Lord—when they were all the while worshiping Baal.[8]

Hypocrisy and deception are never far from each other. That is because people in hypocrisy always try to justify their behavior. In a sense, the Israelites could not 'see the forest for the trees.' Even if they could, it is doubtful that many of them would have been willing to acknowledge the truth. The Lord tried to get their attention many times, but they refused to listen.

MODERN-DAY ISRAELITES

It is easy for us to look at Israel and assume we are nothing like them. After all, they were involved in some bizarre, even horrifying practices. Their sin included worshiping man-made idols, sacrificing to foreign gods, partaking in temple prostitution, burning incense in high places and offering their children in human sacrifices.[9] If we read through the Old Testament without putting ourselves into the mindset of the Israelites, we can easily become self-righteous. We might come to the conclusion that they had some serious issues compared to what we deal with.

However, as believers in Christ who have been given a much deeper revelation of God's plan than Israel had, we might actually be much worse off than they were. Our level of accountability is greater than theirs, because the Israelites did not have a complete understanding of the Lord's plan for redemption.

It is true that most of us are not tempted to bow down to a golden calf or to participate in sexual religious rites, but a proper understanding of Scripture should allow us to see that we are not as far removed from the Israelites' sin as we may think.

Let us examine the concept of idolatry in light of our lives in today's church world. One definition reads:

> Anything which we keep in our hearts in the place which God ought to have is an idol, whether it be an image of wood or stone or gold, or whether it be money, or desire for fame, or love of pleasure, or some secret sin which we will not give up. If God does not really occupy the highest place in our hearts, controlling all, something else does, and that something else is an idol.[10]

Another source defines an idol as "anything that leads to the dethronement of God from the heart."[11] When we define idolatry this way, we can see that Israel's issues with hypocrisy are really the same as professing Christians whose hearts are not fully devoted to the Lord.

In many ways, it is much more difficult to spot a hypocritical lifestyle in today's church culture. It would be much easier if someone could rummage through your house and find figurine idols, or follow you around to see where you burn incense or ask at the temple if you have been visiting its brothel. It is a different matter completely to look into your heart and see if Jesus really has it all. Yet, in the same way that many Israelites were so entrenched in idolatry to the point of spiritual blindness, the Christian who has compromised his walk with Jesus is often deceived into thinking that he is living a good Christian life. However, God looks at our hearts and sees the truth.

DISCIPLINED BY JUDGMENT

The syncretism and idolatry of Israel were a constant cause of God's judgment on the nation. Just like a hammer in the hand of a carpenter is the best tool to bang a nail into a piece of wood, or a wrench in the hand of a plumber best for tightening a pipe, judgment in the hand of the Lord is the best tool to destroy idolatry in the hearts of His people.

The Lord gives the Israelites the choice to repent. If you read further through the Old Testament, you find the nation making the decision to continue on in sin and rebellion despite the many warnings given. So, Jehovah is faithful to His promise, and judgment comes upon the nation in order to discipline them and cause them to repent.

God lays down His expectations clearly to Israel in Isaiah 1:19-20. He says, "If you are willing and obedient, you will eat the good things of the land; but if you resist and rebel, you will be devoured by the sword." The nation has two options. Either they can find mercy through repentance, or they will face discipline through judgment. Herbert Wolf writes:

> Israel's bloodstained hands could be made clean if she repented. The people had to choose between obedience and rebellion…In view of Jerusalem's sinful state, the Lord had no recourse but to pronounce judgment against her. He would take drastic steps to purify the land.[12]

Judgment is always for the purpose of causing repentance. If it is ignored, it can cause a hardness of heart leading to further separation from the Lord. God's will is always to show mercy, but when mercy is rejected, God will allow circumstances to transpire—out of love—to try to wake His people up. Godly discipline is *always* out of a heart of love in hope for repentance and restoration.

The Israelites thought they had a free pass to do whatever they wanted without consequence because they were Jehovah's chosen nation. Yet they found out the hard way that this was not so. In the same way, we can be deceived to think that we have a guaranteed spot in Heaven because at some point we made a decision for Christ. The Bible simply does not teach that. Can I take a moment and plead with you? Please do not wait until judgment day to find out if hypocrites can still make it into God's presence for eternity!

GOD'S MARRIAGE TO ISRAEL

Scripture says in I John 4:8 that God is love. Our relationship with Him is born out of a response to His love for us. Continually in Scripture, the relationship of God and man is compared to a marital relationship. The Old Testament prophets are full of examples of this verbiage. The most vivid is the book of Hosea, when God told the prophet to marry a prostitute as a living illustration of His love for His adulterous people.[13]

This marriage symbolism can be found throughout the Word of God. Song of Solomon paints a beautiful picture of the intimacy enjoyed between a husband and wife (and, allegorically, of God and man). We are called the Bride of Christ and Jesus the Bridegroom in several places in the New Testament.[14] We look forward to the Great Wedding Supper of the Lamb, when we are finally reunited with Jesus.[15] The Holy Spirit could have used any metaphor to describe our relationship with Him, but He chose to relate it to a marriage.

When you think about our relationship with the Lord in this way, you can better understand phrases in the Bible which describe God as "a jealous God"[16] or which depict Israel's idolatry as "committing adultery."[17] God uses this language because creation was an expression of His love. Both the Old and New Covenants were an expression of the Lord's passionate love for people. The most radical display of this great love is found in the giving of God's one and only Son. He has done everything He can to win the hearts of men to Himself, but He never violates our free will. It is our choice to receive and reciprocate this love—or to reject it.

THE PARABLE OF THE JILTED LOVER

Chris and Maria's relationship begins the same as most love stories.

They start dating and everything is wonderful. They begin to learn each other's likes and dislikes. More and more of their time is spent together. Chris used to go to bed early, now he is spending late nights on the phone. He is really falling in love with Maria. Soon, he expresses the way he is feeling toward her. Maria tells him that she has never felt the same way about anyone else before. That is all Chris needs to hear; he develops a plan to propose.

Chris starts searching for the perfect ring. Even though he is not wealthy, the price tag does not matter because his sweetheart is worth it. He will put in extra hours at work and even take a second job if needed. His only concern is that Maria knows that she is everything to him. The fateful day comes and the proposal is given. Maria says, "Yes!" Now all that is left is the wedding and then happily ever after.

But wait. A few weeks pass and there seems to be something on Maria's mind. Suddenly Chris' new fiancé seems distant. He asks her about it but she brushes it off as "a lot on her mind." One day they are out shopping together and they bump into a mutual male friend of theirs. When she greets this friend, Chris can see something in her eyes. That twinkle she had when they first met returns in the presence of another man.

Chris questions her—she denies it. Then strange things start happening. Maria talks to this other man on the phone constantly. She often manages to 'accidentally' bump into him in public. And all the while, she is growing increasingly distant in her relationship with her fiancé.

Chris tries to reason with her. Out of desperation he does everything he can think of. He gets angry, begs and cries—all to no avail. The wedding day is fast approaching, but Maria has said nothing about calling it off. She is not willing to admit she has fallen for another man. So, it seems like she will go through with their wedding plans in spite of her complete lack of love for Chris.

What would you do if you were Chris? Could he possibly go through with the wedding to selfishly try to keep Maria to himself? Not if he really loves her. To go through with the ceremony might make her 'legally' his, but he knows he will not really have her heart.

Compare this to the relationship between God and Israel. Jehovah chose Israel to be His people.[18] He married Himself to her.[19] Although

Israel served Him somewhat wholeheartedly at times, the duplicity of the people's hearts was quickly revealed. The history of Israel throughout the Old Testament is the story of a loving God *relentlessly* trying to call the nation back into relationship with Himself.

Just like Chris, after doing everything possible to try to win God's beloved nation back, He had to let her go. Even though He knew He was the one for her, He could not force her to believe or accept that. The only thing that True Love could do was to let her have what she really wanted in her heart.

God's relationship with Israel is similar to His relationship with us. I found it to be true in my own life. As I slowly drifted out of relationship with Jesus and rejected His many attempts to call me back, my heart hardened. I began to blatantly disobey the Lord and to push the conviction of the Holy Spirit away. At times, it was as if the Spirit of God was pleading with me to turn back to Him—but I refused to listen.

I can remember a day when I was determined to find illegal drugs. I had toyed with the idea for some time, but I had finally made up my mind that I was going to use again. For the first six years after I was saved, I was never offered drugs or had any access to them. I always knew the Lord was protecting me. On that day, the Lord lifted His hand of protection off of me and let me have what He knew I truly wanted in my heart. Thinking back to that time—and the drastic plummet my spiritual life took—it is as if I can hear God saying, "Fine! If that is what you want so badly, I won't stand in your way anymore."

In Hosea 11:7, Jehovah says about Israel, "My people are determined to turn from me." The Lord could say the same about my life a few years ago. Would the Lord speak the same words over yours?

SPIRITUAL HARLOTRY

Hosea 5:4 states about Israel that, "their deeds do not permit them to return to their God. A spirit of prostitution is in their heart; they do not acknowledge the Lord." Because God sees His relationship to His people as a marriage covenant, when we turn our back on Him, it is the spiritual equivalent of a man leaving his wife to sleep with a prostitute. Rex Andrews explains, "Throughout the Bible the love which takes God's place in the hearts of men, cities, or nations, is called fornication and adultery."[20]

Spiritual harlotry is anything and everything that God's people love apart from Him. That is His perspective on what takes place when people turn away from His love. This is not only including those who turn away outwardly and leave the faith completely. It also includes those who have chosen to stay in church and are involved in religious activities, but inwardly have fallen away. It is the same spirit of prostitution in Jehovah's eyes.

Listen to the sound of a heartbroken God calling out to His people through the prophet Micah:

My people, what have I done to you? How have I burdened you? Answer me. I brought you up out of Egypt and redeemed you from the land of slavery.[21]

This is how God feels over every soul who grows cold toward Him. He wonders how we can turn our backs on Him after He has been so faithful to us. If you are a Christian, but you have habitual sin in your life or you are playing religious games, this is what God is saying to you right now through this book. "What have I done to make you walk away from me? Look at all that I've done for you!" If that is not enough to move you inside, you need to ask yourself, "Why?" How is it that the Lord's grief over you is not enough to break you? You need to cry out to God for a softened heart right now. Do not put it off another moment!

FINDING MYSELF IN JEREMIAH TWO

In the beginning of my restoration period with the Lord, He convinced me that I was just like the Israelites. One of the key Scripture passages that He used to show me the truth about the condition of my heart was Jeremiah 2. As I read through this chapter—day after day—the Lord kept highlighting new verses to show me how much I had in common with His people in the Old Testament.

Like many in the church, it was easy for me to point a finger at the rebellious people of God and say, "How could they continually turn away from the Lord when He did so many miracles in their midst?" They were constantly rebuked and chastised for their lack of obedience to God, in spite of all of the times that He bailed them out. I felt like they had a huge advantage over me. After all, they had the Red Sea experience in Exodus 14 and countless other direct interventions from Jehovah.

When hypocrisy had a hold of my life, I was in too much delusion about my own spirituality to ever stop and *really* consider how much like them I was. When I finally came to the Lord in honesty, He used this passage in a powerful way to show me the condition of my heart. Through Jeremiah's prophecy, He showed me how my own rebellion grieved Him.

The Lord speaks through Jeremiah to a people who have turned away. He starts by reminding them that they were once in love with Him. Jeremiah 2:2 says, "I remember the devotion of your youth, how as a bride you loved me and followed me through the wilderness…" Can you hear the sadness in the Lord's voice thinking back to the time of Israel's true devotion to Him? He feels that emotion over each of us who have grown cold in our love for Him in our hearts. He reminded me through that verse: "I have not forgotten how much you loved me. We had a true relationship once." That made the next verses much more painful in light of God's faithfulness toward me.

Then God asks a pointed question: "What fault did your ancestors find in me, that they strayed so far from me?" (v. 5) I had to personally come to grips with the fact that God had been completely faithful to me in every way. I had a list of ways I thought He had failed me, but in reality, the Lord never broke a single promise to me. All of the perceived injustices were just selfish desires that were not being fulfilled. He had been nothing but good to me, and yet I too had turned away from Him to follow my own "worthless idols." (v. 8)

Then He continues:

My people have committed two sins: They have forsaken me, the spring of living water, and have dug their own cisterns, broken cisterns that cannot hold water. (v. 13)

This analysis accurately described my life in hypocrisy. I began to place my trust in things that could never satisfy. I let my love for the things of this world replace the intimacy I had with Him. I can relate to the horrible emptiness of trying to fill the cistern of my heart, but never being able to satisfy it. I tried so hard to cover up the guilt and shame, and I desperately wanted to convince myself that everything was okay. Deep down, I knew that none of those things could ever bring me happiness.

Then Jehovah explains the horrible position His people are in. They became prey to their enemies. (vv. 14-16) As other nations came and caused destruction, many of the Israelites accused God, "You protected us many times in our history, but now you have forsaken us!" To this He replies: "Have you not brought this on yourselves by forsaking the Lord your God when he led you in the way?" (v. 17) It was their choice to forsake the Lord and they were merely reaping the consequences.

This could not have been any closer to my own experience. In my heart, I had forsaken the Lord. Because of that, I had allowed the enemy to come in and attack me. I was dealing with consequences *I brought upon myself*, yet I blamed the Lord for them. As Proverbs 19:3 says, "A person's own folly leads to their ruin, yet their heart rages against the Lord." It is completely irrational thinking, but that illustrates how deluding hypocrisy can be.

Jeremiah 2:19 sums up a truth I have found to be absolutely certain: "Consider then and realize how evil and bitter it is for you when you forsake the Lord your God and have no awe of me…" I can testify to the awful condition I was in as I lost all fear of the Lord and chose to turn my back completely on Him.

In the following verses, God reviews what the Israelites had become. They were in denial and the Lord compares them to a wild donkey in heat, willing to commit spiritual adultery with anyone they could find. (v. 23) They had turned to idols who were unable to save them from trouble. (v. 28) In verse 27, God says, "They have turned their backs to me and not their faces…" Though God brought chastening upon them, still they would not listen. (v. 30) They lied to themselves and said, "I am innocent…I have not sinned." (v. 35) A heartbroken God says in verse 32, "Yet my people have forgotten me, days without number."

If you are in hypocrisy today, I pray the Lord would use these verses in the same way He used them in my life. They tore me to shreds inside. I had to continually confess, repent and cry out for His mercy as I saw my life so clearly displayed before me. It was as if I *truly* saw what I had done to Him for the first time. I understood how I had broken His heart with my rebellion.

I could see myself living in the sixth century B.C. hearing Jeremiah preach that message. There I was among the crowd, just another guilty, backslidden Israelite. All of a sudden, the gap of thousands of years and the cultural differences between ancient Israel and myself seemed so small. It was the Lord speaking those words to me directly—and it shook me.

THE JOSIAH SPIRIT

When it came to fighting against idolatry and syncretism in the Old Testament, there was one king who stood out above the rest. His name was King Josiah, and he took the throne of Judah when he was eight years old. He lived in a time when the land of Israel was divided into a northern and southern kingdom. The country was in a mess. Jehovah repeatedly sent prophets to the nation to try to get their attention and cause them to repent and turn back to Him. As we have discovered, Israel remained entrenched in idolatry and the worship of false gods.

Josiah became king just a few years after Manasseh, who was one of the most wicked kings to ever rule in Israel.[22] King Manasseh pushed the limits on idolatry and sin as far as he could. When Josiah became king, syncretism and idolatrous practices had become the norm.

During his reign, many people made idols for a living. There were full-time priests who served at the altars and temples of the false gods. Many in the land were enjoying the 'benefits' afforded to them by sacred prostitution. So, Josiah's strong stand against these practices would not have made too many people happy. In fact, many would have hated him for it. But Josiah did not fear men, he only feared the Lord—and his actions proved it.

II Kings 22 tells the story. As a priest is going through the temple on an assignment from the king, he finds the Book of the Law, which was the first five books of the Bible written by Moses. He brings it to Josiah, and as the king hears the words written, he immediately tears his garment and humbles himself before the Lord. Seeing God's expectations made him realize the backslidden condition Israel found themselves in. He sends people to find a prophetess to inquire of the Lord for him.[23] She informs him that the Lord is still going to bring judgment on the people for all the sins they had committed, but that He would spare Josiah from it.

Josiah launches an all-out attack on idolatry. Chapter 23 contains an awesome description of how thorough Josiah was in cleansing the country. Look at all that he accomplished in his zeal for the Lord:

- **V. 3)** He pledged to obey the Lord by keeping all his commands, laws, and decrees with all of his heart and soul.
- **V. 4)** He removed from the Lord's Temple all the articles that were used to worship Baal, Asherah and all the powers of the heavens, and had them burned.
- **V. 5)** He did away with all the idolatrous priests who offered pagan sacrifices to Baal, the sun, moon, constellations and powers of the heavens.
- **V. 6)** He removed the Asherah pole from the Lord's Temple and burned it, ground the ashes and threw the dust in a graveyard.
- **V. 7)** He tore down the living quarters of the prostitutes that were in the Temple, and where women wove garments for Asherah.
- **V. 8)** He defiled pagan shrines from Geba to Beersheba, and destroyed the shrines at the entrance to the gate of Joshua.
- **V. 10)** He defiled the altar of Topheth in the Valley of Ben Hinnom, so no one could ever again use it to sacrifice a son or daughter in the fire as an offering to Molech.
- **V. 11)** He removed from the entrance of the temple the horse statues that former kings had dedicated to the sun and burned the dedicated chariots.
- **V. 12)** He tore down the altars the former kings had built on the palace roof, and the altars Manasseh had built in the two courtyards of the Lord's Temple and smashed them and scattered the pieces in a valley.

- **V. 13)** He desecrated the pagan shrines east of Jerusalem which Solomon had built for three pagan gods.
- **V. 14)** He smashed the sacred pillars and cut down Asherah poles, then desecrated the places by scattering human bones on them.
- **V. 15)** He tore down the altar at Bethel that Jeroboam had made, burned it and ground it to dust and burned the Asherah pole there.
- **V. 19)** He demolished all the buildings at the pagan shrines in Samaria.
- **V. 20)** He executed the priests of the pagan shrines on their own altars and desecrated them.
- **V. 24)** He got rid of the mediums and psychics, the household gods and every other kind of detestable practice.

That is quite a resumé in the eyes of the Lord. Verse 25 sums up Josiah's life:

Neither before nor after Josiah was there a king like him who turned to the Lord as he did—with all his heart and with all his soul and with all his strength, in accordance with all the Law of Moses.

This Scripture provides us with a vivid picture of what the pursuit of God is all about. This is a big climax in Israel's story. Finally, a king sees how idolatry offends a holy God and *does something* about it! The spirit that Josiah was in could be boiled down to one thought: "Get rid of every trace of anything that is offensive to the Lord!" Josiah did not just command the people, "Stop doing that!" He became proactive and started smashing, burning, tearing down, desecrating, and demolishing everything that Jehovah hated from the land.

This is the attitude that a Christian coming out of hypocrisy needs to develop. We need to be a people that say, "Whatever it takes—no matter how costly or painful—I am going to smash every idol in my heart!" I am praying that the spirit Josiah was in would come alive in your heart, and cause you to say, "No more hypocrisy; no more hiding. I am getting right with God and I am never turning back!"

In the next chapter, we will discuss how hypocrisy evolved from Old Testament syncretism to a religious façade in the New Testament. We will discover how God's people experienced hypocrisy in Jesus' day after the Israelites returned to their homeland from exile.

Pharisaic:

1. **adjective.** emphasizing or observing the letter but not the spirit of religious law; self-righteous; sanctimonious

2. pretending to be highly moral or virtuous without actually being so; hypocritical[1]

*   *   *

Mark 7:6-9, 13 (NIV)- He replied, "Isaiah was right when he prophesied about you hypocrites; as it is written: 'These people honor me with their lips, but their hearts are far from me. They worship me in vain; their teachings are merely human rules.' You have let go of the commands of God and are holding on to human traditions." And he continued, "You have a fine way of setting aside the commands of God in order to observe your own traditions!…Thus you nullify the word of God by your tradition that you have handed down. And you do many things like that."

*   *   *

"Bended knees while you are clothed with pride; heavenly petitions while you are hoarding up treasures upon the earth; holy devotions while you live in the follies of the world; prayers of meekness and charity while your heart is the seat of pride and resentment; hours of prayer while you give up days and years to idle diversions—are as absurd, unacceptable services to God as forms of thanksgiving from a person who lives in repining and discontent. Unless the common course of our lives be according to the common spirit of our prayers, our prayers are so far from being a real or sufficient devotion that they become an empty lip labor or, what is worse, a notorious hypocrisy."

-William Law[2]

THE HYPOCRISY OF THE PHARISEES

BY THE CLOSE OF THE OLD Testament period, the nation of Israel had returned to their homeland after being held in captivity. Jehovah had allowed northern Israel to be exiled by Assyria in 721 B.C.[3] Eventually, Judah was taken into exile by the Babylonians for 70 years.[4] The period between the Old and New Testaments is a duration of four hundred years of prophetic silence. There was no Word from God to His people during this time.

Then John the Baptist appears on the scene and breaks the silence. Israel was ruled by the Roman Empire at this time and Rome stayed in power throughout the life of Jesus. Though the Israelites had returned to their land, they were still under foreign control.

Thinking back on the hypocrisy of Israel and the consequences they faced raises some questions. Did the people of God learn their lesson from the captivity they experienced? Did the discipline they walked through purge them of syncretism and idolatry? One source answers this for us:

In the [New Testament], references to idolatry are understandably few. The Maccabean war resulted in the Jews becoming fanatically opposed to the crass idolatry of [Old Testament] times. The Jews were never again tempted to worship images or gods other than the Lord.[5]

The Jewish community that Jesus was born into was not the same Israel He would have encountered had He been born one thousand years earlier. A transition had taken place in regard to their spiritual lives. The religious leaders of Jesus' day did not need to be told to tear down their wooden idols or to stop worshiping foreign gods. The discipline that God allowed them to experience purged the nation of these practices, but that did not mean that the teachers of the Law, the Pharisees or the Sadducees led pure spiritual lives. A person could smash a wooden idol and still not love the Lord with their whole heart. Someone could cease visiting temple prostitutes and still be completely driven by lust inside. Remember, hypocrisy is always a heart issue.

It is important to realize that the Old Testament often represents the outward life, while the New Testament focuses on the inner life. The Old Testament believers went to an outward temple to worship, but the New Testament says that our bodies are the temple of the Holy Spirit.[6] Jesus took the Old Testament commandments about adultery and murder and applied them to the inner life.[7] When it comes to idolatry, the Old Testament speaks of golden calves, engraved images, Baal altars and Asherah poles. Idolatry in the New Testament moves from outward objects of stone and wood to inward idols of the heart.

Even though the Jews of Jesus' time might have looked night-and-day different from the Old Testament Israelites, the issue of the heart was still the same. That is why they criticized, argued with, tried to discredit, and ultimately murdered the Messiah they were supposed to be waiting for. Jehovah showed up in their midst and yet they plotted against the God they supposedly had devoted their lives to serve. That is a frightening thought.

FOUR: THE HYPOCRISY OF THE PHARISEES

WHO WERE THE PHARISEES?

The Pharisees were a very influential Jewish party during Jesus' time on the Earth. It is important to understand who they were in order to get a clear understanding of what Scripture tells us about them in the New Testament. C.F. Moore writes:

> The Pharisees were a party whose endeavor it was to live in strict accordance with the Law thus interpreted and amplified by the study and exposition of the Scribes, and the tradition of interpretation which they had established, and to bring the people to a similar conformity.[8]

The mission of the Pharisees was to turn the people's focus onto the Law and to teach them how to follow it. Historically, the people of Israel had broken even the most basic commandments by serving idols and foreign gods. So, the Pharisees—working alongside the scribes—were very legalistic about following the Law in an attempt to counteract the lack of obedience to the Lord that had caused them to be exiled in the first place.

With this in mind, it is important to understand that the sect of the Pharisees had good intentions. It is not fair to assume that every Pharisee was wicked, despite the descriptions given in the New Testament. As one source puts it:

> The picture of the Pharisees painted by the [New Testament] is almost entirely negative, but the discriminating Bible student should bear in mind that not everything about every Pharisee was bad. It is perhaps not just to say that all Pharisees were self-righteous and hypocritical. Many Pharisees actually tried to promote true piety. What we know as Pharisaism from the [New Testament] was to some degree a degeneration of Pharisaism.[9]

The Pharisees tend to be the classic example in the Bible of who we should not emulate. Most Christians have the impression that if they were living in Jesus' time, they would have been able to spot the hypocrisy in the lives of the Pharisees easily. However, to the average Jew in that day, the Pharisees were very respectable. Most would have assumed they were very close to the Lord because they said and did all the right things. We also need to realize that there were some Pharisees who were on the right track. Some did love the Lord and honored Jesus, like Nicodemus[10] and Joseph of Arimathea.[11] However, by the time Jesus was walking on the Earth, hypocrisy was the rule in the community of the Pharisees, rather than the exception.

MODERN-DAY PHARISEES

Pharisaism in the negative sense still exists in today's church culture. Jesus refers to hypocrisy as the "yeast of the Pharisees"[12] and warns us to avoid it. So, what might a Pharisee look like today? Modern-day Pharisees would be very involved in church. They would show up every time the doors were opened. They would give their tithes and offerings. They would involve themselves in church activities, such as joining the deacon board, choir, worship team, Sunday school and other ministries. They might even be pastors. They would sing all the worship songs. They would say "Amen" during the sermon. They would be the people others look at and say, "I wish I was more like them. They seem to have it all together." Basically, they would look a lot like genuine believers.

It is easy for us to read the Gospels and point a judgmental finger at the Pharisees because we get Jesus' perspective on the matter. You may have heard it said, "You can fool anyone, but you cannot fool God." Well, the Pharisees found that to be a true statement. They were used to pulling the wool over the eyes of other people. Their religious show was so believable that they thought themselves to be very godly and close to the Lord. That is one of the very deceptive characteristics about this religious, hypocritical spirit. You tend to think that you are who others believe you to be. Nathaniel Hawthorne once said, "No man, for any considerable period, can wear one face to himself and another to the multitude, without finally getting bewildered as to which may be the true."[13]

Jesus called the Pharisees out by exposing the inside world of their hearts. Throughout Jesus' ministry, the Scriptures record that Jesus knew people's thoughts.[14] The Savior did not only see the outside of a man like we do. He did not make His assessments of a person's righteousness based only on the things he or she did or said. If we were part of that community, we would have been shocked at what Jesus spoke about these religious leaders.

In spite of His harsh words, Jesus *always* confronted the Pharisees out of love. He was strong because He needed to be, but He longed for them to repent and follow Him. It was not only out of love for the Pharisees themselves, but also for the people they were leading astray. Jesus understood the end result of dead, dry religion. He saw it as the counterfeit that it was. He was concerned about those who would be deceived by a 'godliness' that went no deeper than the surface. So, out of love, He called them out. And Jesus is still speaking the truth in love to Pharisees today.

THE PHARISEE IN ME

I used to use the Pharisees in my preaching to illustrate religion at its worst. Here was the Son of God coming to Earth to save them from their sins, and they had Him put to death. How could they not see the Messiah when He was right in front of them? How could they remain in hypocrisy after Jesus publicly exposed them?

That made it a pretty hard pill to swallow when God showed me that I was no different than the Pharisees of Jesus' time. When I had read the stories of Jesus' clashes with the Pharisees, I had always pictured myself in the crowd listening to Jesus rebuke them. Then the Holy Spirit showed me that if I had been there—rather than standing in the crowd of people—I would have been standing amongst the Pharisees. It was a tough revelation, but it was necessary for me to see if I was going to get free from hypocrisy.

Just like the Pharisees, I thought I had achieved a high level of spirituality and godliness. God had to open my eyes to show me that it was merely a delusion. It took the Lord's loving correction to help me see the truth. I had to come to grips with the reality that the *real me* was the person I was when no one else was around. It did not matter how intricate a mask

I wore, hiding behind it did not make it a reality in my life. As I studied the Pharisees in the New Testament, the picture of my own heart's condition became painfully clear. As we examine what Jesus said about hypocrisy in the Pharisees' lives, we need to examine our hearts, and ask, "Is Jesus talking to me?"

JESUS' CONTROVERSIAL STATEMENTS

When Jesus confronted the Pharisees and teachers of the Law, He caused quite a stir. It was not only what He said, but who He was speaking to. Can you imagine Jesus standing up against the leaders of your denomination? You would be shocked! You might think, "These are men and women whom I've trusted for years, and you are calling them a brood of vipers?"[15]

In all of the interaction between Jesus and the Pharisees throughout the Gospels, perhaps the most potent conversation is found in Matthew 23. Jesus opens his discourse by explaining that the people were right to follow the Pharisees' instruction. This is because they were teaching the right principles. The problem was that they were not obeying the Law in their hearts. Jesus told the people to do what they say, but not what they do. (v. 3) Like Christian hypocrites, they used all the right words. They could recite Scripture from memory and give counsel, but they were not living it out.

Matthew 23:5 exposes their heart motives: "Everything they do is done for people to see." These were people who cared more about the opinions of men than the opinion of God. Their religion was a mask, which is always worn for others to see. That is why our character is revealed by who we are when no one else is around. The mask comes off when we feel like there is no threat of being discovered.

This is a common characteristic shared by hypocrites today. The whole goal of wearing a spiritual mask is to fool others. Any true Christian knows in their heart that they cannot really fool the Lord with religious charades. If someone had more concern for what God thought about their life, they would get right with Him and lay the mask down—once and for all. Just like the Pharisees, we have to come to grips with the fact that we *like* what others think about us. We enjoy being seen as wise and spiritual, even if it is not the reality of who we are.

THE SEVEN WOES

Jesus continued His discourse by pronouncing seven woes over the Pharisees and scribes. The Greek word for *woe* (*ouai*) is an exclamation of grief.[16] Jesus was deeply grieved over these religious leaders who turned what was supposed to be a relationship between God and man into a long set of rules. Here are each of the woes with a short summary of their meaning.

> **Woe One:** Woe to you, teachers of the law and Pharisees, you hypocrites! You shut the door of the kingdom of heaven in people's faces. You yourselves do not enter, nor will you let those enter who are trying to. (v. 13)

In the first woe, Jesus addressed the fact that the Pharisees were not living out what they said they believed. Not only were they living without a true surrender to the Lord themselves, but as leaders they were stopping the other Jews from getting right with Him. The Pharisees had become a stumbling block to people who were looking to them for spiritual guidance. The nation should have been able to follow them toward Jehovah. Instead, their hypocrisy was actually keeping people from Him.

> **Woe Two:** Woe to you, teachers of the law and Pharisees, you hypocrites! You travel over land and sea to win a single convert, and when you have succeeded, you make them twice as much a child of hell as you are. (v. 15)

Woe two is referring to the fact that the Pharisees were not content living hypocritical lives themselves. Instead, they were very zealous to spread it to others. As each new convert came, they looked to the life of the Pharisees for guidance on how they should live. Part of discipleship was to follow and emulate their leaders. This made them even more deceived and steeped in hypocrisy than the leaders were.

Both of the first two woes dealt with the effects of hypocrisy on other people. As the saying goes: "Misery loves company." Hypocrites like to have other hypocrites around them because it makes them feel more comfortable. True followers of God with genuine faith are a threat to that comfort. As a hypocrite, I always felt uneasy around people who were really on fire for Jesus, because it showed me what I was lacking. Through these woes, Jesus was warning us that hypocrisy is contagious. Just like the Pharisees were leading people down the same path with their lives, hypocrites tend to do the same.

> **Woe Three:** Woe to you, blind guides! You say, "If anyone swears by the temple, it means nothing; but anyone who swears by the gold of the temple is bound by that oath." You blind fools! Which is greater: the gold, or the temple that makes the gold sacred? You also say, "If anyone swears by the altar, it means nothing; but anyone who swears by the gift on the altar is bound by that oath." You blind men! Which is greater: the gift, or the altar that makes the gift sacred? Therefore, anyone who swears by the altar swears by it and by everything on it. And anyone who swears by the temple swears by it and by the one who dwells in it. And anyone who swears by heaven swears by God's throne and by the one who sits on it. (vv. 16-22)

The Pharisees had many traditions handed down that they tried to push onto the people. In the third woe, Jesus talks about the rules they had for swearing by things. The altar and the temple were sacred, yet the Pharisees were treating small things, like the gold in the temple or an offering, as more sacred than the very things established by the Lord. Their rules made no sense. They were trying to use control tactics to put burdens on the backs of the people by majoring on the minors.

> **Woe Four:** Woe to you, teachers of the law and Pharisees, you hypocrites! You give a tenth of your spices—mint, dill and cumin.

But you have neglected the more important matters of the law—justice, mercy and faithfulness. You should have practiced the latter, without neglecting the former. You blind guides! You strain out a gnat but swallow a camel. (vv. 23-24)

Woe four deals with the tithing practices of the Pharisees. Here Jesus really brings out the trust that hypocrites have in outward observances. The Pharisees took the commandment of tithing to an extreme. They paid such close attention to the Law that they even tithed a tenth of the spices they used for cooking. Jesus did not rebuke them for doing this, but reveals that even though they made such an effort to observe every little ritual, they completely neglected major heart issues: justice, mercy and faithfulness.

Jesus basically says, "You make such a big deal about little things, but you neglect the big issues!" I can hear Jesus saying to the hypocrites of our day, "You are faithful to church and you do all the outward activities, but what about purity? What about holiness? What about being genuine? What about love for others? What about a passion for souls?" Like the Pharisees, hypocrites make a big deal about "all the things I am doing right," because those are the things they are trusting in to make them acceptable to God. They focus on the areas that are easy for them, because they do not require true transparency or sacrifice.

Woe Five: Woe to you, teachers of the law and Pharisees, you hypocrites! You clean the outside of the cup and dish, but inside they are full of greed and self-indulgence. Blind Pharisee! First clean the inside of the cup and dish, and then the outside also will be clean. (vv. 25-26)

Woe Six: Woe to you, teachers of the law and Pharisees, you hypocrites! You are like whitewashed tombs, which look beautiful on the outside but on the inside are full of the bones of the dead and everything unclean. In the same way, on the outside you appear to people as righteous but on the inside you are full of hypocrisy and wickedness. (vv. 27-28)

Woes five and six are similar, but instead of talking about what the Pharisees are lacking, Jesus points out what is truly in their hearts. He again refers to what they are doing outwardly. They clean the outside of the cup, making sure their appearance is intact. Just like the Jews would whitewash tombstones once a year, the Pharisees made sure their lives looked beautiful on the outside. However, Jesus could see the greed, self-indulgence, hypocrisy and wickedness in their hearts. When Jesus looks past your outward actions and sees straight into your heart, what does He see? He will either find a heart that is true to Him, or one that is playing religious games.

> **Woe Seven:** Woe to you, teachers of the law and Pharisees, you hypocrites! You build tombs for the prophets and decorate the graves of the righteous. And you say, "If we had lived in the days of our ancestors, we would not have taken part with them in shedding the blood of the prophets." So you testify against yourselves that you are the descendants of those who murdered the prophets. Go ahead, then, and complete what your ancestors started! (vv. 29-32)

The final woe cuts right to the core of a hypocritical spirit. The Pharisees built nice tombs and decorated the graves of the past prophets. In doing this, they were 'honoring' these men of God, but it was all a delusion. They said they would never have killed the prophets like their forefathers did. It was as if they thought they were far too holy for that. The underlying thought was, "We are far more discerning than our forefathers were. We would recognize a true prophet and honor his ministry rather than kill him." Yet in a short time, they were the ones leading the charge to kill the greatest prophet ever sent by God: Jesus.

It is this type of delusion that keeps hypocrites in deep bondage. They have a superior attitude. They look at others and say, "At least I am not like so and so." Yet the hypocrisy in their lives is often far worse than what others may be involved in. Jesus reserved His strongest words in the New Testament for religious hypocrites, because hypocrisy is not a game to the Lord.

THE PHARISEE AND THE TAX COLLECTOR

Other than direct confrontations Jesus had with the Pharisees, He also used parables to reveal their hearts. One of the most powerful parables is about a Pharisee and a tax collector in Luke 18. Luke points out that Jesus was telling this story to "some who were confident of their own righteousness and looked down on everyone else." (v. 9)

Jesus sets the scene like this: Two men come to God. One is a Pharisee and the other is a tax collector. The first is seen as a holy and respectable person in Jewish culture. The other is viewed as a heathen, typically despised by everyone.

The Pharisee comes before God with an impressive prayer. He highlights his own righteousness by comparing himself with the low-life tax collector standing nearby. His prayer was so centered on his own righteousness that Jesus says he was "praying this to himself."[17] God was not even listening. Have you ever spoken with someone that talked so much about himself, it seemed more like a monologue than an actual conversation? That describes the prayer life of this Pharisee.

Jesus is painting a picture here for us. In the Pharisee, we see a person who is so confident in his own righteous effort that he is not conscious of his great need for mercy. His mask has been on so long and so many are fooled by his supposed godliness, he is deceived into believing that his heart is right before God. He is arrogant enough to look down on others who have not achieved his imagined level of holiness.

Then, the scene switches to the tax collector. He approaches God in complete brokenness, not even willing to look up. Contrary to the Pharisee, the tax collector comes to the Lord asking for only one thing: His mercy. As an outcast in Jewish society—and most likely a thief—he feels completely unworthy of the mercy of God. He sees himself for who he truly is and is not comparing himself to anyone else. He is simply looking at himself in light of a holy God. And Jesus says, "This man, rather than the other, went home justified before God." (v. 14)

In telling this parable, Jesus gives us a sneak peek into the hearts of two characters. Both were approaching the Lord, yet the difference of their heart motives could not have been more apparent. We need to ask ourselves, "Which of these characters best resembles my life?"

SIMON THE PHARISEE

Another story that calls attention to the heart of the Pharisaical spirit is found in Luke 7. We are told about a woman who makes an extravagant worship offering to Jesus at Simon the Pharisee's house. The woman walks into the room, breaks open an alabaster box full of expensive perfume and pours it on Jesus' feet. Then she proceeds to wipe it off with her hair. Approaching a Rabbi like this was a bold move for a woman in that culture, especially one with a reputation like she had. She was a "sinner." Her life was a mess. In today's society, she might represent a prostitute, drug addict, murderer, rapist—fill in the blank. She was a woman of ill repute.

The reaction of Simon gives us insight into the heart of the Pharisee. Scripture records:

> When the Pharisee who had invited [Jesus] saw this, he said to himself, "If this man were a prophet, he would know who is touching him and what kind of woman she is—that she is a sinner."
> (v. 39)

Simon is basically building a case against Jesus in his heart. His underlying thought process was: "Holy men stay away from sinful people. Therefore, Jesus must not really be holy—or He is just ignorant." Simon looked down on this woman from his great pedestal of self-righteousness. He thought, "I would never let her touch me if I was in Jesus' place." Unknowingly, he was passing judgment on God Himself and accusing Him of doing something wrong. Can you imagine the audacity?

In Jewish culture, foot washing was a customary practice. When a guest entered someone's house, their feet would be washed by the homeowner or a servant. This was a common courtesy for people who had traveled with sandals through rough terrain. Guests were also greeted with a kiss. Jesus points out to Simon that he had done neither of these socially expected customs of his day when Jesus arrived. Yet this woman had gone way over and above the customs of that day in her gesture of worship.

Then Jesus—in His meek and lowly way—reveals to Simon that he has a problem with his heart. The Pharisee had his focus on everybody else. He was pointing the finger at Jesus and looking down upon this woman. Jesus wanted to expose Simon's Pharisaical heart in the situation.

Jesus explains the motive behind the woman's extravagant love and the Pharisee's lack of attention to his guest. In verse 47, He says, "Therefore, I tell you, her many sins have been forgiven—as her great love has shown. But whoever has been forgiven little loves little." I do not think Jesus is saying that this woman's sin was greater in magnitude than the Pharisee's, although Simon certainly thought it was. What Jesus is explaining is that the person who *realizes* their sin, and how much they have been forgiven, will love more than the one who does not see it. Jesus had to go to the cross for all sin. The just punishment for even the littlest 'white lie' is still eternity in Hell. There is no sin that does not separate men from a holy God.

This sinful woman did not somehow deserve punishment more than Simon. She just saw her sin more clearly in light of God's mercy. Jesus was trying to show this self-righteous Pharisee that he was completely missing his great need to be forgiven, and instead was looking down on everyone else.

Looking back, I can see how this Pharisaical spirit played out in my own life. In my hypocrisy—even in the midst of blatant and intentional sin—I would look at other Christians around me and could easily spot their faults. It made me feel better to point out their imperfections rather than to admit my own. I had a plank in my own eye, but was quick to look at the speck in theirs.[18] I had the attitude of Simon: "At least I am not like so and so! Look at what they are doing. And they call themselves Christians?"

Yet, in private, the things I was involved in were far more depraved than what I saw in other people's lives. Wearing a religious mask is deceptive. Somehow, I thought my secret sin was less offensive to God than a Christian compromising out in the open. The Lord had to show me that what I was doing was far worse because I was pretending to be someone I was not. Others may have done things that were not right, but at least they were not trying to hide them. I was in sin—*knowing* fully how wrong it was—and even went to great lengths to keep it hidden from the public eye. I was truly a Pharisee.

SINCERELY WRONG

Once again, we need to realize that many Pharisees were sincerely trying to please God with their outward religiosity. Before the Apostle Paul had his experience on the Damascus road, he was a persecutor of the church named Saul. In his own words, he was:

> ...circumcised on the eighth day, of the people of Israel, of the tribe of Benjamin, a Hebrew of Hebrews; in regard to the law, a Pharisee; as for zeal, persecuting the church; as for righteousness based on the law, faultless. (Philippians 3:5-6)

Saul was a great Pharisee. He was well respected for his zeal. He was very sincere in what he did—but he was sincerely wrong. Think about it, he was actually working directly against what the Lord was trying to do on the Earth. He was an enemy of God's people, and therefore an enemy of God. The whole time he was deceived into thinking that he was doing Jehovah's business, yet the devil had him as his pawn.

My sincerity was part of the reason it was so hard for me to realize that I too had become a Pharisee. I was as sincere as I knew how to be in worship. I tried to pray and read the Bible. In my own eyes, I was a sincere Christian—but I was deceived.

As we have seen in this chapter, the Pharisaical spirit is a lot like many Christians in hypocrisy. They both hide behind spiritual masks and put up a great façade. However, in today's church culture it is much easier to appear spiritual than it was for a Pharisee. All that a Christian hypocrite needs to do to blend in with today's crowd is attend church occasionally, know how to speak some Christian words and sing some worship songs. In the next chapter, we are going to examine today's church culture and see how and why hypocrisy is still thriving in our day.

Hypocrite:

1. **noun.** a person who pretends to be what he or she is not; one who pretends to be better than is really so, or to be pious, virtuous, etc. without really being so.[1]

*   *   *

Matthew 24:12 (NIV)- Because of the increase of wickedness, the love of most will grow cold...

II Peter 2:1-2 (NIV)- But there were also false prophets among the people, just as there will be false teachers among you. They will secretly introduce destructive heresies, even denying the sovereign Lord who bought them...

II Timothy 4:3 (PHP)- For the time is coming when men will not tolerate wholesome teaching. They will want something to tickle their own fancies, and they will collect teachers who will speak what they want to hear.

*   *   *

"The Church is filled with hypocrites because people were never made to see that they must make an *entire consecration* of everything to Christ. All their time, all their talents, and all their influence must be given or they will never get to heaven...When they die, instead of finding heaven at the end of the path they are pursuing, they will find hell."

-Charles Finney[2]

5

HYPOCRISY IN TODAY'S CHURCH

WE HAVE LOOKED IN-DEPTH AT HYPOCRISY in the lives of the Israelites in the Old Testament, and we have also encountered the double-minded Pharisees of Jesus' time. Now, I want to build a bridge to modern-day Christianity. Though we have seen some of the similarities that modern hypocrites have with the Israelites and Pharisees, there are many differences as well. Neither the Israelites nor the Pharisees were born again believers, or even had a full knowledge of the New Covenant. The lifestyle of a Christian hypocrite may manifest differently on the outside, yet the root issue is the same. The aim of this chapter is to bring to focus the climate of our church culture and examine false teachings that make it easier for a hypocrite to stay comfortable living a double-life.

IN-BETWEEN CHRISTIANITY

As a whole, the modern church in the West has grown extremely weak. There are some highly successful churches with big buildings and many attendees, but most churches are lacking spiritual power. I believe this is due to the fact that many professing Christians attempt to live between two extremes.

One extreme contains people who have completely walked away from the faith and are in a backslidden condition. It is obvious that they are not living for Jesus and they make no real attempt to hide it. The other extreme is a group that includes completely sold-out believers, who have fully consecrated their lives to Jesus. They are not perfect, but they are willing to obey the Lord in every area. They repent, when needed, to remain in communion with Him. This is the true church of Jesus Christ. They can be found everywhere around the world, in all cultures and in every denomination.

However, most of the people in our modern-day churches are floating somewhere in-between these two extremes. Yet they still believe they are truly walking with God. The problem with this kind of thinking is that it is based on a deception that there is some kind of Christianity that can exist between the two extremes. You will have a difficult time trying to find an 'in-between faith' anywhere in Scripture. That is because a faith that is not red-hot for the Lord is not faith at all. Yet our modern churches are full of people living in this lukewarm state. The commonality of it only aids its growth because it is no longer uncommon to be a wishy-washy Christian.

True believers are often labeled as fanatics in popular church culture. But is it not true that all the men and women of faith in the Bible and church history looked like fanatics to those in their time? Some of those in closest communion with Christ—some of those most consumed with the Spirit of God—were brutally murdered by the so-called 'church' of their day. Would it not be safe to assume that any one of these would be labeled as fanatics in our society? They certainly did not model for us a middle-of-the-road Christian walk.

DEFINING BACKSLIDDEN

I want to submit to you that people living in-between these two extremes are already backslidden and do not even know it. Imagine you are climbing up a mountain and are already at the peak. Suddenly your foot slips and you lose some ground. You would have to admit that you had slid back from where you were, even if it was only a short distance. If someone slipped halfway down a mountain, they would be a fool to say, "I have not really backslidden because I am not all the way down at the bottom." Certainly they have not hit the bottom of the mountain, but they are not at the top either. You would tell that person, "You are denying the truth, you have slid back halfway."

Yet this is how we often talk about backsliding in the faith. Let us say this mountain represents our walk with Jesus. The top of the mountain symbolizes being totally sold-out to Him. The bottom of the mountain represents totally forsaking Him. Sometimes a Christian who is closer to the top begins to get comfortable. They find themselves slowly slipping down. Even if they slide halfway to the bottom, they will often say, "I am not backslidden." They picture a backslidden state as being involved in some gross sin at the bottom of the mountain. They refuse to admit that they may be closer to that point than the top.

The word *backslide* can be defined as, "to lapse back into a less desirable condition."[3] Another source says it is "to slide backward in morals or religious enthusiasm; become less virtuous, less pious."[4] So you can see, to be backslidden simply means we are not where God wants us to be.

Now, I firmly believe that at some point as you slide down the mountain, you cease to be walking with the Lord and are in great danger. Only He knows at what point that occurs, but a sincere believer would not be trying to find out. That seems to be the lifestyle of many in our churches. They endeavor to see how close they can get to the world without really "being of it." There is a point of no return. God's will is for all to move toward the top and stay there, and it happens only through repentance and intimacy with Him.

HELL IN OUR CHURCHES

I used to cringe when I heard unbelievers criticize the church by saying, "The church is full of hypocrites." I always viewed that as a classic cop-out to not go to church, since this is often the excuse people use to never go. However, I was thinking about that in a church service and I felt like the Holy Spirit whispered to me, "They are not wrong." I was stunned. I think the average Christian in America views their church as a majority of sincere believers and a few unbelievers that come from time to time. Everyone seems to be excited about God.

But I have to say, I do not think the Lord sees it that way. In fact, having been on both sides myself, I would say hypocrisy is one of the greatest threats to Christianity today. After hearing those words in my spirit, my thoughts went immediately to Jesus' parable of the wicked servant in Matthew 24. He sums it up by saying, "He will cut him to pieces and assign him a place with the hypocrites, where there will be weeping and gnashing of teeth." (v. 51) It is interesting that Jesus calls Hell a place where hypocrites are.

Could it be that, through hypocrisy, the devil has found a way into our churches? Rather than through demon-possessed men joining a church to try to destroy it, could it be that the enemy is having more success entering through the compromised hearts of professing believers? Could it be that in these last days the enemy is now taking a different approach to render the church powerless?

FALSE TEACHINGS THAT ENCOURAGE HYPOCRISY

The enemy loves to introduce false doctrines into the Christian culture to try to deceive people. He uses truth and distorts it just enough that people will believe it. Heresy is dangerous, and if left undetected and unchallenged, it can become a stumbling block to true faith. As the Apostle Paul told the Corinthian church, "But I am afraid that just as Eve was deceived by the serpent's cunning, your minds may somehow be led astray from your sincere and pure devotion to Christ."[5]

I believe we have a Christian culture that has been deceived by subtle lies. And the evidence of this is the carnality running rampant in our churches. These lies have created an extremely comfortable atmosphere for people to fall into hypocrisy and remain there.

It is time to stand up and begin to engage the enemy in this spiritual battle. The best weapon to combat a lie is the truth. In the remainder of this chapter, we will cover three primary attacks on biblical faith that have gained traction in our day. Although much could be said about each, my intention here is to show how the enemy is using false doctrines, distorted teachings and imbalanced theology in our churches to keep hypocrites comfortable in their hypocrisy.

FALSE TEACHING #1:

A MISREPRESENTATION OF SALVATION

When I first entered the residential program at Pure Life Ministries, we watched a sermon preached by Steve Hill, the evangelist who led the Brownsville Revival in the 1990s. I heard him say something that sounded radical. He basically said that if a Christian was not passionately in love with Jesus, he would question their salvation.

I will admit those words seemed too harsh the first time I heard them. Could it really be true? If so, that would call into question the salvation of so many people in churches. However, just because we do not hear that message spoken from many pulpits or written in popular Christian books, does that mean we should dismiss it as fanatical? It is my deep conviction now—on the other side of hypocrisy—that these words are absolutely true.

The enemy has crept into our church culture and has dulled people's understanding of biblical salvation. In today's spiritual climate, the truth sounds too harsh because church leaders have softened the message in an effort to make the Gospel more appealing.

THE 'ONCE SAVED, ALWAYS SAVED' DOCTRINE

One of the popular, unbiblical teachings in the church world today is known as the 'Once Saved, Always Saved' doctrine. It basically teaches that anyone who has ever made any commitment to Christ in their life is guaranteed salvation forever. One advocate of this teaching describes it this way:

> The Bible clearly teaches that God's love for His people is of such magnitude that *even those who walk away from the faith* have not the slightest chance of slipping from His hand.[6]

> Even if a believer for *all practical purposes becomes an unbeliever*, his salvation is not in jeopardy.[7] *(emphasis added)*

This view sure sounds nice. It is certainly convenient for anyone who is backslidden or who claims to be saved but never produces fruit. But I cannot see these words coming from the mouths of Jesus, Paul, Peter or any of the other New Testament writers. I simply *cannot* find this type of teaching in Scripture. I see many warnings about falling away, admonitions to bear fruit and commands to examine our faith and sincerity, but no comfort offered to anyone whose salvation is questionable.

The 'Once Saved, Always Saved' teaching is based on Scriptures that are true for sincere believers. The problem comes when you apply them to anyone who claims to be a Christian or to have ever been a Christian. I am not against a biblical approach to eternal security, in the sense that a believer can be sure that they are saved, as long as there is evidence in their life. I also do not believe the Lord is in favor of a true believer being made to fear that at any moment they can somehow lose their salvation or step out of grace. However, the Bible never says that God wants to offer the same assurance and security to those who have pushed Him out of their lives, even if that rejection has only happened in their hearts.

CALVIN AND ARMINIUS

The doctrine of eternal security is a debate that has been going on for ages. I do not pretend to have all of the answers. However, I do believe it is crucial—*especially* in the life of a lukewarm Christian—to take a look at the Scriptures used to support both sides and seriously consider what the Bible actually teaches. To really examine what God says—rather than just believing what man teaches—is exercising wisdom. To ignore the issue completely could be detrimental to one's soul.

The two main schools of thought when it comes to the permanence of salvation are Calvinism and Arminianism. Before I touch on this, I want to make a couple of points. First, it is important to realize there are strong arguments on both sides. You cannot just cherry-pick one Scripture and develop an entire doctrine on it. That is called proof-texting and it shows a great lack of discernment when people do it. Horrible heresies that have led many astray have come from pulling Scriptures out of the context of the whole Bible.

Second, there is no easy answer to this complex issue. That is why it has been debated for so long. I think that anyone who says, "This is the side that is right. Here are Scriptures to prove it and I refuse to listen to any other opinion," is unwise. Even with a strong Calvinistic or Arminian theology, an honest look at Scripture will show that only the Lord truly knows the answers to these questions. However, most church people have not really attempted to discover for themselves what the Bible teaches. Like Paris Reidhead once said: "Most people don't know what Calvin taught or Arminius taught, they just have been conditioned to know which word to get mad at."[8]

Our purpose here is not to argue one viewpoint against the other. Instead I want to prove that whether you agree more with John Calvin or Joseph Arminius and their views on eternal security, the modern-day teaching of 'Once Saved, Always Saved' is not supported in Scripture at all.

'Once Saved, Always Saved' is often referred to as *moderate* Calvinism. However, this popular teaching is not *true* Calvinism. I think John Calvin would roll over in his grave to hear what people are teaching and crediting to his name. Contrary to popular belief, Calvinism and Arminianism are not two sides of the theological fence. People refer to them as if they are polar opposites. However, the two theological viewpoints are actually saying the same thing on a practical level.

Let me explain. John Calvin was a follower of Christ with a great understanding of Scripture. He understood what the Bible teaches about looking for spiritual fruit. What he actually taught was that if you are genuinely converted, there has to be evidence of it in your life. He taught that true conversion was an irreversible decision on the Lord's part. Calvin believed that all true Christians had been predestined to become a part of God's elect. He taught that the moment you are converted, your salvation is eternally secure. So, there would be no way for a true Christian to ever go back into habitual sin and fall away. That is not an option in Calvin's teachings.

Joseph Arminius was also a godly man who studied the Word of God. He agreed with Calvin that if you were truly saved, your life would have spiritual fruit as evidence. The major point they differed on—in regards to the permanence of salvation—is that Arminius believed that a person could fall so far away from God that they could 'lose' or 'reject' their salvation. He believed that humans had more free will in cooperating with God in salvation than Calvin did.[9]

John Calvin never taught that someone could pray a sincere prayer, try to live for the Lord, grow cold and fruitless, and yet still be accepted into Heaven. This is a teaching that has led many people into a false confidence under the guise of 'eternal security.' Likewise, the Arminians never taught that a Christian needed to live in constant fear that if they sin, they will be condemned to Hell. There are people who have taken it to that extreme and taught it this way, but that is not the original intention.

To the professing Christian living a fruitless life, without a sincere (undivided) devotion to Christ, Calvinism would have this to say. According to Calvin's interpretation of Scripture, the lack of fruit is in itself *proof* that the person was never truly converted. The Arminians would say to the same person that the lack of fruit is evidence that they either were never saved in the first place, or they are backslidden and in danger of losing (or rejecting) their salvation. The end result on either side of the eternal security doctrinal stance is the same. Either that person needs to repent (and either return to Christ or be saved) or they are in danger of Hell. As Norman Geisler explains:

> Ironically, Arminians and strong Calvinists have much in common on this issue. Both assert that professing believers living in gross, unrepentant sin are not truly saved. Both insist that a person cannot be living in serious sin at the end of his life if he is truly saved. And both maintain that no one living in grave sin can be sure of his salvation.[10]

Regardless of which view you choose to adopt as your own conviction, there is one important point I want to make. If you are reading this book and you have no evidence of true spiritual life on a *daily* basis, you had better throw yourself before the Lord and repent. Plead for His mercy and ask Him to change your heart. He wants to extend mercy to you.

EVIDENCE OF SALVATION

Scripture talks about remembering the Lord's works and what He has done in the past. The Bible also clearly teaches that the way to be sure of our salvation is to look for fruit *now*. Examining your life for evidence of true faith is a present-tense work. We are not told, "Think back to the day you were saved for proof." As one source states, "To assume we possess eternal life based solely on a past experience or on a faith that is no longer vital is a grave error."[11]

Salvation is not a one-time event, but an entrance into a life of devotion and obedience to God. We should be in the process of being sanctified by the Holy Spirit as we grow deeper in love with Him. We are commanded in Scripture: "Examine yourselves to see whether you are in the faith; test yourselves."[12] It is crucial that we honestly evaluate our lives to ensure that we are walking with the Lord.

When I was sinking deeper into sin, I tried to comfort myself with the message of 'Once Saved, Always Saved,' because it was a very convenient belief system. It was the only way I could keep my sin and still believe I was saved. In spite of this, I still preached about the possibility of walking away from the faith. I could not escape the fact that the Bible contains clear warnings of falling away from God. I was totally double-minded, holding to a doctrine for comfort that I did not even believe could be proven with Scripture.

When I found myself in bondage to sin, I made some mistakes in my judgment about my spiritual condition. One of them involved this issue of looking only in the past for evidence of salvation. This is what I was taught early on in my Christian walk. I was told whenever I was struggling in my faith to look back to the day Jesus saved me and hold onto that assurance. Even in a completely backslidden state, my thinking always was, "I know I got saved in Teen Challenge in August 2002. I know God changed my life and I walked with Him. So, I must be a believer who is just going through a hard time."

This is not to say having a born again experience is not part of the equation at all. But if 'Once Saved, Always Saved' is true, this would be all the evidence that is needed. Do not misunderstand, if someone cannot look back to a specific time they were born again, then they need to go no further. They should repent of sin and ask Christ to forgive them and make Him Lord now. However, for those who can remember getting saved and having a relationship with Jesus, looking back alone is not enough.

CHRISTIAN SERVICE IS NOT NECESSARILY SPIRITUAL FRUIT

Another mistake I made was to adhere to a faulty definition of spiritual fruit. I realized that Scripture taught that there should be evidence in our lives to show we are saved. To some degree, I did search for fruit, but the fruit I looked for was not a true indicator of my spiritual state. I made the mistake many make of viewing service to God as spiritual fruit. I told myself, "The Lord is using my ministry and I am faithful to church. Look at everything I'm doing for Him." Serving God is important, but someone who is not even born again could do what I had been doing.

If we are not careful, we can fall into this trap. Many think that all the outward church activities they are involved in prove they are saved. These things have no saving value and are not evidence of salvation. Though we believe we are not saved by works, often when a believer backslides, this is the justification he uses. If you ask them how they know they are Christians, they would be quick to list what they *do* rather than who they *are*. The difference between the two is incredibly important. The kind of fruit that we should be looking for is in our character and walk with the Lord. The remainder of this book will be discussing those areas.

ASSURANCE OF SALVATION

When it comes to eternity, we need to realize that only the Lord truly has all the answers. If He wanted us to know *exactly* how it all works, He would have stated it more clearly for us in His Word. We need to understand that Scripture—as a whole—does provide security in salvation to those who live righteously, walk in the Spirit and fear the Lord. We *can* be sure of our salvation. If you take one side of the argument and build a doctrine, even a sincere follower of Christ might fear losing their salvation every time they sin. Scripture does not place that burden on the backs of God's children.

Yet, Scripture as a whole *does not* reassure a Christian in a backslidden state. In no way does it say that because a person had some kind of spiritual experience, that they are guaranteed to be walking with Jesus. If you take the other side of the argument out of context, you can reassure someone right into their sin, and they can die and go to Hell believing everything is right between them and God. Hell is full of people who were deceived to think they were truly saved.

What type of place would Heaven be if it freely accepted people who have rejected God in their hearts, but continue to display an image of godliness to the world around them? James 4:4 tells us that friends of the world are enemies of God, and certainly Heaven is no place for the Lord's enemies.

FALSE TEACHING #2:
DISTORTING THE CONCEPT OF GRACE

In the book of Jude, we are given a strong warning about false teachings in the church. Jude wrote this:

> For certain individuals whose condemnation was written about long ago have secretly slipped in among you. They are ungodly people, who pervert the grace of our God into a license for immorality and deny Jesus Christ our only Sovereign and Lord. (v. 4)

This Scripture is a warning to the church that we need to reject any teaching that seems to provide a license for Christians to indulge in sin without consequence. In many Christian circles, sin runs rampant and goes unchallenged for the most part because of a distortion in the teaching about grace.

When it comes to sin in the life of a believer, many Christians rely heavily on I John 1:9. It says, "If we confess our sins, he is faithful and just and will forgive us our sins and purify us from all unrighteousness." This verse is true and God is gracious and forgives. However, many Christians use this as a license to sin. They assume they can keep on sinning as long as they ask forgiveness each time.

Yet the same writer who wrote this verse said in 2:1: "My dear children, I write this to you so that you will not sin." John goes on to say, "But *if* anybody does sin, we have an advocate with the Father—Jesus Christ, the Righteous One." *(emphasis added)* Scripture refers to sin as a possibility, not an expectation.

I am not suggesting that we can achieve moral perfection in this life, but the Lord's will is that we live a life *without* sin. Sin in the life of a believer should be the exception—not the rule. In his book *Extraordinary*, John Bevere says:

> ...it is important that I warn you to avoid presumptuous sinning.
> If you say within, "I'm saved by grace, so I'm covered no matter

what my lifestyle. I'm going to forget self-control and live for pleasure," stop! That's dangerous ground. You are deceived! Don't be offended, but you need to ask yourself, "Am I even saved?"[13]

THE DANGER OF DISTORTING THE GRACE OF GOD

David Wilkerson hits this truth home with a strong warning in his message *Turning the Grace of God Into Lasciviousness*:

Satan sells his lie by persuading Christians that grace is simply a never-ending river of forgiveness. He whispers to us, "You can keep going back to your sin, as long as you keep coming back to the altar...Surely your loving Savior will forgive you...As long as you have a repentant heart and keep mourning over your sin, you'll be okay. You can indulge your lust a thousand times and He'll freely forgive you every time." This sounds so close to the truth. Indeed, there is no end to God's forgiveness for those who come to Him with a truly repentant heart. So, this statement truly is ninety-five percent gospel. However, the other five percent is pure poison. And it will eventually destroy your soul.[14]

Many Christians do not believe it is possible to live a life free from the power of sin. But what does Romans 6:2 mean when it says, "We are those who have died to sin; how can we live in it any longer?" Although Christians may sin at times, living in continual sin is completely contrary to the New Testament teaching on the Christian life.

II Peter 1:3 says that God has given us "everything we need for a godly life." In my past Christian experience, I just assumed I was a slave to the power of sin. I believed it was a problem I had to live with. My Christian life was much more about managing my sin than living in victory over it. I gave myself so much slack believing in this false sense of grace that I allowed sinful habits to cause me to completely backslide.

Whenever I would sin, I would tell myself, "Jesus died to forgive my sins from the past, present and future. I cannot beat myself up, I just have to keep pressing on." I would cry out to the Lord to forgive me and things would be good for a period of time. However, when pressure and temptation came back, I would find myself going around the mountain again.

It was a vicious cycle and I detested it. I was living anything but a victorious Christian life. I even went as far to say that Paul's thorn in the flesh was probably a similar sin to mine, and I found comfort in Romans 7. I figured Paul was in the same predicament as I was when he described doing things he did not want to do. But now I have come to realize that in Romans 7, Paul is talking about life outside of Christ—trying to obey the Law. Chapters 6 and 8 are showing what life in Christ should look like free from sin. Romans 7 is not the confession of a habitual sinner, although this is how many have tried to interpret it.

Because of my experience, I assumed the best I could do was put on a mask. I figured I could at least make others believe that I was walking in freedom. Somehow that made me feel as if my secret sin was not so bad. This is a common scenario for many hypocrites.

Once again, I am not saying any of us will ever achieve sinless perfection in this life. God knew before He created us that He would have to rescue mankind from sin. The Lord never expected that any of us would be able to live a sinless life. However, I am saying that a true believer will strive to attain it. Jesus did die for all the sins of the world. He died for our sins even before we commit them, but too many Christians distort this truth into a license to sin. The thinking is, "I am going to sin again, but since all sin is already covered by the blood, I'll just ask forgiveness again." This is not what the Bible teaches at all about sin. The Bible is clear: *Get rid of all the sin in your life!*

I am not trying to downplay the struggle against the flesh. All believers have to learn to fight this battle. I am saying that we can actually learn to die to sin. In the past, my flesh was in control. I tried to conquer my sin in my own strength, but deceived myself into believing that I was fighting spiritually. All of that has changed because of the power of grace in my life.

THE POWER OF GRACE

In Titus 2:11-12, the Apostle Paul writes:

For the grace of God has appeared that offers salvation to all people. It teaches us to say "No" to ungodliness and worldly passions, and to live self-controlled, upright and godly lives in this present age…

This passage clearly tells us that grace actually empowers us to live godly lives. Anyone who treats grace as a license to sin often and be automatically forgiven is missing this essential truth. Bevere writes:

Many in the church today view grace as "The Big Cover-Up" because of the way it has been taught and misunderstood. What do I mean by "Big Cover-Up"? Have you ever heard someone say, "I know I'm not living the way I should, but thank God for His grace!" This is completely contrary to what the New Testament teaches about *grace*. Yes, grace does cover, but in addition to that it is the divine influence on our heart with the reflection of its power in our life. It gives you the ability to live in *truth*.[15]

It would be cruel of God to expect us to live a life of holiness and self-control if He did not give us the ability to do it. It is His grace that gives us that power. Many in the church, however, have watered down the truth about grace and given hypocrites a false sense of comfort in their sin.

FALSE TEACHING #3:
A MISUNDERSTANDING OF GOD'S CHARACTER

Another widespread issue in the modern church has been an imbalanced teaching about the character of God. Much of the popular teaching about the Lord's character is based on *some* truth about who He is. However, by de-emphasizing other aspects of His character, we have created a very unbalanced view of the Lord. I thought I knew Him well even at the peak of hypocrisy. It was not until I repented and really gave my life completely to Him, that I realized I had some serious misconceptions about His personality.

Imagine you have to appear before a judge for committing murder. Before your court date, several people tell you, "This judge has let five murderers go without any penalty this year." You might go into the courtroom with a preconceived notion that you will be dealing with a judge who extends mercy. You might have the attitude, "I'll just state my case and I have a good chance of being let off." You might not even give your defense much thought. You would probably approach the judge with some confidence, expecting him to be kind and compassionate.

The problem is that you do not have all of the facts. In reality, this judge has taken 500 homicide cases in that year and 495 of them served the maximum sentence. He has a reputation of being swift and severe. You would certainly be in for a shock at the outcome if you were served a harsh sentence. You would have approached things much differently and prepared for the worst had you been given the full story. This is because having only *some* facts about someone does not necessarily give you a true picture of their character.

Now, the courtroom illustration is flawed in the sense that, unlike the judge, the Lord really is incredibly merciful. He is willing to let one hundred percent of the cases go free if they ask for mercy! But the point of this illustration remains true and it describes the way many Christians treat God. They zoom in on one aspect of His character and ignore all the rest. Then, they get frustrated when He does not do things the way they think He should.

This illustration is similar to the modern-day teaching about God. It is true that His love, forgiveness, grace and mercy should draw men to Him. However, His wrath, righteousness and justice should cause men to fear Him. Paul Washer talks about this distorted view in his sermon, *10 Indictments Against the Church*:

> Sunday morning is the greatest hour of idolatry in the entire week
> of America because people are not worshiping the one true God—
> the great mass at least—but are worshiping a god formed out of

their own hearts by their own flesh, satanic devices and worldly intelligence. They have made a god just like themselves and he looks more like Santa Claus than he does Yahweh.[16]

It is so vital that we do not become deceived in this area. Satan will do anything to destroy a true understanding of who the Lord is. It is necessary for us as believers to know the God of the Bible. While we cannot go into an extensive discussion about this topic, we need to clarify a few areas that have caused multitudes of people to see a distorted version of the Lord.

IS GOD DIFFERENT IN THE TWO TESTAMENTS?

Many Christians treat the Bible as if the writing of the New Testament made the Old Testament illegitimate. They focus on the aspects of God we see more clearly in the New Testament and reject those that seem to be more prevalent in the Old. The thinking goes something like this: "Thank God I am under the New Covenant. The God of the Old Testament was so harsh and angry!"

It is true that the Old and New Covenants are totally different. In the Old Covenant, the nation of Israel was totally bound by the Law. The New Covenant has made the grace of God available to the world. We should be glad that we are living under the New Covenant. However, to say that the Lord has somehow changed is inconsistent with Scripture.

I can understand where this thinking originates. There are many stories in the Old Testament about Jehovah destroying nations, including women and children. We are told about rebellious people being swallowed up by the Earth and others being consumed by fire.[17] In contrast, Jesus is a clear depiction of a gentle and loving God. He seems to be vastly different from the 'God of the Old Testament.'

But we must learn to see how much love and compassion the Lord shows in the Old Testament and how much wrath the 'New Testament God' displays. Hebrews 13:8 says Jesus Christ (who is God) "is the same yesterday and today and forever." From the foundations of the world, He has never changed and never will.

LOVE AND WRATH CO-EXIST

Atheist Richard Dawkins uses the "cruel Old Testament God" argument against Christianity. He claims that the Old Testament God could not be a God of love. He cites passages in the Old Testament to try to prove his case. He states:

> What makes my jaw drop is that people today should base their lives on such an appalling role model as Yahweh—and even worse, that they should bossily try to force the same evil monster (whether fact or fiction) on the rest of us.[18]

When you take Scriptures out of the context of the whole Bible, a compelling argument can be made that God is not really good. Unfortunately, the general consensus of many in the church is not far off from this. Many think the God of the Old Testament was wicked and cruel and could not be a loving God.

Part of the problem is that many do not realize what wrath is. The Lord is a God of mercy. His will is *always* to grant mercy to people and He is always extending it. But because of His justice, He *has* to deal with sin. It is not that He wants to judge people. He was grieved over the people He destroyed in the Old Testament, because He loved them. He does not enjoy judgment—as if He is a murderous tyrant—but mercy rejected leaves no other alternative. Perhaps one of the most frightening aspects of God is His love. As Jack Deere says:

> Wrath is God's steady, controlled hatred against sin...When the Trinity decided to create the earth, they were committed to the death of the Son...that is due to His wrath against sin and His love for humanity, so both are true...You cannot have a real love without a hatred of sin.[19]

Wrath is a necessary outflow of the love of God. However, what has occurred in our day is a shift in thinking. Nowadays, 'Hell, fire and brimstone' preachers are painted in a negative light. People have rejected those 'old-fashioned preachers,' and have instead turned to those who will preach about the God they want to believe in. Granted, there may have been an imbalance in teaching about judgment and wrath. Many preachers may have painted the Lord in a bad light, because they do not understand that wrath comes from love. But as in so many other areas, the church has gone to the opposite extreme, rather than just balancing out its teaching.

Christians are being taught—in a very subtle way—to focus on the aspects of God that are seen as more positive (love, grace, forgiveness) and to ignore those parts of His character that are supposedly displayed only in the Old Testament (judgment, wrath, anger). What is being presented is an incredibly shallow view of Him. It is a safe, powerless God who does not get angry. In fact, it is not God at all.

Now, before you totally write me off, let me give you a couple of examples from the New Testament to prove my point. The first is Jesus clearing out the temple. This story is hard for some to understand, because they cannot see Jesus getting angry with people. Yet, Jesus actually makes a whip and forces people out of the temple in zealous anger.[20] Many people would rather see Him sitting under a tree holding children or healing people, but there was more to Jesus than that. Jesus' love for His Father caused a righteous anger to rise up when He saw His Father's house being abused.

A second example is found in Acts 5 in the story about Ananias and Sapphira being struck dead. Let us pretend the same two people are living in our time. In many Christian circles, they would be taught about a God who is different now because of Jesus' death on the cross. "He is not like we read in the Old Testament. Now, He is full of only love and grace." They probably would not think it was any big deal to lie to the Holy Spirit. And yet, when Ananias and Sapphira tried to pull the wool over the early church's eyes, they came into a contact with a God who *judged* them fiercely and swiftly, taking their lives.

Did the God of the Old Testament make one last appearance in Acts before turning into a God of only love and grace? If this is what you are thinking, I dare you to read the book of Revelation and see what this 'only loving-never judging' God allows to happen to people like you and I on the Earth.

Now, let me reiterate that God is love.[21] However, the concept of a God of love that is often portrayed today is not true love. Because God poured His wrath out on the cross, forgiveness is available to all of us. God chose to judge Ananias and Sapphira. Obviously, He is not smiting every person who lies in the church, or we would be seeing casualties every week. But God does choose to judge according to His perfect wisdom.

The Lord is able to judge and still be full of love and mercy. He is also able to give grace and mercy freely without overriding His place as Judge of the Earth. Love and wrath are not mutually exclusive, but actually co-exist in the character of our Creator. And we see this correlation most clearly in the death of His Son.

LOVE AND JUSTICE DISPLAYED AT THE CROSS

The classic argument against the existence of the God of the Bible is, "If God is so good, how could He send people to Hell?" There is a fallacy in this statement. The truth is that God allows people to choose their eternal destination. Scripture informs us that the Lord did not even create Hell for people.[22] A true understanding of the justice of God should make us ask, "If He is so just, how could He not send *everyone* to Hell?" After all, the Bible teaches that we have all sinned and turned away from God.[23] We were all once His enemies and therefore, none are worthy to spend eternity with Him unless He makes us worthy. That is the scandal of grace. We receive His righteousness and do not even deserve it!

To understand who the Lord truly is and what love looks like, the only place to look is to the cross. There can be no questioning the love or goodness of God when looking to Calvary where He sent His innocent Son to be tortured and left to die. This happened for no other reason than to save fallen humanity.

One cannot question the justice of God while looking toward the cross either. The perfect wrath of God was poured out on Jesus there. God's nature cannot change. He does not pardon sin without penalty. That penalty was paid at His Son's expense. The Lord's forgiveness for sin—made possible at the cross—must be accepted. Otherwise, everyone would automatically receive eternal life whether they wanted it or not.

LACK OF A TRUE KNOWLEDGE OF GOD

If you asked me about the President of the United States, I could say, "I know who he is." I could tell you quite a bit about his family, what he looks like, his beliefs and where he lives. Imagine if I bumped into him in public. There would be a familiarity to him. I would think to myself, "Hey, there is the President!" I could say, "Mr. President, it is so good to see you. Would you like to go grab lunch?" He would think I was crazy. I might even feel like he should recognize me. After all, I feel like I know him.

Knowing *about* someone can be deceiving. The more you know about them, the better you feel like you know them. In reality, it is only head knowledge without a relationship; it is completely one-sided. This lack of true knowledge often characterizes the lives of professing Christians in relation to God.

When I arrived at Pure Life Ministries, I believed that I really knew the Lord because I had learned so much about Him in theology books. In one of my first counseling sessions, my counselor suggested that my failures came from a lack of truly knowing God. He said if I truly knew Him, I would not have gone astray like I did. At first this idea shocked me. In pride, I thought, "How can he say that I do not know God? I've known Him for years!" As time went on and the Holy Spirit opened my eyes, I began to realize there was a whole lot more to God than I had realized.

Since then, my Christian walk has been a fascinating adventure of discovering who He is. I was guilty of trying to fit the Lord into a box, but a box-sized god is not God at all. I know I have only begun to scratch the surface of who He is, but at least I can admit that I really do not know as much about Him as I previously thought.

How does all this tie in with hypocrisy? One common factor that is true in the lives of all double-minded Christians is a lack of the fear and knowledge of God. A healthy fear of God would prevent someone from faking Christianity. The lack of fear comes from misunderstanding His character. To truly know God, you have to fear Him. A true understanding of His holiness and power creates godly fear. This fear is not a fear of punishment or judgment, but a healthy respect. Just like a good father commands the respect of his children, God's children should respect Him as well. It is a love-based fear.

MISUNDERSTANDING THE CHARACTER OF GOD

Looking back, I can see how my misunderstanding of the Lord's character contributed to my downfall. One example is in the area of my life ambitions. When I first got saved, I really loved God. He had rescued me out of a pit and I knew where I would be without Him. I just wanted to spend time with Him in His presence.

At that time, I felt like the Lord wanted me to start ministering in music. So, I stepped out and began evangelizing at outreaches, concerts and youth groups. Though He never told me that I would become famous doing it, the desire to make a name for myself soon took over. I had developed my own plans and dreams and I expected God to fulfill them. I told myself, "If I do it for Him, there is nothing wrong with making it big."

Well, things did not turn out the way I wanted, and it became a colossal issue in my relationship with God. I realize now that my plans were not actually His plans for me, but I was not willing to believe that then. Instead—out of a bitter spirit—I began to dabble with old addictions that the Lord had set me free from.

Rather than humbling myself before God, admitting my hypocrisy and getting in line with His will, I pushed the blame onto Him. I felt like He was withholding from me the one thing that I really wanted. I desired to become rich and famous and He was standing in my way. It was Satan's old Eden lie: "God is not really good. He is holding out on you."[24] My belief in that lie became a stronghold in my life. As I continued to backslide, I grew more and more despondent in my faith and became desperate to escape. As I began to reach out frantically to the things of this world, I grew increasingly bitter at the Lord for keeping me from them.

God *was* trying to get in the way of my sin and my selfish dream, but it was not because He wanted me to be unhappy. Instead, it was because He loved me and knew those things would destroy me. Like a lot of people, I saw God as some kind of 'cosmic kill-joy' trying to keep me in line to make me bored and miserable. The fact is that He was preventing *my* dreams from coming true. He did not enjoy seeing me suffer, but He knew that was not the path for me to take and He wanted to give me *His* dreams for my life.

Though each situation varies and not everyone's path is the same, I believe similar distorting lies have crept into every life where hypocrisy is present. To truly know the Lord is to fear Him, obey Him and love Him. This is why a balanced understanding of God's character is key to victory over hypocrisy.

FLESH-PLEASING TEACHINGS

We have looked at three areas of teachings in the modern-day church that encourage hypocrisy. There is a misrepresentation of true salvation, a distortion of grace and a misunderstanding of God's character. These are all unbiblical teachings that are very popular today.

One way to test a false teaching is to carry it out to its logical conclusion. All of these false teachings have the same practical application: *I can live however I want to and still be a Christian.* That is the underlying lie and the reason these teachings are so prevalent in our culture. The flesh *wants* to believe them. People in hypocrisy can find a variety of teachers who will make them feel secure in sin by pulling Scriptures out of context. Hypocrites need to examine whether or not their beliefs actually line up with the whole teaching of the Bible.

Too many people in church have settled for what the Lord has never asked them to settle for. The devil is at work in the church, trying to cause Christians to either fall away blatantly or internally grow cold. Satan does not mind if people keep the outward observances and call it walking with the Lord. He wins in either case.

In the next chapter, we will diagnose our spiritual condition and see the areas of our spiritual lives that hypocrisy affects the most.

SECTION TWO

IDENTIFYING HYPOCRISY

Now that we have defined Christian hypocrisy in detail, it is necessary to go deeper. In this chapter, we will learn how to identify areas of hypocrisy in our own lives. How can we know if we have a hypocrisy issue? The following chapter will provide an evaluation to help us answer that question.

Vital:

1. **adjective.** of, concerned with, or manifesting life[1]

*   *   *

II Corinthians 13:5 (MSG)- Test yourselves to make sure you are solid in the faith. Don't drift along taking everything for granted. Give yourselves regular check-ups. You need firsthand evidence, not mere hearsay, that Jesus Christ is in you. Test it out. If you fail the test, do something about it.

Luke 13:6-9 (NIV)- Then he told this parable: "A man had a fig tree growing in his vineyard, and he went to look for fruit on it but did not find any. So he said to the man who took care of the vineyard, 'For three years now I've been coming to look for fruit on this fig tree and haven't found any. Cut it down! Why should it use up the soil?'

"'Sir,' the man replied, 'leave it alone for one more year, and I'll dig around it and fertilize it. If it bears fruit next year, fine! If not, then cut it down.'"

*   *   *

"If you want to break up the fallow ground of your heart, you must begin by looking at yourself...See where you are. Many never seem to think about this. They pay no attention to their own hearts, and they never know whether they are doing well in their faith or not. They do not know whether they are gaining ground or going back; whether they are fruitful or going to waste."

-Charles Finney[2]

6

SPIRITUAL PULSE CHECK

IN THE FIRST FIVE CHAPTERS, WE have defined hypocrisy. We have seen how hypocrisy was intertwined into the lives of the Old Testament Israelites and the New Testament Pharisees. We have also examined how many of the teachings of the modern-day church contribute to the hypocrisy issue. Now we need to bring it a little closer to home. This chapter deals with the symptoms of hypocrisy. I encourage you to read with an open heart, asking the Holy Spirit to illuminate possible traces of this epidemic in your own life.

CHECKING FOR A SPIRITUAL PULSE

When a paramedic arrives on the scene of an emergency, they need to make a quick evaluation to determine if a person is dead or alive. They do this by checking their vital signs. Vital signs are "indicators of the efficient functioning of the body, esp., pulse, temperature, and respiration."[3] These vitals are the signs that a person has life in them. The absence of them is evidence of death.

Spiritually speaking, there are vital signs that we can check to see if the life of Christ is in us or if we are spiritually dead or dying. The sad fact is that there are many in this world whose Christianity looks alive and vibrant, but the signs of true spiritual life are simply not there. It is like the church in Sardis to which Jesus said, "You have a reputation of being alive, but you are dead."[4] Some have never had true life, while others have grown cold. They have contented themselves to live the outward Christian life, but refuse to surrender to the Lord in their hearts.

Take Dave as an example. Dave is a businessman and he and his family are faithful attendees of First Church. He is married to Nancy and has three kids. Dave is an usher and was recently voted onto the deacon board. Nancy sings in the choir and teaches a women's Sunday school class. Their oldest boy attends the youth group, and the two youngest kids are involved in the children's ministry. Everyone sees them as a solid family in the church. They are the kind of family every pastor wants in his congregation. They tithe faithfully, and never fail to lend a hand when needed. If they were being evaluated as quality churchgoers, they would exceed expectations. However, Heaven's scorecard tells a different story.

Dave and his family are in some serious trouble. You see, it is not so much anything blatantly wicked in their lives. Dave is not having an affair or harboring some secret sin. He has not been abusing his kids or embezzling money. In fact, he tries to do the right thing most of the time. So what is the big deal?

Jesus is not the center of their lives.

"But I thought you said they are active in their church?"

I did.

"I thought you said they are pretty good people?"

I did.

These are often the areas we examine when we are trying to evaluate someone's spiritual life, but church attendance and morality do not necessarily equate to walking with Christ. Nice people who faithfully serve their churches die and go to Hell every single day.

If you were to look for signs of spiritual life in this family, you would have to go deeper than the superficial. Otherwise, you could easily be deceived to believe that these were good, God-fearing people, in love with the Lord. The scary thought is that the church is filled with people like Dave and Nancy.

So, what does a life in Jesus really look like according to Scripture? Could it be that God demands more from us than just a moral life, filled with godly activities? Spiritual vital signs go much deeper. In order to search for signs of life, we must look into our hearts. In this chapter, we will look at four vital signs we can use to take our own spiritual temperature.

VITAL SIGN #1: OBEDIENCE

Obedience is inseparable from a true relationship with God. The Bible shows many examples of men and women who obeyed the Lord in spite of what it might cost them. Abraham left his country to go to a land that he never knew.[5] Joseph took Mary as his wife in spite of the fact that she was pregnant with a baby that was not his.[6] People throughout the Bible and history have literally put their lives on the line in order to obey God.

The reality of the importance of obedience really got a hold of me while reading Lee Sheldon's book, *In His Steps*. When I decided to read the novel, I had no idea what I was in store for. Although this is a fictional story, it had a significant impact on my spiritual life.

The story is told through the lives of several characters who attend a church together. The pastor of the church sees a great need in the Body of Christ to obey the principle of I John 2:6 to "live as Jesus did." He challenges everyone to ask, "What would Jesus do?" before making any decisions for one year. Those who accepted the challenge were to obey what they believed Jesus would do, *regardless* of the personal cost.

In response to the challenge, a girl who is destined for fame with a beautiful voice walks away from a chance to fulfill her dreams to lead worship in the slums. A newspaper editor loses a large percentage of his subscribers when he decides to only print what he believes Jesus would print. A high official in a factory is terminated from his job when he decides to confront dishonesty in his company. It is a story depicting what radical obedience to the Lord could look like.

The whole premise of the book haunted me; I could not get away from it. I realized that a fundamental element in the lives of God's people throughout history is obedience. That is the fruit of a true relationship with Him. Jesus said, "Why do you call me, 'Lord, Lord,' and do not do what I say?"[7] In another verse, He says, "If you love me, keep my commands."[8] Doing whatever Jesus says to do shows that we belong to Him.

Hypocrisy often forces a person to break the commandments of God. You cannot truly love people if you are not willing to be transparent. Often, one has to lie and deceive in order to keep up appearances. Many times there are secret sins being covered up, so a life of obedience cannot truly happen until the hypocrisy is dealt with. All-out obedience should not seem like a radical thing. Did Jesus not make Himself obedient to the Father by dying on a cross?[9] Obedience is an integral part of walking with the Lord.

JAMES ON OBEDIENCE

In speaking about obedience, James addresses a core issue that many face in our churches. In James 1, he explains that there is a difference between hearing and doing. To hear only is to deceive oneself. (v. 22) The great danger we all face is to hear God's Word, but not respond. When someone hears the Word of God, whether through reading or preaching, there are only two possible responses. Either they obey it or they ignore it. Every Sunday, many people walk out of church services saying, "That was an excellent sermon; it really spoke to me." However, if they do not allow the truth to change their hearts, they have only heard. Obedience softens the heart toward the Lord, but disobedience will harden it.

A person who hides behind a Christian mask has heard the Word of God, but stopped doing it. Their heart has grown callous to the things of God, but they deceive themselves to believe that hearing the Word and being a part of the Christian community somehow equates with godliness. You would be amazed at the amount of truly convicting sermons I listened to on a regular basis while continuing in sin. Yet somehow, because I agreed with the message and was listening to the Bible, I thought that I was in a good place spiritually.

This is a perfect description of how someone can be in total hypocrisy and still read the Scriptures regularly. The unspoken thought behind my Scripture study was always, "Do I know this already?" I was reading for insight—looking for more information. I wanted to make sure I had my theology right so I could preach with confidence.

In order to avoid being hearers only when reading the Bible, there is a question we need to always ask ourselves. That question is: "Am I *doing* this already?" That is the dividing line between the Pharisee and the true saint. The religious person knows the Word, but the true believer is putting it into practice. The difference may seem subtle, but it is night and day in the spiritual realm.

Asking this question while reading through the Bible could be one of the best ways to see where you line up on the hypocrisy scale. When you come across a command from Scripture, such as, "Forgive as the Lord forgave you,"[10] you first ask yourself, "Do I already know this?" If you answer "Yes," and then immediately move on, you have done nothing more than a mental exercise, which is spiritually unprofitable. The question that you need to follow up with is, "Am I doing this?" Then examine your life in the area of forgiveness. Are you harboring bitterness against someone in your heart? If so, you need to repent, forgive them and continue to walk in forgiveness towards them from this point forward. That is how we learn to be obedient. Then we can truly be doers of the Word.

JOHN ON OBEDIENCE

John—the beloved disciple—knew Jesus intimately. He was a man with real faith and a heart without hypocrisy. In his letters, he wrote in a very simple language with the purpose of defining the distinctive qualities of true believers. He had much to say about hypocrisy, which was a big issue in his day as well. John gives us several powerful tests in his epistles to determine whether or not we are truly walking with the Lord.

John writes in I John 1, "God is light; in him there is no darkness at all." (v. 5) The Lord's nature is completely undivided, without any hypocrisy. Then he contrasts this thought with, "If we claim to have fellowship with him yet walk in the darkness, we lie and do not live out the truth." (v. 6) This is a picture of the Christian hypocrite. They say the right things, but it is a lie because their actions show the truth. John warns us that if we are not honest with ourselves and others, we can fall into deception. He goes on to say:

> We know that we have come to know him if we keep his commands. Whoever says, "I know him," but does not do what he commands is a liar, and the truth is not in that person. But if anyone obeys his word, love for God is truly made complete in them. This is how we know we are in him: Whoever claims to live in him must live as Jesus did. (I John 2:3-6)

In these verses, John does not leave us any wiggle room. He affirms that the true test of a believer is their obedience. He cuts through all of the smokescreens. Anyone can put on a great religious show, but when it comes right down to it, the proof is in the lifestyle. If they obey God, they prove they belong to Him. If they do not do what He says, the truth is not in them.

What does your life look like? Do you look more like the person who is saying the right things, but not doing them? Or are you obeying the Lord and endeavoring to live according to His ways? Obedience is essential. If there is a lack of it in your life, why not make the necessary changes right now?

THE DANGER OF DISOBEDIENCE

When it comes to seeking the Lord, sometimes people in church will say, "I know God wants me to spend more time with him, but..." Then they list whatever they think is keeping them from fully committing. I can understand this struggle myself. I have had to fight my flesh many times in order to keep my relationship with Jesus strong. However, when days, weeks and even months go by and the story has not changed, there is a deeper issue that needs to be addressed.

What that person needs to see is that the Lord is asking for their obedience. If time has passed, and He has given them opportunities to comply, yet they are not doing what He told them, *they are in disobedience!* It is that simple. God said, "Do this," and they said, "No!" Maybe they did not say it verbally, but they did with their actions. They are going directly against what they consciously know the Lord wants.

What a frightening place to be! If you have sin in your life—and you know God is putting His finger on it—but you are refusing to let go, *you are in danger!* How much more obvious could that be? Many people say, "Well, God understands my heart. He knows I love Him and that I want to do it, but it is just too hard. Eventually, I'll obey!" The truth is that disobedience will bring about consequences. Repent and obey what the Holy Spirit is asking you to do right now. He only wants what is best for you, but you have to make the choice to cooperate with Him.

VITAL SIGN #2: PASSION

There are more signs of spiritual life than just obedience. Another clear indicator that a professing Christian is not living a sincere faith is a lack of passion. This is one of the first things to diminish as a Christian backslides in their heart. Of course, they will not consciously admit that they have lost their passion for Jesus. Many will say things to sound more spiritual like, "I'm just going through a dry season." Although there can be such a thing as a spiritually dry season, a season has a time limit.

Typically, a dry time is when we are seeking God, but it seems like He is not near. Maybe His Word does not seem to come alive like it used to. But the passion in a true believer's heart is still alive—even in a dry season. They will continue to seek the Lord diligently in spite of it—sometimes with even greater tenacity. If a dry season has caused you to stop seeking Jesus, you had better stop and check your heart. That is a sign of a backslidden condition. At some point, you should stop calling it a season, because the season should have already passed.

If the Lord sees our passion fading, He will often allow things into our lives to bring our hearts back to Him. Yet our response to what the Lord is trying to do will determine if we draw closer to Jesus or we push Him further away. Many professing Christians will harden their hearts toward Him rather than repenting of backsliding.

Some only cry out to God in times of trouble, as if He is just a 'spiritual handy man.' Often, when lukewarm Christians face tragedy, the Lord wants to use the trials to get their attention. And they may seem to cling to Him when the hardships come. It may look like He finally has their attention. But when the crisis passes, soon the passion wears off and it is back to business-as-usual, half-hearted Christianity.

Just as we observed in the lives of the Israelites, the Lord allows things to happen to us for redemptive purposes. In those times, He is extending mercy to us. However, there will come a time when He says, "If you do not want me, and you want your fake, hypocritical religion, you can have it." At that point, many will never return to Him because they have pushed His approaches off so many times. Their hearts have hardened with each rejection of His offer of mercy. The Lord often uses difficulties in our lives to try to ignite a fresh passion for Him. But we choose how we will react to the trials that come.

EVIDENCE OF PASSION

One evidence of the passion in someone's life is his words. True believers love talking about Jesus. Recently, I was in a fast-food restaurant. I was getting a drink at the soda fountain and a man came up to witness to me. He talked about how Easter was a holiday to celebrate the Savior. I said, "Yes, I believe that brother." His face lit up and we shook hands. He said, "I guess I'll be seeing you again someday."

It was a quick interchange as we both went our own way. We had never met, but it was like we had known each other for years. It was the witness of the Spirit in us. We could sense each other's passion for Jesus. I would have loved to sit and talk with him for a while and hear about how Jesus changed his life and share my own story. His passion for Jesus was so strong, he had to talk about Him even to a stranger at a soda fountain!

In our backslidden church culture, Christians love to talk about all kinds of things. If you want to talk sports, you will find fans excited to discuss stats, scores and upcoming games. They will describe scenes from recent sporting events in detail. They are passionate!

If you bring up the latest reality shows on TV, it will not be hard to find many in church who can talk about all the hottest new episodes. They are in touch with this world's culture. They know all of the juicy details in the lives of celebrities, along with the newest music and movies, and they can talk for hours about them.

Church people talk cars, politics and just about anything you can think of. Often, when you try bringing up the Bible or what the Lord has been teaching you, many will suddenly disengage. Why is that? It is due to a lack of sincere desire. It is exciting to talk about the things of God when that is your passion. However, to those who are not where they know they should be, real passion brings conviction.

Jesus said, "for the mouth speaks what the heart is full of."[11] I encourage you to keep track of the things you love to talk about. Analyze what you spend most of your time discussing with others. Then ask yourself what that indicates about your heart. The passion driving a person's life is not hard to find. Just look at the things they spend their time and money on. What do they talk about when they are not putting on a religious show in church?

PASSION IN OUR DAILY LIVES

Like a fire, passion is something that is kindled. You need to keep adding fuel to keep it burning; doing nothing will cause it to slowly fade. That is why putting your spiritual life on 'cruise-control' is not safe. Your heart will grow harder automatically. That is just our fallen human nature. You do not have to intentionally turn from God and sin to backslide. If you allow the passion to die, you will be heading in that direction already. As

Brother Lawrence once wrote: "We must, nevertheless, always work at it, because not to advance in the spiritual life is to go back."[12]

Hell is full of professing Christians who simply did nothing. They never allowed a passion in their hearts to grow. They pushed off God's attempts to get their attention. Right before their eyes, they found themselves hardened toward the Lord and no longer in relationship with Him. If you are not *continually* feeding your relationship with God, you are on the pathway to indifference; it is just a matter of time.

THE PATH TO INDIFFERENCE

In his book, *The Pursuit of Holiness*, A.W. Tozer once wrote:

Where faith is defective the result will be inward insensibility and numbness toward spiritual things. This is the condition of vast numbers of Christians today. No proof is necessary to support that statement. We have but to converse with the first Christian we meet or enter the first church we open to acquire all the proof we need.[13]

Indifference in the life of a professing Christian should be a strong warning signal that something is not right. As the passion is allowed to dwindle, many find themselves in a place where spiritual things no longer hold the same weight in their lives. Apathy sets in, and though they used to be on fire, now they start going through the motions. As Jesus warned the church in Ephesus, "You have forsaken the love you had at first."[14]

Soon after apathy takes a hold of someone's life, they will start becoming critical and judgmental of true believers. Some even display animosity towards them. This is because encountering people who are still in love with Jesus is a threat to their indifference. Coming in contact with true faith should cause them to repent. But instead, many who were once in love with the Lord lash out at true Christianity. They might do this by making sarcastic comments or jokes about those who are sincere. I have seen true believers in a group try to turn the attention of others to spiritual matters and be ridiculed for it. "Oh, there goes so and so. They always have to be the spiritual one." Those who have lost their first love brush them off as fanatical.

When indifference in someone's life turns into sarcasm and criticism toward people who love Jesus, it should be a major wake-up call to repent. Jesus said, "Truly I tell you, whatever you did for one of the least of these brothers and sisters of mine, you did for me."[15] What we do to those who belong to Christ is like doing it to Jesus Himself. To set yourself against someone who is sold-out to Jesus is to set yourself against Him. Likewise, if you crack a joke, slander, make fun of or talk down to one of His, it is like saying those very things to Jesus. Some would not dare say the things to Him that they say to and about others. Some people do not maliciously attack believers verbally, but in their hearts they harbor bitterness toward them. These are warning signs that they need to cry out to God for renewed passion.

Indifferent people like other indifferent people because they are not threatening. That is why Israel killed the prophets and why the Pharisees hated Jesus and the apostles. The passion of true faith is a threat to indifference. We all desperately need passion in our own lives to keep the fire of love burning in our hearts. Passion goes hand-in-hand with devotion to the Lord.

VITAL SIGN #3: DEVOTION

Sally and Tom have been married for several years. When they first met and fell in love, they could not get enough of each other. They stayed up late at night talking on the phone. They called each other on breaks at work and met for lunch as often as possible. Even when they were not together, their minds were always on each other. Tom made Sally feel loved and secure.

After the honeymoon stage of their marriage, things began to change. Tom's love for Sally never faltered. He always wanted to be with her and longed for her company, but it did not seem to be reciprocated. At first he thought, "Maybe it's just a season we are going through." But Sally continually grew distant. It was not that she was doing anything wrong. She was not seeing another man; she just got busy. Other things became more important than Tom. When he would confront her, she would always promise to try harder. "You know I love you with all my heart and I am yours," she would respond.

At first, Tom was very forgiving. However, as time went on, he became more impatient. He was jealous for his wife's attention. Once after she gave her usual, "I love you, I'm just busy" speech, he slammed his hand on the table and said, "If you love me like you say you do, then spend time with me! Change your priorities. Cancel some appointments!"

To this Sally replied, "But my schedule is just too full. You know I would change things if I could."

Tom—head held low—just replied, "You make time for everything else. Don't lie to me and tell me you cannot make time for me. That is simply not true."

I do not think that anyone reading this story can say Tom is being unreasonable. This does not sound like much of a marriage, does it? No marriage can be very strong without intimacy. This marriage that began strong had really become a one-sided relationship.

Yet, I fear this accurately illustrates the spiritual lives of many in our churches. Tom represents the Lord, and Sally the believer. After first getting saved, many go through a 'honeymoon' stage. They love to be with Jesus. At one point, it was no sacrifice to wake up early, stay up late, give up hobbies or cut off the TV to be with Him—it was their joy. Over time, they grow disillusioned. They get hurt. Promises seem unfulfilled and prayers seem to go unanswered. So, they begin to drift.

God's love for them never changes, but like Sally, these Christians get busy. Without realizing it, their first love begins to dwindle. They get caught up in the affairs of this life. This is not necessarily sinful activity, but other things become a priority over their relationship with God. All the while, they still claim the Lord is truly first in their lives.

Like Tom, God is patient. He continually calls out to us, beckoning us to seek Him. The Bible tells us He is a jealous God.[16] He is jealous for our affection. The whole reason He created us was for relationship. Yet many Christians are just like Sally: full of justifications and empty excuses.

Devotion is ongoing communion with God. Salvation is an event that should lead us into a *lifestyle* of communion.

A professing Christian trying to walk with Jesus without any intimacy is only fooling himself. Intimacy does not come from spending a couple of hours with Him in church services throughout the week. I do not know any marriage that would have a fragment of intimacy in it if both spouses only spent a couple of hours on Sunday mornings together and one or two hours throughout the week. Intimacy requires devotion to a person.

Loss of intimacy is not only one of the first signs of backsliding, but it is also a doorway into hypocrisy. Pursuing and maintaining intimacy is a foolproof way to avoid the double-life. It is also a key factor in restoring a hypocrite to God. Everything in the Christian life flows out of intimacy. If you lose that part of your Christian walk, you are on a slippery slope.

RELIGION OR RELATIONSHIP?

I have often heard it said that Christianity is not about a religion, but a relationship. While this statement is true, a relationship requires devotion and intimacy, which require time and sacrifice. There are scores of people in America today who do not seek the Lord except when they are in a church service.

This could not be further from the Christianity of Bible times. It seems to me that many Christians today are mistakenly living with Old Covenant thinking. In Israel, God's presence dwelt on Earth first in the tabernacle,[17] and then the temple.[18] These were the places Jehovah chose to manifest His presence. If you wanted to go where He was, you had to travel to a specific geographical location to worship Him there.

Many Christians today live as if God only dwells in their local churches. They have a time of worship and prayer once or twice a week in church, but the rest of the week they are ignoring the Lord completely. That is simply not a relationship, but comes a lot closer to a religious mindset. Church services are to be nothing more than the outflow of what is happening in our hearts the rest of the week. It is a time for corporately worshiping God.

If we do not set aside time every day for the Lord, we are showing that He is not Number One in our lives. There can be no other explanation.

Many Christians will say, "I just do not have time for God. I'm too busy." But that is not true. We find time for the things that we really love. Those same professing Christians will find time for their hobbies, entertainment (movies, TV, sports), families, shopping and personal pursuits no matter what. They need to get honest before God and admit, "Lord, I do not really love you and *want* to be with you the way I say I do!" They need to cry out to Jesus for that desire. It is His will to do that for each of us, but if we just make pathetic excuses for our lack of devotion, God cannot do anything to help us. If we believe Christianity is all about relationship, let us live like that is true.

WHAT IS THE DEVOTIONAL LIFE?

When we hear the term *devotions*, many of us automatically think of 365-day books with a quick thought, short prayer and a verse. But a devotional life is so much more than that. The devotional life is a *lifestyle* of living to please God. Like William Law said: "Devotion does not imply any form of prayer but a certain form of life that is offered to God everywhere and in everything."[19]

The true believer who is walking in the Spirit will find that the Lord is constantly pursuing their hearts. He wants all of our hearts because He loves us. A sign of spiritual life is a growing hunger for the presence of the Lord in our daily lives. In the same way, a sign of spiritual death is a lack of devotion to God outside of church. Many people filling our churches have pathetic devotional lives. They look great on Sunday, but if you followed them throughout the rest of the week, you could easily ask the question, "Where is Jesus in their lifestyle?" Some make feeble efforts when they really feel guilty, but soon revert back to spending no quality time with Him.

I was in the same rut when I was living a double-life. There were times I really tried to seek Jesus, but it would never last. Why? Because I did not do it out of love for Him, but an outward commitment to try to be more spiritual. Like everything else in the Christian life, seeking the Lord has to come from the heart, or it means nothing. There will be times that we do not feel like we are connecting, however, outward actions without inward sincerity only harden the heart even more.

By the time I arrived at Pure Life Ministries, I literally had no devotional life. I did not read the Bible and I only prayed an occasional "Help me, Lord" prayer. One of the questions on the application for the program was, "How much time do you spend seeking God?" This question is important to ask because the level of a Christian's spirituality is directly proportional to the quality of their devotional lives. Leonard Ravenhill once said, "Let me live with a man awhile and share his prayer life, and I'll tell you how tall I think he is, or how majestic I think he is in God."[20]

If you want to be like someone you have to get to know them. The more time you spend in the presence of Jesus, the more you will become like Him in your character.

THE LACK OF DEVOTIONAL DEPTH
IN OUR CULTURE

It is a sad fact that Christians who choose to press into the Lord have to swim against the current of the general church population. Many are looking for a shortcut to intimacy with God. They want to read a verse, say a quick prayer and expect to have a deep walk with Him. As A.W. Tozer once wrote:

The idea of cultivation and exercise, so dear to the saints of old, has now no place in our total religious picture. It is too slow, too common. We now demand glamour and fast flowing dramatic action. A generation of Christians reared among push buttons and automatic machines is impatient of slower and less direct methods of reaching their goals. We have been trying to apply machine-age methods to our relations with God. We read our chapter, have our short devotions and rush away, hoping to make up for our deep inward bankruptcy by attending another gospel meeting or listening to another thrilling story told by a religious adventurer lately returned from afar.[21]

What a prophetic word for our generation! Maybe it is time to set this book down a few minutes and get honest with the Lord yourself. Ask Jesus to cause you to fall in love with Him again. That is a heartfelt prayer He *will* answer!

THE BLESSINGS OF DEVOTION

When it comes to our devotional lives, God has made some awesome promises to us. Hebrews 11:6 says that God will reward those who diligently seek Him. Do we really believe this is true? If we do, why are we not more diligent in spending time with Him? Here are just a few references to the blessings of seeking the Lord:

- If you seek Him, He will be found by you. (**I Chronicles 28:9/ Luke 11:10**)
- Those who seek the Lord will lack no good thing. (**Psalm 34:10**)
- We will seek Him and find Him when we seek Him with all of our heart. (**Jeremiah 29:13**)
- The hearts of those who seek Him rejoice! (**Psalm 105:3**)
- If we seek first His kingdom and His righteousness, everything else will be taken care of. (**Matthew 6:33**)

With all of these promises in view, it is amazing to think that so many people who claim to be Christians do not make their devotional time a priority. I used to live like that, and my Christian experience was one of defeat and struggle. Now that I see the difference intimacy makes in my life, I know I have to make my quiet times a priority *at any cost*.

This is the area the enemy will attack the most, because Satan knows if he can get in between us and God in our quiet times, he can defeat us everywhere else. I know for myself, if I do not have quality time with the Lord, I lean much more on my emotions, and things just do not go smoothly. I am less able to look rationally at a stressful situation, and more likely to let the little things sink me. It is imperative for all Christians to spend time with Him every day. Like Martin Luther once said, "I have so much to do that I shall spend the first three hours in prayer."[22] Devotion is a sign of true spiritual life. But there is one more vital sign for us to consider.

VITAL SIGN #4: ETERNITY-MINDEDNESS

The Bible is clear that the heart of a true believer is one that is not at home in this temporal world. The word for *pilgrim* in Greek is *parepidemos*, and it means "a resident foreigner."[23] This term describes a person who resides in a place that they do not belong. The Bible uses this concept to describe a Christian's increasing awareness of eternity. As William Law put it:

> This is the only measure of our application to any worldly business—let it be *what* it will, *where* it will, it must have no more of our hands, our hearts, or our time than is consistent with a hearty, daily, careful preparation of ourselves for another life. Now he who does not look at things of this life in this degree of littleness cannot be said either to feel or believe the greatest truths of Christianity.[24]

I know firsthand how it feels to be out of place as a foreigner in another country. When you first move overseas to a new country with a different language, customs and food, you experience what is called *culture shock*. Culture shock is the feeling of being completely disoriented because of the differences you have from the people and customs around you.

Even after learning some of the language, adjusting to the climate, making friends and enjoying life in another country, you never completely forget that you are a foreigner. You still speak a different first language. You still have friends, family and memories from a different country. You learn to live with that reality and though you might not even notice it very often, occasionally something will remind you of home. Along with that reminder comes the realization that you are not there. This is how every sincere believer should feel in this world. It is an indication that your focus has changed from this life to the next. This world is only a place we are passing through, and we should not feel too much at home here.

IN THIS WORLD, BUT NOT OF IT

In Philippians 3:18-19, Paul talks about a group of people that he identifies as "enemies of the cross of Christ." He gives us a description of the type of people they are. He says their "destiny is destruction, their god is their stomach, and their glory is in their shame." Basically, these are people who are driven by the desires of their flesh.

Then Paul gives a defining characteristic that joins them all together. He says, "their mind is on earthly things." This is one difference between true Christians and false ones. Paul draws a sharp contrast when he writes, "our citizenship is in heaven. And we eagerly await a Savior from there, the Lord Jesus Christ…" (v. 20)

What exactly is Paul telling us? He is defining a completely different perspective on life. Those who belong to this world cannot understand that. Christians who are compromised in their walk do not either. If we are not careful, Heaven can easily become a distant fairy tale to us. Rather than a present reality, it becomes only a hope for the future. It may be something we think about once in a while, but not a reality that affects our daily decisions.

So how should this vantage point influence our lives? Peter tells us, "Dear friends, I urge you, as foreigners and exiles, to abstain from sinful desires, which wage war against your soul."[25] In this verse, Peter explains that being a pilgrim involves keeping ourselves from sinful desires. The unredeemed world is under the bondage of sin. They are slaves to it.[26] In contrast, our relationship with Christ causes us to die to sin.[27] Therefore, the mark of someone who does not belong to this world is a holy life that does not include continual sin. We should stand out in the crowd if we are truly children of God.

This is the type of life that should be normal for every true believer. If living as citizens of Heaven and pilgrims of this Earth is evidence of true faith in Christ, then the inverse must be true as well. The more one feels at home on this Earth—the more comfortable with the world around them—the more evidence there is that true faith is not being walked out in their lives.

THE WORLD WAS NOT WORTHY OF THEM

Hebrews 11 gives us snapshots of some of the greatest heroes of the faith in the Bible. These were men and women who accomplished great feats for God. They were entirely sold-out to Him. The writer is speaking about people like Enoch, Noah and Abraham. He says they admitted that:

> …they were foreigners and strangers on earth. People who say such things show that they are looking for a country of their own. If they had been thinking of the country they had left, they would have had opportunity to return. Instead, they were longing for a better country—a heavenly one. Therefore God is not ashamed to be called their God, for he has prepared a city for them. (vv. 13-16)

These are great examples to us of what living for the Lord should look like. One characteristic that joined them all together was that "they were foreigners and strangers on earth." They knew they did not belong. They were not living for the here and now, but sought an eternal homeland. Their rewards were in Heaven and their minds were set on things above. These were people who lived extremely close to the Lord, made incredible sacrifices and were used mightily of God. They lived as if this Earth was not their home, even without the full revelation of Christ and Heaven that we have. Yet, in their hearts, they knew there was a reality that transcended this world.

Does that attitude characterize your life? If you have hypocrisy in your life, I can tell you that you are far more concerned with your life here on this Earth than you are about your home in eternity. How else could you play spiritual games and gamble with your eternity, hoping that in the end, you will not die out of relationship with Him?

The Bible gives the most amazing testimony about these great men and women of God in verse 38. It says, "the world was not worthy of them." Think about that for a moment. The world was not worthy of them because they were so eternity-minded. That is an incredible statement. Then ask yourself, "Is the world worthy of me?"

WHAT DOES YOUR PULSE CHECK REVEAL?

I would encourage you to check each of these spiritual vital signs and prayerfully consider your own spiritual state. Where do you rate in the area of obedience? What are you most passionate about in life? How healthy is your devotional life? Where are your eyes set, on things above or below? Answering these questions will help gauge your spiritual temperature.

SECTION THREE

OVERCOMING HYPOCRISY

At this point, we have not only defined Christian hypocrisy, but we have also examined our own lives for traces of it. The obvious question to ask is, "What do we do about it?" The following six chapters will give us powerful tools to help overcome hypocrisy in our lives. Hypocrisy has enemies. They are spiritual principles that chip away at its power. We can enlist them to fight on our side as we battle for victory from hypocrisy's grip.

Repent:
1. **verb.** to feel sorry or self-reproachful for what one has done or failed to do; be conscience-stricken or contrite
2. to feel such regret or dissatisfaction over some past action, intention, etc. as to change one's mind about[1]

*   *   *

Acts 3:19 (NIV)- Peter: "Repent, then, and turn to God, so that your sins may be wiped out, that times of refreshing may come from the Lord…"

Acts 26:20 (PHP)- Paul: "…I preached that men should repent and turn to God and live lives to prove their change of heart."

*   *   *

"New Testament repentance is about *truth* and represents a complete change of mind or heart. It is when we are deeply sorry we've hurt the heart of God and are now committed to obeying His desire in this area."

-John Bevere[2]

"The true meaning of the word for 'repentance' was a revelation to me when I first learned it. For years the Church has tried to limit the definition of repentance to the words, 'I am sorry,' with a promise not to repeat the offense. In reality, repentance is a more comprehensive term. It is complete submission of one's mental processes to God, which results in a transformation by His pervasive power. Repentance leads to an in-depth change of both attitude and activity."

-Marvin Gorman[3]

7

HYPOCRISY'S ENEMIES: REPENTANCE

REPENTANCE IS A WORD I HAD heard frequently throughout my Christian life. I had a basic understanding of what it meant, but I did not realize its importance in a believer's life beyond conversion. Many Christians understand that repentance is a requirement of salvation. We know that a sinner must turn away from his sinful life and turn toward God. He must repent of breaking the Lord's commands and endeavor to live a life for Him. However, what I have learned through my experience at Pure Life Ministries is that repentance is not a one-time event, but a *lifestyle*.

A true understanding of repentance is greatly lacking in today's churches. Partially, I think the 'Once Saved, Always Saved' teaching (see page 110) has influenced this. If I can take one trip to the altar or pray a quick prayer and live the rest of my life however I please, then repentance is not essential. I also think we lack clear teaching on biblical repentance.

The concept of repentance can be found in the Bible from the beginning to the end. You could say repentance is one of the biggest themes in Scripture. Why? Because the only way for sinful men to come into relationship with a holy God is through repentance.

Every major figure in the Bible carried this message. Noah preached repentance. Moses demanded it from Israel. All of the prophets carried repentance in the themes of their messages. John the Baptist, Jesus and His disciples all preached it. Scripture references which command us to repent and describe the blessings of repentance are too numerous to list. Here are just a few:

Ezekiel 18:30-32- Repent! Turn away from all your offenses; then sin will not be your downfall. Rid yourselves of all the offenses you have committed, and get a new heart and a new spirit. Why will you die, people of Israel? For I take no pleasure in the death of anyone, declares the Sovereign Lord. Repent and live!

Matthew 4:17- From that time on Jesus began to preach, "Repent, for the kingdom of heaven has come near."

Mark 6:12- They [the disciples] went out and preached that people should repent.

Luke 3:8- John the Baptist: "Produce fruit in keeping with repentance."

Luke 15:10- Jesus: "In the same way, I tell you, there is rejoicing in the presence of the angels of God over one sinner who repents."

Acts 2:38- Peter: "Repent and be baptized, every one of you, in the name of Jesus Christ for the forgiveness of your sins."

Acts 17:30- Paul: "But now [God] commands all people everywhere to repent."

Acts 26:20- Paul: "I preached that they should repent and turn to God and demonstrate their repentance by their deeds."

Romans 2:4- Or do you show contempt for the riches of his kindness, forbearance and patience, not realizing that God's kindness is intended to lead you to repentance?

II Corinthians 7:10- Godly sorrow brings repentance that leads to salvation and leaves no regret, but worldly sorrow brings death.

II Timothy 2:25-26- Opponents must be gently instructed, in the hope that God will grant them repentance leading them to a knowledge of the truth, and that they will come to their senses and escape from the trap of the devil, who has taken them captive to do his will.

II Peter 3:9- The Lord is not slow in keeping his promise, as some understand slowness. Instead he is patient with you, not wanting anyone to perish, but everyone to come to repentance.

Revelation 3:19- Jesus: "Those whom I love I rebuke and discipline. So be earnest and repent."

The preachers of the New Testament saw repentance as the central message of the Good News, and they taught it as the only way to be born again. Repentance is a big deal to God because sin is the thing that separates people from Him. Repentance turns people from sin to the Lord.

WHAT IS REPENTANCE?

The Hebrew word for repent in the Ezekiel passage listed above is *sub*. It means "to turn back, turn to, return, restore, recover, bring back."[4] The Greek word often used in the New Testament is *metanoeo*, meaning "to think differently, to reconsider."[5] One commentator puts it this way:

Theologically, it means to change one's mind or disposition toward God. More specifically, to repent is to undergo a moral reorientation of the soul in which one acknowledges the error of his ways and turns toward the divinely prescribed way of truth and righteousness.[6]

You can see from these definitions that repentance is not something only needed once at salvation. Repentance is the process of getting every area of our lives in line with the Lord's will.

How often should repentance take place? As often as we need to turn away from doing things our way instead of God's. How often do we rise up in pride? How often do we demand our own way? Disobey the Lord? Do not do the good we know we should? Repenting is coming to the realization: "In this area of my life, I am not submitting to God," and then committing to obey Him in that area.

Please understand, I am not talking about living under continuous guilt and condemnation. Nor am I encouraging a life of constant self-examination. Our eyes should be on Christ and His grace, not on ourselves and our sin. God's grace is sufficient for us. However, we ought to be living holy lives. Whenever our consciences are violated from one of our thoughts, words or actions, repentance is necessary.

REPENTANCE: TOWARD AND FROM

It is important to realize that repentance is not just turning away from something, but it is turning toward Someone. If you only turn *from* sin but do not turn *toward* God—while you may have cleaned yourself up on the outside—true heart transformation did not occur.

Trying to give up a habit without turning toward the Lord brings to mind the saying 'dry drunk.' This phrase refers to an alcoholic who has quit drinking, yet they are just as depressed as before they stopped because they miss their addiction. Many Christian hypocrites are in a place like that in their spiritual lives. They are essentially 'dry sinners.' They do not have peace and joy in Christ, because they are constantly looking back to the 'good old days' before they became a Christian. They are buying into the same lie that the Israelites did concerning Egypt. God's people were constantly looking back as if Egypt was paradise, when in fact they were miserable slaves when they lived there.[7]

I have experienced this firsthand. There came a point where I started to long for sin again, and I turned away from Jesus. Since I was not finding any fulfillment in my Christianity, I began to imagine how satisfying it would be to go back to my sin. I had only done half of repentance. I had given up some sinful practices, but I was not turning toward God with all my heart. It is no wonder I ended up going back into sin. Repentance that only turns away from sin, and not toward the Lord, is not biblical repentance.

CRYING OUT TO THE LORD

One of the first things I was taught at Pure Life was that I needed to cultivate a cry for God in my heart. My counselor advised me to begin crying out to Him throughout the day. He explained that it would feel mechanical and forced at first, but to continue doing it. In the beginning, I wondered how it could help. It did not even feel sincere. The words seemed so lifeless and I did not enjoy the feeling of admitting I was in need. Even though I did not feel like my heart was in it, something happened—God responded.

As He began to help me, the cry in my heart grew more sincere, and eventually became a lifestyle. I do not know how many times a day I say in my heart, "Lord, I need you." It has become such a part of my life, I do not even realize I am doing it. I can testify that God has developed a real cry in my heart for Him. I still do not enjoy feeling needy at times, but it is much easier now to ask for His help than it used to be. I have seen how the Lord responds to a needy cry.

I discovered that this area was a key issue in my heart. I wanted to be self-sufficient. To admit that I had needs—even simple things like asking someone for prayer—meant weakness. For example, I was freezing cold the first couple of nights in the program because I was too proud to ask for an extra blanket. To ask for help meant admitting I could not do it on my own. Human nature does not like feeling needy or weak.

Yet, this is exactly how God designed us to be. We are meant to be totally dependent on our heavenly Father for everything. Matthew 5:3 says, "Blessed are the poor in spirit." The Greek term for *poor, (ptochos)*, is the same as the word used for *beggar*.[8] This verse literally means, "Blessed are the spiritual beggars." There is something about the simple cry of our hearts that attracts the Lord's attention. Most of us try to be strong in ourselves and wonder why our relationship with God is so shallow. Developing a cry in our hearts for Him is an essential element of the repentance process.

I TOLD GOD I WAS SORRY!

Repentance is not merely apologizing to God, asking forgiveness and continuing in sin. This is an area where a lot of Christians—especially those in habitual sin—get confused. As Charles Finney once said:

> Many suppose that remorse or a sense of guilt is repentance. Then hell is full of repentance because it is full of unutterable and eternal remorse. Others feel regret that they have sinned, and they call that repenting. But they only regret their sin because of the consequences, not because they abhor sin. This is not repentance... Repentance is a change of mind toward God and sin. It is not only a change of views, but a change of the ultimate preference or choice of the soul and of action.[9]

I was stuck in this endless cycle for years. I would sin and then beg God to forgive me—often with tears. Then I would promise to do better. But the next time the temptation would come, I would commit the same sin all over again. I thought that by saying I was sorry, things would automatically change, but I could not find the freedom I longed for.

A trip to the altar only goes as far as the lifestyle that follows it. One moment of *sincere* repentance can do what a thousand trips to the altar without follow-through cannot. I am not minimizing the importance of altar calls. There can be something special about making a tangible commitment to the Lord. But the altar is just the means to an end. The end is a heart change that must result in an altered lifestyle. An apologetic person is not necessarily experiencing biblical repentance.

WORLD SORROW OR GODLY SORROW?

Paul gives a great illustration of the difference between being sorry and true repentance in II Corinthians 7. What Paul is describing in these verses are two kinds of sorrow. The word for sorrow in Greek is *lupe*, which means, "sadness, grief, heaviness."[10]

There is a sorrow that Satan loves and a sorrow he hates. One will drag a person deeper into darkness and one pulls a person up into the light. In this chapter, Paul is discussing a previous letter he wrote to the Corinthian church. In it, he had rebuked them about specific areas in their lives, but Paul rejoices because that sorrow caused them to repent. (v. 9) He explains that *godly* sorrow produces repentance which leads to salvation. (v. 10) Can you see why the devil hates it?

There is another sorrow, referred to as the sorrow of the world. This is the emotion most people feel when they get caught doing something wrong. We have all seen public figures getting exposed for secret sin. The exposure may cause consequences to their reputations, families, marriages and careers. They often make public apologies, but sometimes you can tell they are not truly sorry. They are just sorry they got caught. This type of emotion is *worldly* sorrow.

Worldly sorrow can be sincere, but it is sincerely the wrong kind. Godly sorrow is a gift from the Lord to cause us to realize our need to repent and turn to Him. But the enemy loves to get people to experience worldly sorrow. It is extremely deceptive because it feels like legitimate remorse. We may even wish things were different. But worldly sorrow will not cause any change in our lives. In fact, Paul tells us that it leads to death. (v. 10)

So the question that might come to mind is, "How can I obtain godly sorrow?" II Timothy 2:25 says that repentance is a gift from God. It does require action on our part, but ultimately it is God who grants it to us, so we should ask Him for it.

Godly sorrow is a blessing. If someone feels sorrow over his sin, the worst thing another person can do is say, "Don't be so hard on yourself." Our self-esteem culture suggests that people just need enough positive reinforcement to get out of their problem. Tell that to Jesus when he openly rebuked the Pharisees or told Peter, "Get behind me Satan!"[11]

The hypocrite needs to see the ugliness of his ways. That is the process the Lord uses to bring us into a broken state so we will repent. In James 1, the Bible is referred to as a mirror. When we compare God's standard of holiness to our lives, we are supposed to see what does not line up so we can cooperate with the Holy Spirit and change. Who will stop sinning if they do not see the ugliness of it first? It is not until we see sin for what it is that God can help us overcome it. His plan is to bring us into a brand-new, unified life in Him. Godly sorrow is not where the Lord wants us to live as His children, but hypocrites must pass through this wilderness on the way to the Promised Land of freedom.

THE FRUIT OF REPENTANCE

Continuing in II Corinthians 7:11, Paul shows us what the evidence of godly sorrow is. He says:

See what this godly sorrow has produced in you: what earnestness, what eagerness to clear yourselves, what indignation, what alarm, what longing, what concern, what readiness to see justice done.

What Paul is saying is that there is evidence when true repentance has occurred. Luke 3:8 tells us to "produce fruit in keeping with repentance." We should be able to look at our lives and point to changes and say, "This is how I know I've repented."

The fruit of repentance was lacking in my life when hypocrisy fixed its roots in me. I may have attempted to pretend I had fruit, but there was no evidence deep down inside. If you are wondering whether a trip you took to the altar was true repentance or merely lip-service, just look for the proof of it. True repentance should cause a desire to rid your life of sin. The sin should not be something you can run right back into without a second thought. Although temptation may still come, there should be a godly fear that prevents you from giving in, and a vehement desire to stay in good standing with God.

When I was in Bible college, I struggled with a particular habitual sin. My solution was to respond to every altar call that was given and cry out to the Lord; but that is where I drew the line. I was not really prepared to do what was required to rid myself of the idol. I thought I was sincere, but the fact that I continued in that besetting sin proved that sincerity was not enough. There were plenty of practical steps that I could have taken to eliminate the sin, but I refused. My repentance was proven false by the fact that there was no fruit from it.

It is like the saying, "Put your money where your mouth is." If you really mean business with God, you will do whatever it takes. People who have wet eyes on Sunday, but no change on Monday, need to examine the sincerity of their repentance.

Some would propose that sinning less is fruit of their repentance. A trip to the altar may serve to delay their sinful activity temporarily, so they point to that as evidence that they have repented. However, the fruit of true repentance is a discontinuation of the sin, not just a change in its frequency.

Think about it. Imagine someone telling his spouse, "I am only committing adultery once a year now—it used to be a lot worse!" Would a spouse be quick to forgive and sweep the matter under the rug? Of course not! They would be headed to divorce court and it would be hard to find a sympathetic ear to comfort them and say, "Once in a while is no big deal."

Sadly, this is what too many Christians do to God. He is forgiving, but there is a vast difference between slipping up occasionally in an area and intentionally sinning. I am not advocating that He is ready to divorce us every time we sin. It is true that we are human and will sometimes make mistakes. However, too many Christians use the "I am just human" argument to stay in habitual sin. The fruit of biblical repentance is that one no longer partakes in the sin they repented of.

REPENTANCE: AN ONGOING PROCESS

One of the tragic consequences of the false grace teaching in our churches (see page 116) is a huge down-play on the concept of repentance. After all, why would any believer need to repent if grace just covered all of their sins before they committed them? Ongoing repentance becomes unnecessary if it is only important at salvation. Yet, repentance was never meant to be a single experience that covers us for a lifetime—or even a series of isolated events in a believer's life—but rather a lifestyle. Anyone who argues that they never have a need to repent should study James 4:17. This verse says, "Anyone, then, who knows the good he ought to do and doesn't do it sins." I do not know any Christian who cannot apply that to his or her life at least some of the time. As the Holy Spirit brings conviction to an area in our lives, we are to repent, ask forgiveness and forsake that sin.

It is important to realize that once we have repented, we can move on in victory. We do not need to live in shame and condemnation once we have done business with the Lord. Imagine a husband who sins against his wife. He confesses to her and she forgives him. Then he comes back a week later and says, "I am so sorry for what I did last week, please forgive me." So she nicely responds, "I've already forgiven you." What if that husband went to his wife every week, always asking forgiveness for the same thing that he was already forgiven for? The wife would say, "Stop it! I forgave you right after you confessed the first time!"

Many Christians are like this in their relationship with God. He does not want us to live in constant guilt over what *He has already forgiven and is in the past*. He wants us to enjoy our life with Him. When the enemy comes to try to bring condemnation, we need to realize we have been forgiven and move on. However, whenever there is sin that we have not dealt with, repentance becomes a necessity.

NO EXCUSES BEFORE GOD

So how do we approach the Lord in repentance? A.W. Tozer said the repentant man:

...should put away all defense and make no attempt to excuse himself either in his own eyes or before the Lord...Let the inquiring Christian trample under foot every slippery trick of his deceitful heart and insist upon frank and open relations with the Lord.[12]

This advice is especially true with a hypocrite coming to the Lord in repentance. Honesty is *critical*. The person who has been hiding behind a spiritual mask has had to constantly justify his behavior in order to push off the guilt that comes from living in guile. I used to regularly try to rationalize even blatant sin and disobedience. I would try to convince the Lord that I was powerless to fight it. Obviously He was not fooled, but I comforted myself with my list of excuses. It was not until I was totally honest with the Lord that change began to happen.

King David is a great example of a man who went from rationalizing sin to having no excuses before God. When he saw Bathsheba on the roof in II Samuel 11, he gave into the temptation to lust after her. That lust in his heart found expression in the outward act of adultery. We are not told how it all unfolded. I cannot imagine he brought her into his palace and said, "I am the king and I command you to sleep with me." I envision he probably talked with her, gave her attention and made her feel special. I doubt Bathsheba went to the palace with sex on her mind. Maybe she just got caught up in all the riches and power. Either way, Bathsheba ends up pregnant.

If you want to see extreme justification, just look at the fact that David had Bathsheba's husband killed in order to cover up his sin. Can you imagine the thoughts going through his mind? A person does not just plot a murder overnight. He must have thought through every angle. First, he brought Uriah back from the battlefield to try to get him to sleep with Bathsheba to make it look like it was his own baby. The most heartbreaking part of the story is that Uriah is so loyal to David, he refuses to go home in spite of David's attempts to get him drunk.

David's plans go from bad to worse when he justifies the murder. "If I cannot make Uriah think it is his baby, he has to die." I am sure this is where David's thoughts must have been. However, there was another way: confession and repentance. However, according to Mosaic Law, David could have been put to death for adultery, so confession was a risky option.[13] There is a period of at least nine months where David chooses to live without repenting. In his eyes, the problem has been taken care of. Bathsheba is his wife and no one knows what happened.

But Someone does know.

I cannot imagine a day went by that David did not feel guilt in his heart, but he kept rationalizing.

"It's better this way."

"We were meant to be together."

"Uriah probably would have died in battle either way..."

I am sure he had a list of justifications a mile long. Then, Nathan the prophet knocks on David's door. (II Samuel 12:1) I wonder if the king was nervous about seeing a man who had a reputation of hearing directly from Jehovah. Or maybe his heart was so hardened at this point that he was overly confident that everything had been swept under the rug. I remember times in my own life during church services that I was afraid of the speaker calling me out for my hypocrisy in front of everyone through a revelation from God. Then, there were other times that, in my arrogance, I took pride in how well I could fake it.

Regardless of what David thought when Nathan entered the room, he was confronted by the prophet and something beautiful took place: King David repents. He throws out all of the lies, justification and rationalization and just comes to God in brokenness.

PSALM 51

When King David repents, he writes a beautiful psalm to pour out his heart to God. Psalm 51 is perhaps the greatest repentance prayer ever prayed. David really does business with the Lord. He comes in brutal honesty and gets right with the One he sinned against. When reading through the psalm, you get the impression that this is a man who is no longer in denial. He takes ownership of his sin and says, "Against you, you only, have I sinned." (v. 4)

His highest priority is re-establishing his relationship with God. He has seen his sin, and now he makes the following requests:

Create in me a pure heart, O God, and renew a steadfast spirit within me. Do not cast me from your presence or take your Holy Spirit from me. Restore to me the joy of your salvation and grant me a willing spirit, to sustain me. (vv. 10-12)

This is the cry of the truly repentant heart. A repentant person needs to see how their sin affects their relationship with God. A sincere believer will long to do whatever is necessary in order to make things right. David does not ask for the Lord to change his circumstances. He does not try to make excuses. He only asks for his relationship with God to be restored and for the strength to walk in purity.

In verse 17, David makes a powerful statement when he writes, "My sacrifice, O God, is a broken spirit; a broken and contrite heart you, God, will not despise." The Lord will always respond to a truly repentant heart. If there are areas in your life that you need to repent of, Jesus is just waiting for you to do it. It is His desire that your relationship with Him be restored.

This is where every hypocrite must get breakthrough in order to find freedom. If someone stops at this point and chooses to harden his heart toward God, he will not make it out. This is a lesson I learned the hard way. When we returned home from the mission field after my confession, what I needed was to come to the Lord in true repentance. But rather than repent, I was willing to go to counseling, take medication and do just about anything to try to side-step it. The eight months that I spent unrepentant were some of the darkest, most frightening months of my entire life. Please take it from someone who knows from experience: *Do not put repentance off another minute!* You are only hurting yourself if you do.

TWO RICH MEN MEET JESUS

Two rich men in the Gospels were given a chance to respond to Jesus in repentance. The first one was Zacchaeus. Most Christians know the story about the short tax collector who climbed a sycamore tree in order to see the Messiah. I had read this story many times, but because I had a 'children's church' level of understanding, it never had the full impact on my heart. What takes place in this story is a powerful picture of repentance.

Zacchaeus was a chief tax collector. We are told he was a wealthy man in Luke 19. Tax collectors in those days were slaves to money. They were extortionists and they ripped people off to make a comfortable living for themselves. Zacchaeus clearly references that this was his lifestyle when he vows to pay back anyone he cheated four times what was stolen. (v. 8) Obviously, he had overcharged people on their taxes.

Money was an idol for Zacchaeus; it was his drive. His love of money caused him to live a sinful life. When he not only chooses to repay everyone he cheated, but also gives half of his possessions to the poor, you see a dramatic heart change. Here was a man who saw his sin and was zealous to make it right however he could. He got the idol out of his heart and became a changed man.

The rich, young ruler in Matthew 19 had the exact opposite reaction. He came to Jesus and asked, "Teacher, what good thing must I do to get eternal life?" (v.16) Jesus responded by saying that he must keep the commandments. The man was probably hopeful at this point when he replies, "All these I have kept...What do I still lack?" (v. 20)

You can tell from his response that this ruler followed the Torah his whole life. He must have grown up in a Law-abiding Jewish home. Jesus did not argue with him and say, "No, you have not obeyed the commandments." Instead, He simply says, "If you want to be perfect, go, sell your possessions and give to the poor, and you will have treasure in heaven. Then come, follow me." (v. 21)

This ruler asked a loaded question. He asked Jesus what was standing in his way spiritually. However, he got an answer that he did not like. Just like Zacchaeus, this man was a slave to money and possessions. Unlike Zacchaeus, he walked away upset because he was not willing to give the 'one thing' up. (v. 22) These two rich men had a lot in common when they met Jesus. Coming into contact with the Savior only produced life-changing repentance in the life of one of them.

Take a moment right now and imagine that you were the rich, young ruler. You ask Jesus, "What is standing in between me and total surrender?" What would He tell you? What are you holding back from Him? When God puts His finger on something in our lives, we need to respond like Zacchaeus. We do not want to refuse and remain in bondage like the rich ruler. The way we respond may very well determine our access to eternal life.

Now we have taken the first step. Without repentance, the rest of this book will accomplish nothing. Take some time to pour your heart out to the Lord. Then, we will examine another key area in overcoming hypocrisy: *Exposure*.

Secret:

1. **adjective.** kept from public knowledge or from the knowledge of a certain person or persons

2. concealed from sight or notice; hidden[1]

*   *   *

Jeremiah 16:17 (NIV)- My eyes are on all their ways; they are not hidden from me, nor is their sin concealed from my eyes.

Isaiah 29:15 (NKJV)- Woe to those who seek deep to hide their counsel far from the Lord, and their works are in the dark; they say, "Who sees us?" and, "Who knows us?"

Isaiah 29:15 (MSG)- Doom to you! You pretend to have the inside track. You shut God out and work behind the scenes, plotting the future as if you knew everything, acting mysterious, never showing your hand.

*   *   *

"The double life must be dismantled no matter what. Satan knows the power he has within secrecy. The man who wants to remain in his sin avoids exposure at all costs. However, the man who is serious about overcoming it exposes his sin so that he is less likely to succumb to the temptations when they arise later. Living a double life prevents a solid foundation of godliness from being formed."

-Steve Gallagher[2]

8

HYPOCRISY'S ENEMIES: EXPOSURE

EXPOSURE IS ONE OF THE MOST potent weapons against hypocrisy. Yet it is also the one that requires the most courage to carry out. Many people fail to realize that exposure is immanent. Everyone will be exposed—there is no way around it. Whether in this life or in the throne room of God, every man's heart will be "laid bare before the eyes of him to whom we must give account."[3] We might be able to cover up a pseudo-faith and fool others enough to say nice things about us at our funeral. But on the other side of this mortal life, we will appear before a God who is completely holy. We will have no religious mask to hide behind and our true selves will be revealed.

Who did we *really* live for? Did we *really* know Jesus or was it just a game? Was our life *really* motivated by self-love or self-less love? The answers to these questions determine if we truly knew God and our eternal destination will be decided in that moment. We will not have a chance to take anything back. There will not be an opportunity to repent. There will be pleading for mercy, but none will be extended. It will be a horrifying moment for many, though the Lord never wanted it to be that way. There is still time if you are reading this book. No matter how you have lived or what you have done, there is a loving God ready to respond to your cry for mercy right now!

The thought of judgment day should make us think. In Revelation 20:11-15, we are given a glimpse into the great throne room of judgment:

> Then I saw a great white throne and him who was seated on it... And I saw the dead, great and small, standing before the throne, and books were opened. Another book was opened, which is the book of life. The dead were judged according to what they had done as recorded in the books...Anyone whose name was not found written in the book of life was thrown into the lake of fire.

Do we really want to wait until we stand before God to come clean about hypocrisy? Although no one would want that to happen, refusing to expose our double-lives will only reinforce the likelihood of that outcome.

In hypocrisy, the number one fear that plagued me day and night was that I would be exposed for who I truly was. I believed the lie that no one could possibly love me after that. That is one of the greatest tactics of the enemy to keep us in bondage. He whispers in our ear, "You cannot come clean. Think of what it will do to your family. What about your reputation? You will bring shame to Jesus. You cannot show the world you are a hypocrite." On and on he goes. The more we try to avoid exposure, the deeper the darkness grows. Then, the walls between us and other people grow thicker.

GOD THE EXPOSER OF DARKNESS

In Revelation 21:23, John writes a description of Heaven: "The city does not need the sun or the moon to shine on it, for the glory of God gives it light, and the Lamb is its lamp." Think about that. If the sun was ever extinguished, the whole sky would be pitch black because we depend on it for light. In Heaven, we will not need a powerful light source like the sun because the Lord is the light.

Light exposes darkness. We cannot hide anything from the Lord's all-seeing gaze. Look at these passages that confirm this:

I Corinthians 4:5- Therefore judge nothing before the appointed time; wait until the Lord comes. He will bring to light what is hidden in darkness and will expose the motives of the heart.

Jeremiah 23:24- "Who can hide in secret places so that I cannot see them?" declares the Lord. "Do not I fill heaven and earth?"

If God had to write a resumé, you would find one position that He has always held is 'Exposer of Darkness.' The Lord's light will always penetrate the darkness of sin and secrecy. His desire is that we allow Him to expose the darkness in our lives on Earth, so that we can walk in His light. Every deed will be exposed for what it is one day. Allowing Him to expose the truth about ourselves now or choosing to carry sin and secrecy to our graves, has eternal implications.

Jesus makes a powerful statement about light and darkness in John 3:19-21. He says:

This is the verdict: Light has come into the world, but people loved darkness instead of light because their deeds were evil. Everyone who does evil hates the light, and will not come into the light for fear that their deeds will be exposed. But whoever lives by the truth comes into the light, so that it may be seen plainly that what they have done has been done in the sight of God.

Jesus—the light of God—came into the world to expose darkness. Yet those who do evil hate the light for *fear* that their deeds will be exposed. This is the fear that keeps many hypocrites from coming into the light. Allowing the light of the Lord to shine into the darkness of our lives brings liberation from it.

Light and darkness cannot co-exist. When you enter a dark closet and turn a flashlight on, the darkness is immediately dispelled. By allowing the darkness in our lives to be exposed to the light, God can help set us free from anything we are hiding. It is something that comes naturally for Him, but we choose whether or not we allow His light to shine in the dark places of our hearts.

What if you knew that facing your fear of exposure was the only thing standing in your way to freedom? What if you knew that even though you might need to walk through a difficult season, there was a vibrant, unified life in Christ just on the other side of it? Would you do it? Is it not worth paying any price for freedom?

THE VANITY OF HIDING

Many hypocrites are masters of disguise. They secretly take pride in how well they can fool other people. However, wearing a mask is always in vain; there is no true secrecy. Isaiah 29:15 says clearly:

Woe to those who go to great lengths to hide their plans from the Lord, who do their work in darkness and think, "Who sees us? Who will know?"

This is an exact description of the hypocrite's attitude. They go out of their way to cover up their lifestyle and may think God does not notice. But He sees it all.

Listen to how Jesus describes Himself to the church of Thyatira in Revelation. He says, "Then all the churches will know that I am he who searches hearts and minds, and I will repay each of you according to your deeds."[4] To those whose walk with the Lord consists of nothing more than going through the motions, you need to stop and ask yourself some questions. Do you expect to escape the One who searches hearts and minds? Do you really think He will miss any area of your life?

Many hypocrites live their lives as if the person they are portraying to others is the only person anyone can see. As long as they keep their true selves hidden, they feel safe. What they fail to realize is that Scripture clearly tells us in Proverbs 5:21, "For your ways are in full view of the Lord, and he examines all your paths." So it does not matter how great someone is at making other people think they are spiritual, God still sees their true motives.

To think that the Lord cannot see what is happening is a delusion. I can remember how deceived I was, even in the midst of gross sin. When I looked at my own life and who I thought I was, I automatically viewed myself from the perspective of what others saw. I was a missionary. I had a testimony of salvation. I was active in church and people generally thought of me as a godly person. What I refused to see was that the *real me* was the person I was when no one else was around. I was not a sincere, devoted follower of Christ who just had a few struggles in his life. I was hiding behind a cardboard cut-out of spirituality. It took a great deal of breaking down to be able to see what should have been obvious to me all along.

When I played with my daughter when she was little, she used to cover up her eyes to hide from me. Her little mind could not understand that just because she could not see me did not mean I could not see her. Yet that is exactly how God sees our foolish attempts to hide. Think of how pointless a spiritual mask looks to Him. These truths should cause anyone in hypocrisy to cry out to God for mercy. So come out and expose the hypocrisy! Be done once and for all and be free!

EXPOSURE IS MERCY

I want to say something here that might not seem to make sense: Exposure is the mercy of God. Most people do not view it that way. You might ask, "How can that be? I have seen people exposed and their lives are often destroyed."

When I had drifted from the Lord and was living in blatant hypocrisy, I wanted to find some way to get out of the mess I was in. I was willing to confide in one person who I knew would not tell anyone else. I was willing to read books, do Bible studies, and try all kinds of different approaches to get free. However, I was not willing to do anything that involved exposing my double-life. Looking back, I *fully* believe that I could not be set free from the bondage until I allowed the Lord to expose it. There was never any other possibility available to me.

I twisted Scriptures in order to appease my conscience. I told myself, "If I confess to God, I am forgiven, so I do not need to tell anyone else." I also said, "Eventually things will change, so it would only hurt people unnecessarily if I confessed." I would swear, "This is the last time I'll ever do that. As long as I quit after this, there's no need to expose it."

I cannot say that my fear was not based on some reality. The truth is, I had a lot to lose. I had spoken at countless churches, youth groups, outreaches and concerts and shared my testimony with thousands of people about how Jesus had set me free from drugs and sexual immorality. I continued to share publicly even after that ceased to be a reality in my life. I had relocated our family to the foreign mission field and we had sold most of our belongings. I knew that if I confessed, we would be asked to step down and return home. We did not have a backup plan. A career in missions was our goal and we were taking the necessary steps to continue on that path. Our first daughter had just been born, and I sincerely believed my wife would leave me if I confessed to my secret life. When I thought of exposure, my perception that it could cost me dearly was not just my imagination. It was almost a guarantee that I would pay an enormous price.

Whenever the guilt and shame would rise up inside me, the reoccurring thought would come: "If only I would confess, this nightmare could be over." However, it was the fear of exposure that I continued to succumb to. I thought about what my wife, family, church and all the people I had falsely testified to would think. I thought about the unbelievers in my life who would be pushed even further away from the faith at my confession. I wondered where we would live, what our future would hold and what my kids down the road would think of their struggling dad. Those fears were so strong that, even though I longed to cry out for help, I just could not bring myself to do it for many years.

What I have found is that exposure can be the greatest blessing that a hypocrite could ever receive. Exposure is not God's way of trying to put someone to public shame so that they will get what is coming to them. It is His way of opening a door of escape from living with a divided heart.

I have met many friends in the last few years who have gone through horrible public humiliation. On the other side of it—although they had to walk through some extremely challenging seasons—they can look back and testify: "It was the Lord's *mercy* that I was exposed." This is because they could not enter into a rich relationship with Jesus or an intimate relationship with a spouse, family or friends, while still wearing a mask.

WALKING IN THE LIGHT

If exposure is an enemy of hypocrisy, one of its greatest allies is secrecy. Anyone who has ever lived a double-life is well aware of this fact. The two go hand-in-hand. Show me a Christian with a secret life and I will show you a hypocrite. A person who lives a life of secrecy does not fully disclose themselves to others. They project a false image to those around them. The moment someone decides in their heart that they are going to keep something secret from everyone else, they automatically put a mask over their face. What they are saying is, "I do not want anyone to find out about this because _____." Fill in the blank for your situation (I do not want to feel rejected, no one will like me, understand me, etc.). The reasons may vary but the intent is always the same. Hypocrites choose to keep themselves hidden so that no one will be able to discover who they truly are.

If there is one key that would help set a person free from hypocrisy, it is this: *You have to let the secrets out!* I know just thinking about that sent some readers into a panic. It was my fear of doing this that held me captive for years. If I even considered telling my wife even small things, I automatically had a defensive wall of excuses and justifications pop up:

"Things will eventually change."

"She is better off not knowing."

"The truth will only hurt her more…"

And on and on the excuses went. Each of them assisted in justifying my choice to live a secret life.

Scripture tells us plainly we are to "walk in the light, as he is in the light."[5] This means true Christians should not have areas of darkness in their lives. We should not be a people with skeletons in our closets. Jesus paid the highest price so that we can be completely free. If there are areas of darkness in your life now, bring it into the light and let God help you with it. Then, learn what it means to walk continually in the light.

SECRECY BREEDS DECEPTION

A secret kept leads to lies. During my high school years, I was a drug addict. I still lived at home, so I could not do whatever I wanted, whenever I wanted. In order to go out and party, I had to come up with a story. I would tell my parents that I was going out with some friends to watch a movie. It seemed like an innocent lie, but in order to keep the partying a secret, I had to start lying all the time. They would ask about the movie, and I would have to make something up. The stories got more detailed as I grew more paranoid that I would be found out. Pretty soon, I was in such a web of lies, I did not know what the truth was anymore. I would 'remember' things and then find out later they never happened.

That is what secrecy causes. If not confessed, one 'little white lie' will need other lies to reinforce it. Then the stories grow more sophisticated until the secret has caused a domino effect of lying and deception. This is how double-lives are built. They are formed one secret at a time, fortified by all of the supporting lies that go with it. The more secrets and lies one has, the greater the separation between who someone really is and who they are pretending to be to everyone else.

There is only one escape route: exposure through *full* confession. Some try to partially confess that they are living a double-life, but they are unwilling to fully disclose everything. They may admit to sin in their lives, but lie about the frequency or depth to which they are involved. The problem with a partial confession is that whatever area remains unconfessed will suck them right back into secrecy. They may feel at peace for a short time, having let some of the burden off of their chest, but darkness always breeds darkness. If you do not deal a deathblow to it, it will grow. You will be more hardened in your heart than before your partial confession. We need life-changing exposure because a secret life is similar to a cancerous tumor. Just like morphine can temporarily relieve the pain of a cancer patient, partial confession can take the edge off of the guilt. To kill the tumor, you need full disclosure, which is like radiation to secret sin.

Roy Hession nicely sums up the importance of transparency with others in his book *Calvary Road*:

> We must be willing not only to know, but to be known by [them] for what we really are. That means we are not going to hide our inner selves from those with whom we ought to be in fellowship; we are not going to window-dress and put on appearances; nor are we going to whitewash and excuse ourselves. We are going to be honest about ourselves with them. We are willing to give up our spiritual privacy, pocket our pride, and risk our reputations for the sake of being open and transparent with our brethren in Christ.[6]

HOW FREE DO YOU WANT TO BE?

To the degree that you are willing to be transparent, you can be free from hypocrisy. I am not talking about letting everyone in your life know everything. It is imperative that certain people know all of the details, like a spouse, a parent if you are under their care, or a pastor who is counseling you. However, there are many who have no business knowing every detail of your struggles. Exercise wisdom and find someone to guide you through the process. However, to be free, there should be someone with whom you are *totally* transparent.

Obviously God fits this role, but there are many who would say, "I've confessed everything to the Lord and He forgave me, so I do not need to tell anyone else." For a hypocrite, I do not believe this is ever an acceptable option. All they need to do is look at how they have ended up where they are to understand the reason why. How many times have they confessed to the Lord and asked His forgiveness? Probably more than they can count. Can they honestly look at their lives and say, "I do not need to tell anyone else?" This might be an easy way to let themselves off the hook, but they will stay in bondage thinking like this. Confession to God is certainly essential, but it cannot stop there. James 5:16 says plainly we are to confess our sins to *each other*.

Just how serious are you about getting free from hypocrisy? How much do you really want to live a whole life for Jesus? Some would agree with this chapter in their heads and say, "That is true." However, if you show your unwillingness to follow through in this area, I would seriously question your heart. It is one thing to agree, and an entirely different thing to follow through. Ask the Lord to break you and make you willing to do whatever it takes, no matter how painful or costly it may be. Freedom in Him is totally worth it!

THE ROLE OF ACCOUNTABILITY

Hypocrites despise true accountability. They just want to be left alone. They do not want anyone probing too closely, because it puts the mask into focus. A religious mask is like a Monet painting, which looks great from a distance. But as you get closer, you can see all the little brush strokes that make up the bigger picture. In the same way, as you get closer to the life of a hypocrite, you begin to see inconsistencies. They have the talk down and can play the religious game. From the surface, everything looks great, but if you try to press deeper, they will grow uncomfortable and withdraw.

For the person who is committed to rid their lives of hypocrisy, accountability is crucial. While the first step into freedom is to expose the darkness, there is a need to maintain that freedom. Having someone to help them along the process will prove to be an invaluable asset. However, this should never replace our reliance on the Holy Spirit. We need to learn to walk in the Spirit and allow Him to ultimately keep us accountable. There is a danger in putting too much emphasis on a person or program to depend on. This can make us become dependent on someone or something other than God. What happens if you really need to talk to someone and your accountability partner is not available? The Holy Spirit is always with us.

That being said, as I am learning to live free from hypocrisy and besetting sin, I have found that talking to a person is often needed. There are thoughts that may be tempting in my head, but if I say them out loud,

I realize how foolish they are. We need to have people in our lives that we can be totally honest with. This is a perfect way to ensure we are walking in transparency and not hiding anything.

An accountability partner cannot be just any person in your life. It must be someone who is walking humbly with the Lord himself. It makes no sense to find someone on the same level that you are. It is true that you really cannot take someone further spiritually than you have gone yourself. Find someone who is in a place spiritually that you want to be. It might be a minister, a family member or a friend. Do not waste your time with an 'accountability partner' who is not going to demand honesty and growth in you. Pick someone who is dependable and consistent. They need to be able to ask you the tough questions like, "Are there any areas in your life that you are hiding something?" or "How much time are you spending with God?" It does no good to have someone who is not going to push you to be true to the Lord.

Accountability has been a huge blessing for me. There are people in my life who I know are fighting for me. If I mess up, I can confess to them and they will hold me accountable. They push me to really seek the Lord and stay strong in Him. It is important to find someone who can fill this role in your life. Then submit yourself to that person so you can continue to walk in the light.

A TRANSPARENT LIFESTYLE

For years, I grew accustomed to always being fearful of exposure. Learning to go from a lifestyle of complete secrecy to living like an open book has not happened overnight. A hypocrite's mindset is in constant self-protection. They are continually thinking, "What if someone finds out what I am really like?" Secrecy becomes a very treasured thing and exposure becomes the ultimate threat.

The amazing thing that occurs when your secrets are exposed is that you no longer have that fear hanging over your head. Once I exposed my hypocrisy, I did not have to worry about what people would think if they knew because it was out in the open. The shame that I initially felt gradually faded and the experience I feared the most ended up being the greatest thing that could have happened to me. It was the very *doorway* I had to walk through to eventually arrive at freedom. For so long I had tried to sidestep that door. I was willing to do anything but expose the secret life. I read books, pleaded with the Lord and tried to get free in my own strength, but found it impossible. The whole time, it was as if God was saying, "You can try anything you want, but the only door to freedom and repentance is through confession."

So coming into a transparent lifestyle from one that was so secretive was very intimidating. I am continually learning the extreme importance of transparency. I see now that the old hypocritical life will always be there calling my name. Secret sins and old ways of coping are always going to be temptations to some degree. But one of the best ways to maintain freedom from the grips of hypocrisy is to learn to live a transparent lifestyle.

Exposing hypocrisy is key to getting total victory over it. In the next chapter, we will examine another strong enemy of hypocrisy: *Consecration*.

Consecrate:
1. **verb.** to set apart as holy; make or declare sacred for religious use
2. to devote entirely; dedicate[1]

*   *   *

I John 2:15 (NIV)- Do not love the world or anything in the world. If anyone loves the world, love for the Father is not in them.

*   *   *

"The time has passed when we need to go out into the world in order to make contact with it. Today the world comes and searches us out. There is a force abroad now which is captivating men. Have you ever felt the power of the world as much as today? Have you ever heard so much talk about money? Have you ever thought so much about food and clothing? Wherever you go, even among Christians, the things of the world are the topics of conversation. The world has advanced to the very door of the Church and is seeking to draw even the saints of God into its grasp. Never in this sphere of things have we needed to know the power of the Cross of Christ to deliver us as we do at the present time."

-Watchman Nee[2]

"I looked for the church and found it in the world.
I looked for the world and found it in the church."

-Andrew Bonar[3]

9

HYPOCRISY'S ENEMIES: CONSECRATION

ONE POWERFUL TOOL THAT THE LORD has used to keep me free from a hypocritical life is consecration. In a church culture where worldliness is creeping in at an alarming rate, we need to have a way to counteract it in our lives; consecration is the key. Worldliness intensifies hypocrisy. This is because trying to live for the Kingdom of God *and* the kingdom of this world reinforces division in a Christian's heart. In order to understand the importance of this spiritual discipline, we must first discuss the concept of worldliness.

THE CHURCH AND WORLDLINESS

In today's church culture, the idea of worldliness is a difficult concept to define. Just like a fish that does not realize it is immersed in water until it is taken out, someone who is surrounded by a worldly, religious culture will not easily identify it around them. However, the concept of worldliness was not always so obscure to the Christian community. Not too many years in the past, the church—as a whole—was very concerned about becoming too worldly. I have talked to many saints from previous generations that were taught that going to a movie theatre, playing cards and other activities that are commonplace in church today, were sins and should have no part in a believer's life. Although I believe that many of those rules became legalism, there was an attitude behind them that I think we have lost.

The thinking of many in the church used to be, "I want to stay as far away from compromising with the world as possible." What happened to that attitude that once so permeated our Christian circles? Despite the church's bent toward legalism, there was much more emphasis placed on the dangers of partaking of the things of the world. We do not see much of that thinking in the American church today. It seems that we have swung too far to the other side of the pendulum.

I understand that those reading this book are from a variety of backgrounds. There are parts of the church that still hold very legalistic views. I had a conversation recently with someone who came from a church that had a strict dress code and taught that if you owned a TV, you would go to Hell. In no way am I in support of such teachings, which put people into bondage and fear. On the other side are segments of the church that claim we can live any way that we want—even in direct opposition to Scripture—and that the Lord has no problem with that. Both of these sides have gone way off balance from true holiness. In my experience in the Christian church, I have seen much more of the latter.

Most church cultures have a list of unspoken expectations that are common to many in the Evangelical community (i.e. no drinking, smoking, cursing, etc.). However, outside of these general guidelines, most Christians seem to live the way that they want to without much consideration about becoming too worldly.

The heart of this chapter is not to make legalistic rules and impose them on anyone. It is to show how I came into the revelation of the worldliness in my own life, and how the Lord has helped me overcome it. Each of us will have to make our own decisions about our lifestyles. And although worldliness may not be a common characteristic of all Christian hypocrites, it contributed so heavily to my own experience that I cannot neglect this area.

HOW CLOSE IS TOO CLOSE?

The question that we each need to ask ourselves as we examine the topic of consecration is, "Am I compromising in any area of my life?" Webster defines compromise as to "accept standards that are lower than is desirable."[4] Anytime we allow anything into our lives that is lower than God's desire for us in His Word, we are compromising in that area. When we are confronted with the things of this world and their unbiblical values—regardless of the level of enjoyment they may offer—we make the choice to either compromise or obey the Lord.

It seems that Western church culture has shifted from an almost phobia-like fear of compromising, to a lifestyle that encompasses it. Steve Gallagher accurately defines the attitude of average American churchgoers in reference to holiness when he said:

> The basic attitude of most American Christians is to go after and get every kind of pleasure they can possibly get their hands on short of obvious sin; and to enjoy every form of entertainment they can possibly enjoy short of obvious sin; to indulge every desire of the flesh they can possibly indulge short of obvious sin; to pursue every personal idol that they have built up in their heart as long as it's short of obvious sin.[5]

This 'How close can I get?' type of thinking is not a way to get closer to the Lord, but instead will bring you closer to the world. As William Law once wrote about true believers, they do not "ask what is allowable and pardonable, but what is commendable and praiseworthy."[6] Or John Bevere says it this way:

A person who is truly saved has God's heart and doesn't say within,

"How much can I sin and get away with?" Rather, an authentically born-again believer says, "I don't desire to sin because it hurts the heart of Him who died for me as well as those He loves."[7]

At the heart of consecration is a desire to get as close to Jesus as possible. If our hearts are given over to the things of this world, consecration will be a very undesirable spiritual discipline.

WHAT IS CONSECRATION?

To consecrate means "to set apart as holy," or "to devote entirely; dedicate."[8] A church is just a building unless you consecrate it as a church. Abstaining from food is just a diet unless you consecrate it as a fast. Here I want to define consecration as a lifestyle where you pour your time, passion and energy into the things of God rather than the things of this world. That is the foundation of the consecrated life, and I saw it displayed clearly at Pure Life Ministries.

In the beginning of my time there, I was surprised when I discovered that the staff had strict parameters about the movies they watched and that they had no network television. Before this, I cannot remember ever meeting any person or family who did not watch TV or secular movies. Although some people I knew were not really 'TV people,' even they did not live completely without it. On that ranch in Dry Ridge, Kentucky, I was faced with some lifestyle choices that seemed nothing short of radical at best, and unnecessary in my estimation.

When I began to hear teaching about worldliness in the program, I was beyond skeptical. When I learned how the staff lived, I thought, "You have to be kidding me. These people are living like it is the year 1900. Someone needs to tell them it's 2011!" Yet there was an *unmistakable* quality about their lives that I had rarely seen in my eight plus years as a Christian. As they began to explain the correlation between ridding their lives of compromise and the joy, wisdom, discernment and depth they had in their lives, I wondered if it could really be true.

It took months of being challenged in my thinking in this area before

I really began to take it seriously. When you hear something no one else is saying, your automatic reaction is, "That cannot be true. Why haven't I heard that before?" As the Lord began to soften my heart and open my eyes, I began to see the reason this teaching is not popular. It is because our church culture is *permeated* with worldliness. It is not just affecting laypeople, but many ministers are just as carnal as their congregation. Do not get me wrong, there are some sincere, deeply spiritual pastors and ministers who love Jesus and have forsaken this world, but they are sadly becoming a rare breed.

I am not saying this with a condemning spirit. I was there once, and I would still be there, if not for the great mercy of God in my life. Because of my sinful life, I had the incredible opportunity to get plucked out of the world and be put into a place where all its attractions (TV, radio, internet, electronics, media, magazines, movies, sports, video games, etc.) had been stripped away from me. Although none of these things are necessarily evil, when I did not have those distractions, I was left with nothing but Jesus and the Bible—and it was amazing.

I was put into an atmosphere and lifestyle of consecration by the design of the program; it was not a decision I made for myself. I was only living that way because I was there and had no choice. But after time, I began to consecrate my life in several areas by my own volition.

LEGALISM DEFINED

When I was first confronted with this type of separation from the world, I did what most Christians would do: I called it *legalism*. The definition of legalism is: "strict, often too strict and literal, adherence to law or to a code," or "the doctrine of salvation by good works."[9] Legalism essentially means to depend on obeying rules for the sake of following rules. From a religious standpoint, it is depending on obedience to those rules for salvation. We have seen the devastating effects of legalism throughout church history. True legalism puts people in bondage when Jesus clearly came to set people free.

We have already discussed in detail the legalists of Jesus' time. The Son of God directly opposed the Pharisees and teachers of the Law for their legalistic lifestyles. They even used their rules and distorted traditions as a reason to crucify Jesus! Legalism leads to spiritual death. While there are still many in the church who struggle with legalism, I believe one of the greatest issues the Western church faces today is not legalism, but a spirit of permissiveness.

Frequently in our churches today, the word *legalism* is used when something threatens to expose someone's love for the world or their lack of holiness. I cannot tell you how many times I have heard things called legalistic that are not necessarily so. It is difficult to differentiate between legalism and consecration because both are determined by *heart motive*.

Two people can perform the same action with different motives and one can be a legalist and the other is making a sincere attempt at consecration. Both might look the same from the outside. Let us say you meet two professing Christians and you invite them out to eat. Both of them refuse to go to a restaurant that serves alcohol. The first one feels that because he has attained a certain level of spirituality, he could not stoop to that level. He condemns any Christian who goes to these places, even if just to eat. That is legalism and it always wants to place its demands on others.

The second person is a sincere Christian. He has made the same lifestyle choice as the legalist. However, he does it because he feels that alcohol creates a worldly atmosphere and it bothers his conscience. He does not like being in a place where there is temptation and where there are people around him partaking in things he does not want in his life. He does not condemn others who do go to these places, but he does feel strongly he is doing everything he can to please God.

I do not think you can label the second person a legalist. I am not advocating that this choice of lifestyle is or is not better for a Christian. I tried to pick an uncommon example to prove my point. However, many Christians would quickly label both as legalists without a second thought. Certainly in the life of the first professing Christian, they would be correct.

However, many times when Christians label people as legalists, it is more of a defense mechanism than true discernment. When they meet someone who has chosen not to do something that they are comfortable doing, it may bring to light an area of compromise. It is easier to brush that person off as a fanatic than to take a moment and consider whether there is some credibility to their lifestyle choices. Many Christians do not want their lifestyle to be challenged because they are comfortable in it.

I say all of that to try to paint a picture of consecration in light of legalism. An action done from the heart in order to please God cannot be legalism because that person's heart is motivated by love for Him. Legalism is often doing the right things for the wrong reason. Consecration is doing things for the right reason, even if it is not something God clearly requires of other Christians. Sometimes God will call us deeper and ask us to consecrate areas of our lives in different ways than others.

This is a vital area that the Lord has to deal with if a compromising Christian is going to repent of hypocrisy and come into a single-minded wholeness in Christ. You can do a lot of what this book teaches, but if you keep your heart open to the kingdom of this world (whose prince is Satan[10]), your loyalty will be divided and you will leave a door open for duplicity to take root again.

THE DRIVING FORCE OF YOUR LIFE

There are many Scriptures dealing with separation from the world. Yet one that stands out above all the others is James 4:4, which says:

> You adulterous people, don't you know that friendship with the world means enmity against God? Therefore, anyone who chooses to be a friend of the world becomes an enemy of God.

The amazing thing is that I used to read this verse and believe that I was living it out. I would tell myself, "I live in the world, but I am not of it." Yet, the driving force behind my life was to pursue the comforts, possessions and entertainment of this world. This is not to say that we cannot have nice things in this life or enjoy being entertained. But if the things of this world have our heart, we have a serious problem.

How can you tell what the driving force of your life really is? One incredibly helpful tool is to take an honest inventory of your life. This happens between you and God. The point is to answer truthfully—not what you want other people to see, or how you wish you were living. Take a real, 'raw-data' inventory of your everyday life. Answer the following questions prayerfully. Journaling would be very beneficial:

MONEY:

1. If you had $100 given to you today—and you had to spend it on something other than daily necessities—what would you spend it on? (And do not give the easy Christian answer, "I would give it all away to charity," unless that is really what you would do).
    -What if it was $1,000?
    -What about $10,000?
2. What do you spend most of your spare money on?
3. How often do you find yourself wishing you could attain to a greater level of wealth?
4. How convinced are you that if you just had more money, your life would be more satisfying?
5. How much of your income goes to the Kingdom of God? (tithes, offerings, missions, etc.)

TIME:

1. How many hours a week do you spend on personal enjoyment (hobbies/ watching TV/ movies/ games/ sports/ etc.)?
2. How many hours a week do you spend with Jesus personally (excluding church services and activities)?
3. When is your daily time for devotions?
    -How often do you set that time aside?
    -How much time do you spend reading Scripture?
    -How much time do you spend in prayer?
    (Do not answer these questions with what you intend to do, but what are you actually doing. Be detailed. Give actual increments of time in minutes.)

WORDS:

1. Think about your normal conversations throughout the day with family, friends and co-workers.

    -What do you find yourself talking about the most?

    -What would they say your favorite topics to talk about are?

2. How often do you talk about the Lord?

3. How does it make you feel when others talk to you about the things of God?

THOUGHTS:

1. What topics do you think about most throughout the day?

2. How much of your thoughts are taken up with spiritual things versus the things of this world?

3. What do you love thinking about?

4. What do you hate thinking about?

If you answer these questions honestly, you should be able to get a general idea of what force is driving your life. There is a difference between enjoying things in this world and being controlled or influenced by them. God wants us to enjoy life. I am not suggesting that a Christian should do nothing but pray, read the Bible and talk about Jesus. Nor should every Christian get rid of all entertainment and hobbies. However, we would all do well to examine whether or not the spirit of this world has our hearts. As we look at our lives, we will discover what is most important to us. For people struggling with hypocrisy, Jesus is not the center of their lives. So the first step is to see it, acknowledge it, and then work toward making more time for Him.

Many of us do not take the time to examine these areas. You can *believe* all the right things. Most hypocrites can agree that all Christians should spend substantial, quality time in prayer and Bible study, but they do not do it. If anything, they may have a 'devotional time' which involves merely giving God a quick greeting, grabbing a verse-for-the-day and then rushing on to what they really desire. There needs to be real intimacy if it is a true relationship.

In my case, prayer and study became formal, lifeless religious activities in an attempt to do the right thing. They did not come from a heart devoted to Jesus. Since I was a preacher, studying the Bible became nothing more than, "How can I preach this to people?" I should have been asking, "How is this preaching to me?" I was deceived to think I was spiritual because, after all, I read the Bible almost every day. Yet, my love for the world and all it had to offer *greatly* overpowered my love for Jesus.

COMMON COMPROMISE

One of the greatest areas of compromise in the Christian church is in the area of entertainment. Multitudes of professing Christians are willing to watch things in movies and TV that are completely against the Bible, but do not think much of it. My wife and I used to live just like this. Other than my secret sin, for the most part, we lived a lot like the other Christians we knew. However, we thought we took holiness a step above many of our friends, because we were very 'careful' about what we watched. Many times, I remember family and friends rolling their eyes as my wife and I had to meticulously look online at the content of each movie option before viewing it. We really thought our lives *must* be pleasing to Him.

When I think back to our discussions about movies we were interested in viewing, I see compromise all over them. We would say something like this:

"How many curse words are in the movie?"

"Well, they only say the 'F word' once. They do take the Lord's name in vain three times…so that is not too bad."

"How about nudity?"

"Well, there is a promiscuous sex scene, but they don't show anything."

When I examine our rationale now, it seems obvious to me that we were pushing the moral envelope as far as we could. How could we have been so blind to see that we were drawing an imaginary line of what *we* thought was acceptable? Certainly, Jesus wanted no part in that kind of entertainment. Many of the shows and movies we watched contained sexual innuendos, adultery, fornication, course jokes, violence and profanity. Jesus had to go to the cross for these things and pay the price of His blood—yet we viewed them as entertainment.

Unfortunately, compromise in the area of entertainment is very common in much of today's church culture. Many Christians are trying to live with one foot in the world and one in the church and are left wondering why their spiritual life is dry and unsatisfying. This is the type of lifestyle that contributes to hypocrisy in our lives and that is not the kind of life Jesus shed His blood on the cross for us to have.

LIMITING ENTERTAINMENT

One thing that our family decided to consecrate to the Lord is secular entertainment. We realized how much of the world's philosophy and values come through television, secular movies and music. We also saw how easy it is to compromise with the type of things that come out of Hollywood. So, our solution was to cut it out completely. I can testify that this has been one of the best spiritual decisions we ever made. We will watch an occasional Christian movie, but we have so filled our lives with other things that we do not have time for entertainment anymore. I understand that not everyone in the church will make a decision like that, but I do want to present it as an option that the Holy Spirit may lead some to pursue.

I know that this kind of lifestyle is very rare, except in some legalistic church circles. When I was first confronted with the thought of living a life void of entertainment, I thought, "There is no way I should live like that. Every Christian I know watches TV. How could God require that of me?" In reality, I was simply saying in my heart, "I refuse to go there."

The only reason that limiting or eliminating TV from our lives is such a strange concept is because television has become such a normal part of our existence—believer and unbeliever alike. To many, even suggesting we can or should live without it is both unreasonable and undesirable. It reminds me of a conversation I had with my wife after trying to convince her that the Lord wanted us to get rid of the television connection. She was just as skeptical about it as I had been. I tried to explain it this way. She grew up in a house that did not allow secular music to be played. It is not uncommon to find a believer who listens only to Christian music. I asked her, "Don't Christians do this because they do not want to be influenced by the world?" She agreed and I asked, "Then why is it that Christians who refuse to listen to secular music have no problem watching secular TV which is filled with the same worldly spirit?" She replied, "Because there isn't a Christian substitute."

That is the heart of the problem. For the sake of pleasure and entertainment, many Christians are willing to compromise in areas where it is convenient. We assume television is just a part of life. It is as if we just have to put up with what the networks dish out. Christians will compromise in this area and act like they are powerless to change it because, after all, "there isn't anything better available." I believe television is the most socially acceptable idol in modern Christianity. If there is one area that causes the greatest degree of compromise, it is entertainment.

I had an experience with the Lord that confirmed this in my heart. It came out of a conversation I had with someone who was talking about a particular talk show that many Christians think is harmless. They were telling me that an episode they watched had frightened them because it made them realize how depraved people can be. The following morning, I was in prayer and that conversation popped into my mind. I found myself asking, "Why in the world would someone want to think about the wicked things people can do? Why would they willingly let that fear in?" As quickly as that thought came, the Holy Spirit spoke to me:

Television and movies are a medium of meditation. My people meditate on wickedness and ungodliness and lie to themselves that it does not affect them. But through their meditation, they are letting these things affect their hearts.

That one revelation reaffirmed our decision to live without television in our home. To watch a movie or TV show is to meditate on its contents. Some feel that even blatant sin will not affect them if it is just on the screen. They reason that since they are not partaking in it, they are not a part of it. After I received those words from the Lord, He brought to my attention Philippians 4:8:

Finally, brothers and sisters, whatever is true, whatever is noble, whatever is right, whatever is pure, whatever is lovely, whatever is admirable—if anything is excellent or praiseworthy—think about such things.

In that moment, God gave us a principle for testing entertainment and deciding what we would allow to enter our home. This Scripture was to dictate the way we lived, no matter what anyone else did. If every believer took this biblical command and applied it to the area of entertainment, many would have no choice but to make some drastic changes.

Another way to think about it is to ask yourself if you would be embarrassed about what you were watching if a godly person—like Billy Graham—knocked on your door and entered your home. Many Christians would be making a mad dash for the remote control to flip the channel or mute the TV if someone like that sat down on their couch. Even if they claim that there is nothing wrong with what they are watching, the fact that they would feel the need to turn it off speaks volumes. Now what if Jesus was on your couch? How would this influence what you watched?

Yet, Jesus *is* on your couch if you are a born again Christian! The Holy Spirit dwells in you. You are His temple.[11] It is horrifying to think of the things believers indulge in with no regard to the Holy Spirit. They have grown so desensitized to it, they are no longer able to sense the very real evil presence behind it. Now, after years of separation, having the TV on in a house seems strange to me. When I hear cursing on someone's TV (even if it is bleeped out) it grieves my spirit. What used to be just background noise is now shouting at me.

It is like a person with a caffeine addiction. They are not really affected by the caffeine because they consume it so often. However, if they quit drinking coffee for a month, the first cup is going to really affect them. Why? Because their system has been acclimated to constant caffeine intake. Their bodies just expect it.

It is the same with the things of this world, especially when it comes to entertainment. Our spirits become desensitized to the compromise much of it contains. Things that should really bother us—like violence, immorality, profanity and coarse joking—become so commonplace, they just do not trouble us anymore.

I am not saying that everything in this world is evil. God gave humans the ability to create. Good creations can be used for evil (like the internet or money), but that does not mean we are not to use them. It is the love of them or misuse of them that can be wicked. Even something that is not inherently sinful can still be an idol if we love it too much.

I am also not saying that every Christian needs to get rid of all technology, secular entertainment and music. However, if the Lord leads you to, then you should. I firmly believe *any* Christian who does give up anything in this world to pursue God, love others and fellowship with His people, will *always* be better off for it. That is a guarantee.

A PRICE TO BE PAID

Can consecration be taken too far and become legalism? Of course. A counselor once warned me that you can force yourself into a corner if you start eliminating all technology and hobbies from your life, hoping to become more holy. The pain of sacrifice should always be dulled with the joy of doing it for the Lord, not out of some religious duty that makes us miserable. However, in the church cultures that I have been a part of, I have not run into many who were making this kind of radical attempt at consecration. I think that a good dose of true consecration could radically alter the condition of the church as a whole. Lord, send us a hunger for righteousness!

Jackie Pullinger was a missionary who moved into a lawless city slum in China. Gangsters, drug pushers and pimps were running the city. Once she was asked:

"What's the cost of doing something like that? What's the cost in your life?" And without thinking, [she] said, "There's no cost. It costs nothing! Nothing. What you give up is nothing in comparison with the joy that you have in serving the Lord."[12]

This was a woman who followed the Lord into a very dark place and worked in an area that others had turned their backs on. Yet, what an amazing statement she made when she said the joy of walking with Christ far outweighed the difficulties.

This has been my testimony in the area of consecration as the Lord has led us as a family: *The joy outweighs the pain.* The Lord has given us an exceedingly greater life than we could ever have had if we would have been unwilling to separate further from this world. I can look back over the last few years of living a separated life and also say: "What sacrifice? It was nothing for the joy of knowing Him more!"

I believe the Lord is looking for believers in our churches who are willing to make a painful separation from this world. I am not suggesting that it will not hurt. Consecration and sacrifice were never meant to be comfortable decisions. This is because our flesh hates not getting what it wants. There is a price tag for a deeper walk with Jesus, but I truly believe many reading these words right now will *never* experience true intimacy and a deeper walk with Him without some kind of further separation.

AN ILLUSTRATION OF TRUE CONSECRATION

Speaking about consecration brings to mind a story from the book, *The Cross and the Switchblade.* This book describes the birth of a worldwide ministry for drug and alcohol addicts called Teen Challenge. The ministry of Rev. David Wilkerson has made a tremendous impact in the lives of countless people globally. All of this started with a simple response to the Lord's prompting to consecrate his life. He explains it best:

It was late, Gwen and the children were asleep, and I was sitting in front of the set watching the "Late Show." The story somehow involved a dance routine in which a lot of chorus girls marched across the set in just-visible costumes. I remember thinking suddenly how dull it all was. "You're getting old, David," I warned myself.

But try as I would, I could not get my mind back on the threadbare little story and the girl—which one was it?—whose destiny on the stage was supposed to be a matter of palpitating interest to every viewer.

I got up and turned the knob and watched the young girls disappear into a little dot in the center of the screen. I left the living room and went into my office and sat down in the brown swivel chair.

"How much time do I spend in front of that screen each night?" I wondered. "A couple of hours, at least. What would happen, Lord, if I sold that TV set and spent that time—praying?" I was the only one in the family who ever watched TV anyway.

What would happen if I spent two hours every single night in prayer? It was an exhilarating idea. Substitute prayer for television, and see what happened.

Right away I thought of objections to the idea. I was tired at night. I needed the relaxation and change of pace. Television was part of our culture; it was not good for a minister to be out of touch with what people were seeing and talking about...

...My life has not been the same since. Every night at midnight, instead of flipping some dials, I stepped into my office, closed the door, and began to pray...It was during one of these late evenings of prayer that I picked up *Life* magazine.[13]

The spiritual journey that led to the founding of Teen Challenge came out of David Wilkerson's encounter with that magazine. The Lord put an unrest in his soul and a short time later, this country preacher found himself on the streets of New York City. He began witnessing to drug-addicted, murderous and perverse young gang members without any prior experience of this type of culture. Most of us would shudder at the thought of walking in that kind of faith.

Yet the Lord did all this through Brother Wilkerson's response to cut off the television and seek His face. It was a choice he had to make. He could have resisted the Holy Spirit and missed all that God wanted to do through his life. This story gives a great picture of what consecration looks like in a practical sense and the great blessings it brings.

MAKING YOUR HOME A SANCTUARY

I want to challenge you to make your home a sanctuary. How is that accomplished? By limiting the amount of the world that comes in. There is a way to set the atmosphere in your home for the presence of the Lord to rest.

First, examine what you have in your house that does not glorify God. Then take anything that does not pass the test and get rid of it. Go through your movies, music, magazines, books and internet sites. Ask yourself, "Is the Lord pleased that I have this?" If the answer is "No," get rid of it immediately. Why would you want to hold onto anything that could grieve the Holy Spirit?

Make no provision for the flesh. I remember when I gathered every secular DVD we had in our house to throw them away. I hesitated for a moment, asking, "Am I going overboard? This is too radical, isn't it?" I knew the Lord was leading me to do it, but I wondered how I could live without them. Many of those movies had been very special to us. Although it was difficult at the time, we do not miss them at all now. They simply are not a part of our lives anymore. But it took some tough decisions on our part to get to that point.

The second step is to set boundaries on what you decide to keep. You may decide to only watch Christian movies, like we have. However, even if you were only watching clean movies, but were watching them every night and neglecting other important priorities, then you would still be out of balance. If you spend hours every week on social networking sites when you could be using that time in a more God-honoring way, your priorities need adjusted. Even if you are not blatantly sinning, you still need to learn to discipline yourself. Our family has an internet connection, but we set boundaries on what it is used for. Take time to prayerfully consider lifestyle adjustments that would make more room for Jesus and others.

Lastly, set the atmosphere. I love coming home and turning on worship music. It gives me peace and draws me closer to the Lord. Maintaining an atmosphere where the Holy Spirit can dwell should be a priority in our homes. We need to be intentional about making our homes into sanctuaries.

There is so much more I could say about consecration. This is such an important and often neglected area in today's church culture. It is important to state that this chapter is not meant to be a list of do's and don'ts, or a formula to copy. So seek the Lord for His will in the area of consecration for your life and obey as He leads.

Consecration is an extremely important way to fight off hypocrisy. We cannot be a people who try to live with one foot in the church and the other in the world. Next we will learn about another weapon in our arsenal to fight off hypocrisy, and that is *Humility*.

Humble:
1. **adjective.** having or showing a consciousness of one's defects or shortcomings; not proud, not self-assertive; modest
2. low in condition, rank, or position; lowly; unpretentious[1]

*   *   *

Philippians 2:3-7 (MSG)- Don't push your way to the front; don't sweet-talk your way to the top. Put yourself aside, and help others get ahead. Don't be obsessed with getting your own advantage. Forget yourselves long enough to lend a helping hand. Think of yourselves the way Christ Jesus thought of himself. He had equal status with God but didn't think so much of himself that he had to cling to the advantages of that status no matter what. Not at all. When the time came, he set aside the privileges of deity and took on the status of a slave, became *human!*

*   *   *

"A true understanding and humble estimate of oneself is the highest and most valuable of all lessons. To take no account of oneself, but always to think well and highly of others is the highest wisdom and perfection. Should you see another person openly doing evil, or carrying out a wicked purpose, do not on that account consider yourself better than him, for you cannot tell how long you will remain in a state of grace. We are all frail; consider none more frail than yourself."

-Thomas A Kempis[2]

HYPOCRISY'S ENEMIES: HUMILITY

O NE MAJOR OBSTACLE THAT KEEPS CHRISTIAN hypocrites from true faith is *pride*. If repentance is the key to coming into a unified life, pride is the key to staying divided. If exposure is a tool the Lord uses to help a hypocrite come into the light, pride is the tool the devil uses to keep them in darkness. If the Lord is calling a believer to deeply consecrate his or her life, the devil uses pride to keep them in carnality.

True repentance, exposure and consecration all require humility. For us to experience repentance, we must admit we are doing things wrong and choose to change and live God's way. A proud person will not do that. Though they may put on a good show to fake these qualities in their lives, deep down they have not changed. The fruit of their disobedience will come to the surface again; it is just a matter of time.

Christian hypocrites are extremely prideful people because they are choosing to deliberately disobey the Lord and go their own way. Remember, these are people who know enough of what is expected of them to pretend like they are living right. The more realistic a person's spiritual mask is, the more they prove their accountability to the Scriptures. Due to the fact that they are able to project exactly what they know they should be doing, they prove they know the right path to walk. So, to remain living in opposition to it in their hearts is dangerous ground.

WHAT IS PRIDE?

I had a very shallow understanding of pride for most of my Christian life. I thought all proud people were arrogant and haughty. Since I never really displayed these qualities, I figured I must not struggle with pride like others I knew. Yet, I have found this concept to be so much broader than that. Steve Gallagher defines pride this way: "Having an exaggerated sense of one's own importance and a selfish preoccupation with one's own rights."[3]

When you think of pride in that light, you can see how much the lives of professing Christians in today's church culture are affected by it. What I learned about pride has forever changed my perception on the reality of it in my own life. I learned that this sin ran deep into many areas of my heart.

Pride is the sin that turned the beautiful archangel, Lucifer, into the evil, twisted Satan. Ezekiel gives us a glimpse into what happened to Lucifer, the anointed Cherubim, in Ezekiel 28:17. It says, "Your heart became proud on account of your beauty, and you corrupted your wisdom because of your splendor."

Basically, there was a point in history when Lucifer took his eyes off of the beauty and wisdom of God, and began to look at himself. It all boiled down to pride. He focused on himself and thought, "I really am beautiful." He probably compared himself with the other angels around him. Verse 15 says, "You were blameless in your ways from the day you were created till wickedness was found in you."

The original sin did not take place in the Garden of Eden, but in Heaven long before. This sin of pride changed Lucifer forever. Pride has the same ability to turn a believer into a backslider. It is no wonder Satan loves to trip Christians up in this area. After all, pride cost him everything.

At its very core, pride is an attitude of the heart. It is thinking, "I am going to do things my way instead of God's." It is a self-focused life. The prouder a person is, the bigger he or she becomes in his or her own mind. It is not necessarily the conscious thought: "I am better than everyone else." It is just the attitude of the heart that exalts itself above others. This is the deceptive nature of pride to which I was ensnared without even realizing it.

There were two resources I received at Pure Life Ministries that really opened up my eyes to pride's nature and how to identify it. The first was Steve Gallagher's book, *Irresistible to God*. In this book, he highlights seven forms of pride. These are: a haughty spirit, vanity, self-protection, unapproachable pride, know-it-all pride, rebellion and spiritual pride. I strongly recommend this book for every believer, as it gets down to the root of pride and provides a pathway into lowliness.

The second resource that really challenged me was a booklet called *From Pride to Humility*. It lists thirty manifestations of pride. My counselor advised me to read it and write down how I had displayed each manifestation of pride in my own life. My first thought was, "I'm sure I won't be able to find an example for all thirty areas. I don't struggle with pride as much as other people."

I was terribly wrong. As I looked at the ways pride could manifest itself in my life, I was overwhelmed by what I saw of it in my heart. Due to the significant impact this booklet had on my life, I will list the thirty areas that the author had identified as signs of pride. For more details—along with Scriptures and examples—I would encourage you to get a copy of this resource for yourself.

"Manifestations of Pride" by Stuart Scott

1. Complaining against or passing judgment on God.
2. A lack of gratitude in general.
3. Anger.
4. Seeing yourself as better than others.
5. Having an inflated view of your importance, gifts and abilities.

6. Being focused on the lack of your gifts and abilities.
7. Perfectionism.
8. Talking too much.
9. Talking too much about yourself.
10. Seeking independence or control.
11. Being consumed with what others think.
12. Being devastated or angered by criticism.
13. Being unteachable.
14. Being sarcastic, hurtful, or degrading.
15. A lack of service.
16. A lack of compassion.
17. Being defensive or blame-shifting.
18. A lack of admitting when you are wrong.
19. A lack of asking forgiveness.
20. A lack of biblical prayer.
21. Resisting authority or being disrespectful.
22. Voicing preferences and opinions when not asked.
23. Minimizing your own sin and shortcomings.
24. Maximizing other's sin and shortcomings.
25. Being impatient or irritable with others.
26. Being jealous or envious.
27. Using others.
28. Being deceitful by covering up sins, faults and mistakes.
29. Using attention-getting tactics.
30. Not having close relationships.[4]

I would encourage every person reading this book to take the time to prayerfully review this list and ask the Lord to show you how pride manifests in your own life. The greater degree of hypocrisy someone lives in, the more areas they will find pride appearing. Then, repent of each one and ask the Lord to help you. He longs to do that for every one of us.

TALK FAST

One of the greatest pivotal moments in my spiritual life at Pure Life came through a talk fast. Talk fasts are commonly used in the program as a time set apart where you talk to nobody but God. Sometimes a week would be given where no talking was allowed on campus. What this did was create solitude and forced us to seek the Lord, because we had no one else to go to with issues. It was a very valuable spiritual discipline.

Sometimes the staff would put individuals on a personal talk fast for various reasons, such as pride. Like I said earlier, I did not think I had a pride issue when I entered the program. In fact, throughout my ministry, people commonly told me how much they appreciated how humble and un-assuming I was…and I believed them. But because of the pride in my life, my counselor put me on a personal talk fast for nearly six weeks.

What happened in that time radically changed my view of myself. I began to hear others in conversations and would think about all the things I would say if I could talk. I realized I had a horrible habit of hijacking conversations. I would just interrupt and put my two cents into someone else's discussion without even being asked for it. I saw how much I wanted everyone to know my opinions and how little I cared about what others thought. I saw how I used humor to draw attention to myself, and it was incredibly difficult for me to not say anything. The temptation to spout off at the mouth was almost unbearable.

The Lord used this talk fast to show me my heart. This happened in the first few weeks of my time in the program and was part of a breaking down process the Lord brought me through. He began to reveal to me the areas of my life that I was not willing to see. One of the main areas was pride. I began to see how much my selfishness manifested itself in the way I would constantly talk about what I thought. As the Lord revealed these things to me, I could do nothing but repent and cry out for mercy.

God will use situations in this life to try to get our attention. For the hypocrite who truly asks the Lord to reveal his or her heart to them, He will bring them through a similar process. We have to see our pride in order to allow Him to change it. He does not do it in a condemning, 'look how messed up you are' way. Instead, He does it gently—yet firmly—so that we know He means business. It might be painful, but He has to get the poison out of us.

Think about it. God knows the devastating effects pride has on His children. He knows how dangerous it is. In fact, Scripture teaches that it repels God. I Peter 5:5 says, "God opposes the proud but shows favor to the humble." Pride actually puts us in a place where we set ourselves against the Lord. As Brother Jerome once said: "Think, brother, what a sin it must be which has God for its opponent."[5] In God's great mercy, He wants to help us overcome pride, but we need to surrender ourselves to the process of allowing Him to humble us.

SPIRITUAL PRIDE

While pride can manifest in different ways, one of its most deceptive forms is spiritual pride. This is also the form which many hypocrites will wrestle with the most. Spiritual pride can be difficult to keep in check, because it is a heart issue and is therefore often hard to detect. Jesus highlights three specific areas to guard from spiritual pride in His Sermon on the Mount. He gives us a practical look at the manifestations of spiritual pride in the areas of giving, praying and fasting:

> Be careful not to practice your righteousness in front of others to be seen by them. If you do, you will have no reward from your Father in heaven. So when you give to the needy, do not announce it with trumpets, as the hypocrites do in the synagogues and on the streets, to be honored by others. Truly I tell you, they have received their reward in full.[6]

> And when you pray, do not be like the hypocrites, for they love to pray standing in the synagogues and on the street corners to be seen by others. Truly I tell you, they have received their reward in full.[7]

> When you fast, do not look somber as the hypocrites do, for they

disfigure their faces to show others they are fasting. Truly I tell you, they have received their reward in full.[8]

Jesus exposes the heart motives behind the spiritually proud people of His day in these verses. They made a big show of their generosity because they wanted to be noticed. When they prayed, they wanted other people to hear it. When they fasted, they made sure they walked around looking weak and in pain so people would say, "Are you alright?" Then they could reply, "Oh, I'm fine. I'm just fasting like usual." Spiritually proud people want recognition from others. They are looking for people to notice their spirituality.

In all three of these passages, Jesus shows us that if we do things for the praise of men, we get the reward we are searching for. The hypocrites of Jesus' time were well-respected for their giving, praying and fasting. Jesus goes on to tell us that we will only be rewarded by God if we do such things in secret.

A great test of spiritual pride is to do a good deed confidentially. Give a big gift to someone and remain anonymous. Then, see how badly you wish someone knew it was from you. Do something behind the scenes that you think you deserve recognition for. Then see how much it bothers you when you do not get the credit you want.

Hypocrites are often very spiritually proud people. Part of the mask they hide behind involves spiritual practices. They may be the ones who seem to be doing much of the work in the church. They may know how to sound impressive when they pray. They may seem to be very generous. But all of these things are only surface-level if they are doing them to appear spiritual. If they were doing them from their hearts, they would not care if anyone noticed but the Lord.

A MAN WHO HUMBLED HIMSELF

Naaman is a great example of a proud man who was willing to humble himself. We are introduced to Naaman in II Kings 5. He was the commander of the army for the king of Aram and he had a big problem: He had leprosy, an incurable and contagious skin disease. The interesting thing to notice in this story is that God uses the servants of Naaman to open his eyes to the solution. There is something about being lowly of heart that connects us to the ways of the Lord.

In verse 3, one of his wife's servants suggests that Naaman go find the prophet Elisha in Israel. So Naaman brings his team of horses and chariots and arrives at Elisha's house. The prophet's messenger comes out to him and tells him to wash himself in the Jordan River seven times and he will be healed. Naaman's response reveals his heart:

> But Naaman went away angry and said, "I thought that [Elisha] would surely come out to me and stand and call on the name of the Lord his God, wave his hand over the spot and cure me of my leprosy. Are not Abana and Pharpar, the rivers of Damascus, better than any of the waters of Israel? Couldn't I wash in them and be cleansed?" So he turned and went off in a rage. (vv. 11-12)

Naaman lived a prestigious life, so he expected to be treated as royalty. He thought Elisha would come out and make a big scene and heal him so all could see. Instead, the prophet does not even come out of the house. He simply sends a messenger to tell him what to do. What God is requiring Naaman to do to be healed does not look like what he had hoped it would. The Jordan was a dirty, unimpressive river. He wanted to go to a river with a reputation. This proud man did not want to do anything humiliating and he almost missed his chance to be healed. Once again, the Lord uses his servants to get his attention. They tell Naaman:

> My father, if the prophet had told you to do some great thing, would you not have done it? How much more, then, when he tells you, "Wash and be cleansed!" (v. 13)

Naaman's servants remind him of the fact that he would have been willing to do some heroic feat that would make him look important if the prophet had required it of him. The issue comes down to the pride in his heart. But Naaman chooses to humble himself and listens to the servants.

He dips himself seven times in the Jordan River and is miraculously cured. (v. 14)

Naaman's pride is like many hypocrites. They already know in their hearts that they need to repent and come into the light, but their pride keeps them from stepping out and obeying. They want the pain-free way out. They want the Lord to wave His hand over them and make it all go away, but God's way requires humility. It might mean you have to get into the Jordan River and get a little dirty. You might need to confess to people and walk through some painful circumstances. The great news is that there is a miracle waiting on the other side!

The story of Naaman is a great example of a man who sets his pride aside, obeys in humility, and experiences the power of God.

THE LOWLINESS OF GOD

The lowliness of God is one of the great mysteries of His character. The Bible is full of examples of His lowly nature. Anyone who says that the 'God of the Old Testament' is a God of only wrath and judgment is leaving out countless examples of how He reveals Himself as a lowly servant to His people, Israel.

Jesus makes a powerful statement when Philip asks to see the Father in John 14. He says, "Anyone who has seen me has seen the Father." (v. 9) Theology is the study of the nature of God. In order to have good theology, we must look to the Son to discover who the Father is. I like how Bill Johnson puts it: "Jesus is perfect theology."[9] In order to understand the character of God, one needs to look no further than the life of Christ.

In Matthew 11:28, Jesus invites all who are weary and burdened to come to Him. Then he reveals something about Himself. He says, "for I am gentle and humble in heart." (v. 29) If you ask the average churchgoer to describe the character of God, I wonder how many would come up with that description of Him. The NKJV translation says He is "lowly in heart." The word being used is the Greek term *tapeinos*, which means "humble, lowly, particularly of attitude and social position."[10] This is who Jesus was and still is. It is not that Jesus just humbled Himself when He came to

Earth but He already was of a lowly nature. Jesus did not just come to serve mankind; He already was a servant. It is true that He is also a reigning King, but a servant King.

This is a hard concept for us to grasp because our natural perspective is that the common man should be the one to serve royalty. However, that is not who God is. The Lord is all-powerful, yet lowly at the same time. He is drawn to the humble but repelled by pride. Look at what Scripture says about God's perspective on humility and pride:

Job 5:11- The lowly he sets on high...

Psalm 18:27- You save the humble but bring low those whose eyes are haughty.

Psalm 25:9- He guides the humble in what is right and teaches them his way.

Psalm 138:6- Though the Lord is exalted, he looks kindly on the lowly; though lofty, he sees them from afar.

Psalm 149:4- For the Lord takes delight in his people; he crowns the humble with victory.

Proverbs 3:34- He mocks proud mockers but shows favor to the humble and oppressed.

Isaiah 57:15- I live in a high and holy place, but also with the one who is contrite and lowly in spirit...

Isaiah 66:2- These are the ones I look on with favor: those who are humble and contrite in spirit, and who tremble at my word.

I Corinthians 1:28- God chose the lowly things of this world...

Scripture is full of promises for the humble of heart. If you want to get the Lord's attention, humility is the thing that attracts it. The Bible clearly teaches that pride will keep Him at a distance from us.

A PICTURE OF TRUE HUMILITY

One of the most beautiful and vivid pictures of humility comes from Philippians 2. It is hard for us to grasp what it meant for God Almighty to come to Earth as a man. In this passage in Philippians, Paul is writing to the church to tell them about the attitude that every Christian should have. In verses 3-4, he says,

> Do nothing out of selfish ambition or vain conceit. Rather, in humility value others above yourselves, not looking to your own interests but each of you to the interests of the others.

Paul is showing us that humility is demonstrated through selfless love. Humility is viewing the needs of others as more important than our own. Then he gives us a perfect picture of what he is describing. He says we should "have the same mindset as Christ Jesus." (v. 5) And what did Jesus do that we should imitate? Verse 6 says, "Who, being in very nature God, did not consider equality with God something to be used to his own advantage..."

This verse communicates that Jesus chose to lay His deity aside when He came to Earth. The phrase *equality with God* means "the status and privileges that inevitably follow from being in very nature God."[11] Rather than coming to Earth with trumpets blaring and a legion of angels, the Scriptures say Jesus made Himself nothing and took on the nature of a servant. (v. 7) Why would Almighty God come as a servant? He could have come as a king, dictator or ruler, but it is because His nature is that of a servant already. The passage goes on to say, "And being found in appearance as a man, he humbled himself by becoming obedient to death—even death on a cross!" (v. 8)

Jesus was willing to 'stoop' to any level in order to become the servant of all mankind. What more humiliating act could anyone do on behalf of another but to die as an innocent man for someone else's sin? Like Greg Boyd says, "How God flexes His muscles is by dying on a cross."[12]

Jesus chose to come to the Earth in a humiliating way. Think about who He is. Before Jesus came to the Earth, He was in Heaven being continually worshiped by the most majestic beings ever created. He had all power. He spoke all of creation into existence with the word of His mouth. He said, "Let there be," and it happened.[13] In Colossians 1:16, Paul tells us that all things were created *by* Him and *for* Him. That is an incredible statement. Yet it is even more amazing to think about how someone so absolutely powerful could be born in a manger in a baby's body. Could all that majesty really be confined to the womb of a poor woman in an impoverished town?

This is one of the greatest mysteries of the incarnation of Christ. The One who sits on the Throne—the One who created the universe by His Word—came to Earth in a smelly stable. God was born like we were and was once just a dependent baby. When I look at how helpless our own kids were when they were infants, it amazes me to think that the Lord was once this way Himself. Just like all infants, God needed to be clothed, nursed and raised by Jesus' earthly parents. What a crazy thing for Almighty God to do! But He did it because of His love for us. Paul explains that this is a true picture of humility that should characterize our lives as well.

THE GREATEST IN THE KINGDOM

In spite of the example that Jesus set for the disciples, they often tried to jockey for position. They were always trying to one-up each other. Look at the following passages:

Matthew 18:1- At that time the disciples came to Jesus and asked, "Who, then, is the greatest in the kingdom of heaven?"

Mark 9:33-34- When [Jesus] was in the house, he asked them, "What were you arguing about on the road?" But they kept quiet because on the way they had argued about who was the greatest.

You can discern where the disciples' hearts were from these passages. They made following Jesus into a competition. In Matthew 20:21, the mother of two of the disciples approaches Jesus and asks, "Grant that one of these two sons of mine may sit at your right and the other at your left in your kingdom." It says in the story that when the other ten disciples heard about it, they got angry. They felt like she was getting in their way of rising to the top. The disciples were constantly comparing themselves to each other to see who was moving up in rank with Jesus. They were still thinking of an earthly kingdom. In essence, they were expecting Jesus to take over as President, and they were fighting to become the Vice President and Secretary of State.

Jesus continually tried to get His disciples to comprehend Kingdom principles. He tried to express to them that the Kingdom works opposite of the world system. In the world, we try to promote ourselves. In the Kingdom, we humble ourselves and the Lord gives promotion to us. When Jesus gave the parable of the feast in Luke 14, He said:

> But when you are invited, take the lowest place, so that when your host comes, he will say to you, "Friend, move up to a better place." Then you will be honored in the presence of all the other guests. For all those who exalt themselves will be humbled, and those who humble themselves will be exalted. (vv. 10-11)

In spite of lessons like these, you can tell by the way the disciples persistently fought for the top spot that they were not embracing Jesus' teachings on humility. Jesus tried to tell them that the first will be last.[14] He told them if they wanted to become great they had to become servants.[15] And it was on the night before His death that Jesus gave them a visual illustration that I am certain they never forgot.

THE SERVANT OF ALL

Jesus did not come to us demanding the worship that He is worthy of. He came to die the death that we deserved. Other than becoming the servant of all through His death, one of the most beautiful pictures of the servant leadership of Christ is found in John 13. In the first verse, we see the nature of Jesus' heart. Jesus—knowing that his time with his disciples was short—decided to show them how much He loved them.

When someone is on their deathbed, the things they discuss are often the most important words they will ever speak. When death is in view, the little things do not matter anymore. Jesus decided to spend the last night of His life on Earth displaying what true love looks like. However, His display of love did not resemble what the disciples would have expected.

Throughout His earthly life and ministry, Jesus had proven that He was God. The disciples had seen many miraculous signs. They had seen crowds of people following Jesus everywhere He went. They had proclaimed Him to be the Messiah and were looking toward His reign as King. Peter and John had witnessed His transfiguration on the mountain.[16] There was not much room for doubt in their minds that He was the Son of God.

When Jesus took a basin of water and began to wash the feet of His disciples, it was a shock to them because foot washing was the role of slaves in Jewish culture. It was the last thing the disciples would have expected from their leader. That is why Peter reacts so strongly: "No, you shall never wash my feet." (v. 8) Peter is not being obstinate. In fact, he thinks he is being reverent. He is basically saying, "Lord, there is no way someone like you could wash the feet of someone like me. You are not my slave!"

However, Jesus washed feet as a lesson to the disciples. He wanted them to understand how much He loved them. He also washed their feet to foreshadow His death on the cross; a death that would cleanse them from sin. There was another reason as well. He says,

Now that I, your Lord and Teacher, have washed your feet, you also should wash one another's feet. I have set you an example that you should do as I have done for you. (vv. 14-15)

There were many times in Jesus' ministry when the disciples did not understand Him. They were constantly asking Him about the meaning of His parables after the crowds were gone. However, I doubt any of the disciples had trouble understanding what Jesus was expressing to them on that night. He was saying, "If you are my followers, you are going to live as servants to others." History records that almost all of the apostles were martyred for their faith in order to share Jesus with the world around them. They took Jesus' words seriously...are we?

Humility is a powerful force in keeping people free from hypocrisy. In contrast, pride strengthens it. As you consider the necessity of humbling yourself before the Lord, there is another enemy of hypocrisy to be discussed: *Mercy*.

Mercy:
1. **noun.** a refraining from harming or punishing offenders, enemies, persons in one's power, etc.; kindness in excess of what may be expected or demanded by fairness; forbearance and compassion.
2. a disposition to forgive, pity or be kind[1]

*　　*　　*

Matthew 12:1-3, 7-8 (NIV)- At that time Jesus went through the grainfields on the Sabbath. His disciples were hungry and began to pick some heads of grain and eat them. When the Pharisees saw this, they said to him, "Look! Your disciples are doing what is unlawful on the Sabbath." He answered, "...If you had known what these words mean, 'I desire mercy, not sacrifice,' you would not have condemned the innocent. For the Son of Man is Lord of the Sabbath."

*　　*　　*

"...a word so significant that without it there simply is no Word of God to man. And that means: without the word mercy-lovingkindness the Bible is a dead book, in which is no revelation of God at all. Stated another way: Take the word mercy-lovingkindness out of the Bible and there is no Bible, no salvation, no Saviour, no kingdom of God, no eternal life—nothing."

-Rex Andrews[2]

11

HYPOCRISY'S ENEMIES: MERCY

MERCY IS A STRONG OPPONENT OF hypocrisy, yet the biblical concept of mercy has lost the richness of its meaning in our culture. We have given it an oversimplified definition. Most people in church can easily recite the popular definition of mercy: not getting what we deserve. This is true, but the depth of mercy goes way beyond this description. Even more important is being able to understand what mercy actually looks like here on the Earth. If mercy is a crucial weapon against hypocrisy, it is important that we get a clear understanding of what it is.

HESED

If you study mercy in the Bible, you will quickly run into an amazing Hebrew term. The word is *hesed*, and it has such a deep meaning that translators have a hard time narrowing it down to just one word. For example, look how *hesed* is translated in Numbers 14:18 in the following translations:

- The Lord is longsuffering and abundant in mercy (*hesed*) (**NKJV**)
- The Lord is slow to anger, abounding in love (*hesed*) (**NIV**)
- The Lord is slow to anger and abundant in lovingkindness (*hesed*) (**NASB**)
- The Lord is slow to anger, and abounding in steadfast love (*hesed*) (**RSV**)
- The Lord is slow to anger and filled with unfailing love (*hesed*) (**NLT**)
- God, slow to get angry and huge in loyal love (*hesed*) (**MSG**)

From these verses, you can see that *hesed* is a very rich term. It involves mercy, love, kindness and loyalty all in one word. I only had a cursory understanding of what mercy was when I entered Pure Life Ministries. When they told me we would be doing a Bible study called the "Mercy Studies," I assumed it would just be a review for me. When they handed me a copy of *What the Bible Teaches About Mercy*, I had no idea about the significant role that book would play in my life. I wondered how a whole book could be written on such a narrow topic. I was shocked by what I learned in the following weeks.

What the Bible Teaches About Mercy was written by a man named Rex Andrews. Jesus revealed Himself to Brother Andrews in a powerful way after seven years of sexual sin as a backslidden minister. The way He did this was through a revelation of mercy. This book explains this revelation and shows how the word *hesed* is used throughout Scripture.

When the Pure Life staff talked about mercy, they made it seem like one of the most important themes of the Bible. I decided to look it up to see if they were just making a big deal out of nothing. I reasoned that if it was so important, why was that the first time I had really heard it emphasized? I found the Hebrew word in my NIV Keyword Study Bible and was surprised at the length of the definition for *hesed*. The first line stated:

Hesed: to be merciful, faithful. Love, kindness, mercy. One of the most important words in the [Old Testament], *hesed* essentially denotes an act of kindness, love or mercy.[3]

When I read in a lexical aid that *hesed* is one of the most important words in the Old Testament, I was shocked. As weeks went on, I discovered just how valuable this concept would be in my own walk out of hypocrisy. Here are a few of the numerous references of *hesed* in the Old Testament:

Exodus 33:19- I will have mercy (*hesed*) on whom I will have mercy, and I will have compassion on whom I will have compassion.

Deuteronomy 7:9- Know therefore that the Lord your God is God; he is the faithful God, keeping his covenant of love (*hesed*) to a thousand generations of those who love him and keep his commands.

Psalm 57:10- For great is your love (*hesed*), reaching to the heavens; your faithfulness reaches to the skies.

Psalm 107:1- Give thanks to the Lord, for he is good; his love (*hesed*) endures forever.

Isaiah 54:8- In a surge of anger I hid my face from you for a moment, but with everlasting kindness (*hesed*) I will have compassion on you.

Daniel 9:4- ...Lord, the great and awesome God, who keeps his covenant of love (*hesed*) with those who love him and keep his commandments...

Essentially, *hesed* is the desire to do good to someone, regardless of whether they deserve it or can pay you back. *Hesed* is God's mercy, which is love in action. Our heavenly Father showed mercy to us on such a grand scale that He did not withhold the life of His own Son, but I learned it does not stop there. As recipients of the Lord's great mercy, we are called to give that mercy out to everyone, everywhere.

Rex Andrews explains that mercy is the opposite of coveting lust. To covet, or lust, is a desire to take something from somebody else because we want it. Mercy is to give from our hearts and to fulfill the needs of others.

This is the definition of mercy that Rex Andrews received from the Holy Spirit; a revelation that changed his life:

> But after seven lost, hopeless years away from God the Lord came to me when there was nothing left—utterly nothing. And He showed me what His mercy really is by doing it in me and to me and through me. He revealed its true meaning on the earth, and in the heavens, and in eternity…In that year, 1944, was given to me by the Holy Spirit this definition: "Mercy is God's supply system for every need everywhere. Mercy is that kindness, compassion and tenderness which is a passion to suffer with, or participate in, another's ills or evils in order to relieve, heal and restore. It accepts another freely and gladly as he is and supplies the needed good of life to build up and to bring to peace and keep in peace. It is to take another into one's heart just as he is and cherish and nourish him there. Mercy takes another's sins and evils and faults as its own, and frees the other by bearing them to God. This is the Glow-of-love. This is the anointing."[4]

As we continued to study this area week after week, this definition became much more than just words on a page. I started to understand what mercy meant and saw it displayed all around me.

The first time I read Rex Andrews' definition, I struggled with the part that says we should accept others freely and gladly *as they are*. That immediately shot an arrow of conviction into my heart. I knew that this was an area the Holy Spirit was after. I realized I had always played the judge in my mind. I was not accepting and loving of others, especially if they did not meet up to my acceptance or approval. This journey into the heart of God would prove to be difficult, but it was necessary to help me with the battle against hypocrisy.

THE MERCY PRAYER

Based on this definition of mercy, we were taught a powerful prayer called the *mercy prayer*. We were encouraged to make it a part of our daily lives. In the prayer, the words *mercy* and *life* are used as verbs because that is the way they sound in the original Hebrew. I will insert my own name into the prayer as an example of how it would be prayed. It prays like this:

1. <u>Lord, I thank You for Dustin.</u> I thank You for saving him. Thank you for what You have done and are doing in his life.

2. <u>Make Dustin to know Jesus.</u> Help him to increase in the knowledge of God. Destroy speculation and every lofty thing raised up against the knowledge of God and help him to bring every thought captive to the obedience of Christ.

3. <u>Make Dustin poor in spirit.</u> Bring him down, Lord, but please do it gently. Help him to see his neediness. Help him to see himself in light of You. Put him in his rightful place, Lord.

4. <u>Fill Dustin with Your Holy Spirit.</u> Immerse him in Your Spirit, Lord. Come to him in power and in might. Baptize him in fire, Lord.

5. <u>Life Dustin.</u> Life him according to your loving-kindness. Pour out Your life-giving mercies into his soul.

6. <u>Bless Dustin.</u> Lord, bless him in everything he touches. Bless him spiritually, physically and financially. Bless his loved ones. Do for him, Lord, instead of me.

7. <u>Mercy Dustin.</u> Flood him with need-filling mercies. Pour them out in super abundance. Find and meet every need in his life as You see it, Lord.[5]

This is an awesome prayer for all Christians to learn because it is a totally selfless prayer. It is a great way to pray for anyone, anytime. You can pray this prayer for loved ones and enemies alike. What I found is that as I prayed this for people—even those I did not get along with—my heart began to change for them. The prayer is for others, but it changes your own heart in the process as well.

Jesus says, "Freely you have received, freely give."[6] Each of us has received great mercy from the Lord. Regardless of what material resources we may have to give, we are always able to give mercy from our hearts. The mercy prayer is a great tool to give away mercy. This prayer conditions our hearts to give unconditional love to others.

Just like the Pharisees, modern-day hypocrites often set themselves above other people. Their religious pride and self-centeredness cause them to find fault in everyone. Praying for God to have mercy on others overthrows a judgmental, critical spirit and replaces it with love. Mercy is all about meeting needs. As a hypocritical Christian begins to give mercy from their hearts, they will find that other people's needs will become more significant than their own. They will find freedom in giving that mercy away.

THE GOD OF MERCY

In Exodus 33, God is angry with the disobedient Israelites. He offers to send them into the Promised Land with an angel escort rather than for Jehovah to go with them Himself. Moses makes a powerful statement showing his commitment to the presence of God in verse 15: "If your Presence does not go with us, do not send us up from here." The Lord grants his request because of His relationship with this great man of God.

Then in verse 18, Moses makes a bold request of God. He says, "Now show me your glory." Moses was only permitted to see His back so that he could survive. When the Lord passed by in front of Moses, Scripture says that the Lord proclaimed His name. This is a powerful moment. God Almighty—the Creator of the heavens and the Earth—is about to declare who He is in His own words. In chapter 34, the Scripture records:

And he passed in front of Moses, proclaiming, "The Lord, the Lord, the compassionate and gracious God, slow to anger, abounding in love (*hesed*) and faithfulness, maintaining love (*hesed*) to thousands, and forgiving wickedness, rebellion and sin..." (vv. 6-7)

Notice that God points to mercy as one of the chief characteristics that make up His character. Mercy is more than just something the Lord offers to us; it is His very nature! This is a repeated thought throughout Scripture. The Lord is often referred to as a God who is full of *hesed*. Here are two other verses that echo this thought:

Psalm 86:5- You, Lord, are forgiving and good, abounding in love (*hesed*) to all who call to you.

Psalm 145:8-9- The Lord is gracious and compassionate, slow to anger and rich in love. (*hesed*)

The Scriptures reveal to us a God who is overflowing with mercy. He always extends mercy to those who will receive it. He is not a God who wants to send judgment. But judgment must be sent when mercy is rejected, because God is also just. People who preach that the Lord wants to send sinners to Hell do not understand who He is. Just look at the following Scriptures to find evidence for that:

Ezekiel 18:23, 32- Do I take any pleasure in the death of the wicked? declares the Sovereign Lord. Rather, am I not pleased when they turn from their ways and live?...For I take no pleasure in the death of anyone, declares the Sovereign Lord. Repent and live!

II Peter 3:9- The Lord is not slow in keeping his promise, as some understand slowness. Instead he is patient with you, not wanting anyone to perish, but everyone to come to repentance.

Together these passages provide us with a clear picture of a God who wants nothing else than to give mercy to all people. It is as if He is looking down over the Earth, waiting for someone to ask for it. Many people do not realize this about the Lord, but it is important to realize that He is a *hesed* God. And the responsibility that comes from knowing the God of all mercy is that we are expected to give mercy away to others as the following parable clearly depicts.

A PICTURE OF MERCILESSNESS

The parable of the unmerciful servant is perhaps the best illustration of what mercy is all about. It is found in Matthew 18 and tells the story of a servant who asks to be forgiven of a huge debt. His master shows him mercy and spares him and his family from going to debtor's prison. Then, the servant who was just forgiven an enormous debt immediately goes out and finds someone who owes him very little and demands it back. In spite of the man's plea for mercy, the unmerciful servant has him thrown into debtor's prison until he can repay him.

There is an underlying question being asked at the very heart of this story: "How can someone who has been shown so much mercy turn around and withhold it from someone else?" The implications of this parable are extremely important. Every born again believer has been forgiven a huge debt of sins. We should be aware of how much mercy the Lord has had on each of us. The problem is that we are often too busy comparing ourselves to other people. Many Christians have the attitude, "Well, I've never killed anyone. I know people who were saved out of way worse." It is as if they feel they *deserve* God's mercy more than the next person.

The truth is that even the most moral person on Earth deserves eternal punishment in Hell. God is a holy, perfect Being and He must judge sin. It does not matter how good of a life we have lived, Scripture says in Isaiah, "Our righteous acts are like filthy rags."[7]

Only when we come into the reality of who we are apart from Jesus' blood, can we begin to comprehend the free mercy poured out on us. The challenge I have found in my own life is *staying* in view of that mercy. I can tell when I have lost sight of my need for God's mercy by the way I treat others and the thoughts I think about them. I find myself occasionally going back to studying mercy to get re-aligned.

So how does this relate to hypocrisy? Hypocrisy is all about self-preservation and self-protection. It is impossible to love and be merciful when your focus is completely on yourself. As someone in hypocrisy begins to change their lifestyle from self-protection to becoming a giver of mercy, they will find that hypocrisy will begin to loosen its grip. Deep down we all want to be known, loved and accepted for who we truly are—not who we pretend to be. The parable of the unmerciful servant is a picture of hypocrisy. If we want to experience mercy from the Lord, we need to be willing to show it to others.

COMING DOWN AND GOING LOW

In order to describe how mercy plays out in a practical way, it is easiest to explain through my time spent at Pure Life Ministries. This is where I saw mercy become much more than a word from theology books. It was a concept deeply interwoven into the atmosphere of the program. In hypocrisy, my whole focus was on my own image. I was extremely selfish. So encountering an atmosphere of mercy was a sharp contrast to what I was used to.

There are phrases that I learned in the program that illustrate the kind of culture we lived in. Whenever someone would get irritated with another student, you would often hear people say:

"Just be willing to come down."

"Go low."

"Take the low road."

These phrases mean that rather than retaliate against other people, we need to respond like Christ.

In Western society, we live in a self-centered culture, so the lowly ways of Christ are often the exact opposite of the way we think things should be. The ways of Jesus are paradoxical to the ways of the world. He says to save our lives we must lose them[8] and that the last shall be first.[9] As we choose to take 'the lower road,' we will find His presence nearer to us than we ever thought possible. I like the way Misty Edwards refers to this mystery when she calls it, "The inside-outside-upside-down Kingdom."[10] God's Kingdom just operates in a completely different way than human nature does.

The principle of going low or coming under is found in the definition of meekness, which can be defined as "the willing submission of one person to the will of another."[11] The greatest example we have of meekness is when Jesus willingly submitted to the will of His Father in the garden of Gethsemane. Luke 22:42 records Jesus' prayer that His Father would show Him some other way than the agony of crucifixion. Jesus prays, "Father, if you are willing, take this cup from me; yet not my will, but yours be done." In spite of the fact that He did not want to go through with it, Jesus submits His will to His Father's will for the sake of you and I. That is a true picture of meekness.

To live in this kind of love and humility requires us to pay attention to what others want or need. Paul said we should be looking "to the interests of the others."[12] This is the heart-motivation of the merciful person. They live their lives looking for needs they can meet for other people. They do not live just for themselves, but to bless and alleviate the burdens of their neighbors and enemies alike.

MERCY AS A LIFESTYLE

The culture I encountered at Pure Life Ministries was so different than anywhere I had ever been. We were taught to live our lives for each other. You could walk into the kitchen and say, "I'm hungry," and three men would offer you something to eat without a second thought. We had chore sheets listing our responsibilities around campus. Each day, after work, we needed to have them checked off before a certain time. I cannot tell you how many times after a long day's work, I would come home to check the chore sheet and find the word *MERCY* where my initials should have gone. This signified that someone else 'mercied' the chore for me. It was contagious! Whenever you received mercy, you would want to go do the same for someone else. Mercy was much more than just a theological concept, it was a verb to live by.

This type of attitude did not come easily, especially for a hypocrite like I was. My whole life was designed to serve myself. So to try to begin living life for others was a very difficult transition. I had spent years living the opposite way. Self-satisfaction and self-preservation were the two great goals of my life. My counselor encouraged me to start doing mercy and not wait to feel like it. That was a valuable lesson I had to learn: Do not wait to feel like obeying. Obey and eventually your feelings will follow your actions.

It is a sad thing that this type of attitude seems so uncommon to us in today's church. This is because we live in an extremely self-centered culture. Non-believers in other countries around the world are better at loving their families, friends, neighbors and communities than many believers in Western society. We have allowed our culture to dictate our lives more than the commands of Scripture.

Acts 4:32 describes the lifestyle of the early church. It tells us, "All the believers were one in heart and mind. No one claimed that any of his possessions was his own, but they shared everything they had."

We read this and think, "Wow. That is radical!" However, in the Kingdom of God, that is just normal. Reading Scriptures like this should cause us to be convicted of how tightly we hold onto our lives and how little concern we have for others. We should not write it off as if it is some rare occurrence. That is the mercy life on display. Could it be that the Bible is setting the standard for the church by including this passage?

STAYING IN SIGHT OF YOUR NEED

We were created to be completely dependent on God, our Father. Jesus said we need to become childlike to enter the Kingdom of Heaven.[13] One characteristic children share is their dependency on their parents. Children realize that there are things they just cannot do at their age. When my daughter was three years old, if she found something she could not do, she would ask, "When can I do that? When I am 4...6...14?" She had an understanding of her inability due to her age.

This is how God designed humans to be. We were never meant to be self-sufficient. That desire came as a result of sin in the human race. This is extremely important in regards to mercy because you can only receive mercy when you admit that you need it. When I first entered Pure Life, I refused to ask for help with anything, so I blocked mercy from coming into my life. I did not want to be helped because of my extreme pride and self-sufficient attitude. Then, as brothers in Christ began to find ways to show me the love of God, it began to break me. As I was bombarded with mercy, I began desiring to show the same love to others.

In Mark 10, a blind man named Bartimaeus is begging on the roadside. When he hears that Jesus is passing by, he immediately begins to cry out. He knows that he needs mercy and he also knows where to find it. Though the crowd tries to silence him, he keeps on crying out, "Son of David, have mercy on me!" (v. 48) Bartimaeus understood his need, and his faith put his heart in the right posture to receive a miracle.

Anyone with hypocrisy in their lives needs to get in sight of their need for the Lord. It does no good to pretend that everything is okay. You cannot fight this battle in your own strength and God does not expect you to. You do not need religion or some kind of mask, but a true relationship with Him.

Just like Bartimaeus, I had to learn to cry out to Jesus for mercy. Just like He did for a blind man two thousand years ago, He heard my cry and had compassion on me. A cry for mercy has the ability to get God's attention. When we walk around with a religious mask—trying to cover up a lukewarm Christianity—we give the Lord very little to work with. When we see our need and cry out for His mercy, He is always faithful to respond. A heart crying, "Jesus, I need you! Have mercy on me!" is a beautiful sound to the ears of our Savior.

I love a story I heard about Rex Andrews. He had such an incredibly soft heart for God because he saw how much he needed His mercy. Steve Gallagher tells the following story in his book *Living in Victory*:

One day, as Rex Andrews led a ministerial training class, he had his interns practicing how to give an altar call. Standing at the podium was a young girl pouring out her heart to an imaginary group of sinners, pleading with them to repent. Right in the middle of her altar call, much to her shock, she looked up to see Mr. Andrews, now in his eighties, rolling his wheelchair toward the altar with tears streaming down his cheeks. "I'm coming, Jesus," he cried. "I'm coming!" This man lived with such an overwhelming sense of his need for Jesus, that he completely lost track of his surroundings and broke before the Lord.[14]

How can a man who is walking with God be so sensitive to the Lord as to respond to a mock altar call with tears? He had learned to stay in sight of His great need for God.

Allowing the Lord to form a mercy-ing heart inside of us is a process. It is something that we agree to let Him do, but we must cooperate in the process He brings us through. If you commit to this area of spiritual growth, I guarantee He will bring you into situations that give you opportunities to show mercy. Sometimes it will be with people that you really do not feel deserve it. Remember, none of us deserved mercy from God, and He still poured *hesed* on each of us.

We have considered the implications of the mercy of God and how powerful it is to set us free from selfishness. There is one final enemy of hypocrisy that must be discussed. It is *the Fear of God*.

Fear:
1. **noun.** respectful dread; awe; reverence[1]

*   *   *

Proverbs 9:10 (AMP)- The reverent *and* worshipful fear of the Lord is the beginning (the chief and choice part) of Wisdom, and the knowledge of the Holy One is insight *and* understanding.

*   *   *

"There is a slavish fear of God, springing from hard thoughts of him, which is contrary to religion. There is a selfish fear of God springing from dreadful thoughts of him, which may be a good step towards religion. But there is a filial fear of God, springing from great and high thoughts of him, which is the life and soul of all religion. And, whenever this reigns in the heart, it will appear by a constant care to *depart from evil.*"

-Matthew Henry[2]

"It is only the fear of God that can deliver us from the fear of man."

-John Witherspoon[3]

HYPOCRISY'S ENEMIES: THE FEAR OF GOD

THE **FEAR OF GOD IS AN** area that can bring massive breakthrough for those who apply it. It is also an area that has to be a part of anyone's life who is going to be free from hypocrisy and maintain that freedom. However, in order to understand what the fear of the Lord is, first we need to examine the fear of man.

THE OPPOSITE OF THE FEAR OF GOD

The fear of man—which is the opposite of godly fear—is a potent tool in the hands of the enemy. Every hypocrite has a fear of people finding out the truth about who they are. This is a manifestation of the fear of man. This fear encompasses more than just fear in the physical realm. The Israelites dealt with the physical fear of man when they were faced with

Goliath.[4] He was terrifying in the natural. However, you do not have to be facing a giant—or even a violent person—to fear someone. As I grew in my understanding of the fear of man, I began to see how directly related it is to hypocrisy.

When People Are Big and God is Small by Edward T. Welch is a book that opened my eyes to the destructive force of the fear of man in my life. That title basically sums up the main point of the book in one phrase. I learned that any time I allow the opinions of others to be the driving force behind my actions—rather than God's opinion—I am being controlled by the fear of man.

At the very root, the fear of man occurs when other people become idols in our lives. We allow them to dethrone Jesus from our hearts. This is a very serious matter, because we can fall into many failures, sins and hypocrisy when we are controlled more by what others think than by what God's Word says.

There are many ways that the fear of man can manifest itself in our lives. The primary reason that drives people to live behind a mask of spirituality is that they fear people because they can expose and humiliate them.[5] Because of this crippling fear, many Christians stay trapped in hypocrisy. They are trying to protect themselves from that type of hurt. Unfortunately, not one of their problems will ever be fixed by projecting a false image of themselves. They may be able to avoid some of the humiliation that might occur if everyone could see who they really are, but a host of other problems are created along the way.

MY STRUGGLE WITH THE FEAR OF MAN

I lived in such bondage to the fear of man that I was willing to compromise my values in order to avoid conflict. If I was having a conversation and someone disagreed with me about something, rather than stand up for what I believed in, I would cower down. I would just go along with whatever other people said in order to try to prevent rejection. This fear caused some huge problems in my life.

The fear I had was based upon assumptions I made about other people.

I constantly lived my life trying to please others; I wanted everyone to like me. That desire often came into direct opposition with the Christian life I was trying to live. Jesus made it pretty clear when He said, "If the world hates you, keep in mind that it hated me first."[6] I was trying to make my Christian beliefs peacefully co-exist with the world system. It is no wonder I lived such a miserable Christian life! I was trying to do the impossible. Eventually something had to give, and it was my faith that suffered for it.

One clear example of this happened early on in our marriage. We were on vacation with some people and we decided to go watch a movie. My wife and I did not know much about it and we did not do our usual content check beforehand. As the movie began, we became increasingly uncomfortable with its content, and we knew we should not be watching it. The problem was that I was so afraid of what the other people would think of us that I was willing to just sit through it despite my own convictions. But my wife—who was more concerned about what God thought—decided to get up and walk out.

I do not know how long I waited to follow her. It was probably just a minute, but it felt like a lifetime. I was so afraid to walk out of the theatre because I feared that the people with us would think we were just judgmental, close-minded Christians. I almost let my wife take the shame and stayed in the theatre, but I finally got up and went to the lobby and berated her for getting up and leaving. I told her, "Don't you know what they are going to think about us?" It ended up becoming an unresolved issue in our marriage for years.

The problem was that if it were just the two of us in the theatre, I would have left the movie in the first ten minutes, as soon as I saw what it was about—there would have been no question. There was no doubt in my mind that the Lord wanted us to walk out of that movie. I was not at all confused about what I should have done.

But since we were with people who did not agree with our views, suddenly I was willing to compromise on my values. Wanting to stay in the theatre was totally fear-driven. I later came to the realization that my wife had done the God-honoring thing, and I had cowered in the fear of man. What the Lord thought about the movie was not as important to me as what people thought about *me*. This is just one example of how I allowed the opinions of others to control my own actions.

THE FEAR OF MAN CONFRONTED

This was the primary attack the devil used in my life to keep me in bondage. Every time I considered coming clean, the single thought that prevented me from confessing was always, "What will other people think?" I wondered how my wife would respond. What would our children think? What about our church? What about our financial supporters? What about those I had been trying to witness to? What about those closest to me like my parents, siblings and in-laws?

When I finally confessed my sin, I found out that most of my fears were only in my imagination. Most of the people I was convinced would reject me ended up being more supportive and willing to help me than I could have ever imagined.

One example of this was the day I had to contact the leaders of our denomination about my moral failure. We had just come back from the mission field and I was petrified to hear how they would respond. The only reason I made the calls was because I had no choice. I would have done anything to run away and hide from my problems, but I knew I had to follow through.

I recall contacting the pastor from the church we had attended for several years before going overseas. I also contacted the man in the credentials department in our district and the head over our missions department. These were all my denominational leaders who had put their stamp of approval on me. They had taken my word that I was living a moral life, not realizing I had a secret life of sin.

I remember vividly how overwhelmed I was at the love they each showed me. Rather than judging and coming down on me, they ministered to me. They wanted to make sure that our family was taken care of. I still had to face the consequences of my actions and I still felt ashamed and embarrassed. However, I had expected that everyone would reject me and the exact opposite happened. I found everyone to be on my side and willing to fight for me.

Now, I understand this is not always the case. In many situations, it is different when men and women have finally thrown up the white flag and said, "That's it. I am not going to live this lie anymore." Many of them do have people reject them. Personally, I know many who have lost marriages, relationships with friends and family and faced other consequences when exposing secret lives.

The point I want to make is that, in my situation, I allowed the fear of man to push me deeper into darkness. I used it as an excuse and justified my actions to myself. I told myself, "No one would understand. No one could ever love me if they knew." These are the kinds of lies the enemy will whisper to make people stay in hypocrisy. I am praying this book will give some the courage to make a decision in their hearts that they will not allow the fear of man to dominate their lives any longer.

WHAT IS THE FEAR OF GOD?

Hypocrisy and the fear of man go hand-in-hand. You may be asking, "What is the answer? Is there an antidote to the fear of man in our lives? Do I have to live paralyzed by the opinions of others the rest of my life?" The answer is "Yes," there is an antidote, and "No," you do not have to be controlled by the opinions of others any longer. The solution to the problem is the fear of God.

Scripture is full of references about this godly fear. Here are just a few:

Deuteronomy 6:13- Fear the Lord your God, serve him only and take your oaths in his name.

Joshua 24:14- Now fear the Lord and serve him with all faithfulness.

Job 28:28- And he said to the human race, "The fear of the Lord—that is wisdom, and to shun evil is understanding."

II Corinthians 7:1- Since we have these promises, dear friends, let us purify ourselves from everything that contaminates body and spirit, perfecting holiness out of reverence (*fear*) for God.

Hebrews 12:28-29- Therefore, since we are receiving a kingdom that cannot be shaken, let us be thankful, and so worship God acceptably with reverence (*fear*) and awe, for our "God is a consuming fire."

I Peter 1:17- Since you call on a Father who judges each man's work impartially, live your lives as foreigners here in reverent fear.

These passages explain what the Bible states about the fear of God. What does that look like when applied to our lives? I found the following principles in an article explaining what the fear of the Lord entails:

1. A steadfast disposition that takes God extremely seriously in every area of my life.
2. Loving what God loves and hating what God hates.
3. The response of my heart to the holiness of God.
4. Making God's opinion of me more important than anyone else's opinion of me.
5. A conscious awareness of God's presence wherever I go, whatever I do, whoever I am with, all day long.
6. My security, safeguard and protection against intimidation, manipulation and rejection from people.
7. A personnel agent that chooses my companions, friends and associations.[7]

All of these are safeguards from hypocrisy. If we can learn how to walk in these important truths, we will become much more grounded in the fear of the Lord.

THE PURPOSE OF THE FEAR OF GOD

Shortly after the exodus from Egypt, God invited Moses to come up onto Mount Sinai so that He could provide the nation with the Ten Commandments. He told Moses to have the people ceremonially cleanse themselves. He also gave a clear directive that they were to put boundaries around the mountain. This was because if a person or animal touched the mountain, they were to be stoned or shot with an arrow. It was pretty serious business.

On the morning of the third day, the presence of the Lord appeared on the mountain. What the Israelites experienced would cause anyone to tremble. Exodus 19:16-18 says:

> On the morning of the third day there was thunder and lightning, with a thick cloud over the mountain, and a very loud trumpet blast. Everyone in the camp trembled. Then Moses led the people out of the camp to meet with God, and they stood at the foot of the mountain. Mount Sinai was covered with smoke, because the Lord descended on it in fire. The smoke billowed up from it like smoke from a furnace, the whole mountain trembled violently.

After the Israelites panicked for their lives, Moses spoke: "Do not be afraid. God has come to test you, so that the fear of God will be with you to keep you from sinning."[8] Moses explained here that the chief purpose of the fear of God is holiness.

This is a key to understanding how to avoid falling into sin as a Christian. If you can willingly compromise in sin, you are proving that you lack the fear of the Lord. I think this is a huge issue in the modern church. All the hyper-grace, loose-living, 'God does not really care about sin' teaching, has the opposite effect that fearing the Lord should have in our lives. I did not fear the Lord when I fell away from Him. As a result, I kept pushing the boundaries further until my conscience was seared. Eventually, I no longer felt the Holy Spirit's conviction in my life.

The fear of God is a hypocrisy-repellent. Just like water-repellent keeps moisture away from an object, staying in the fear of God will keep hypocrisy away from our lives. It will cause us to stay true to our relationship with Him.

NOT A PUNISHMENT-BASED FEAR

The fear of the Lord we are talking about is a reverence for Him in our lives. The Hebrew word often used for fear is *yare*. It means "to be afraid; to fear, revere; to terrify, make afraid."[9] It is used sometimes in the context of being frightened of something. When the Scriptures use this term in reference to the fear of the Lord, it is defined as "a very positive feeling of awe or reverence for God, which may be expressed in piety or formal worship."[10] The Greek word for fear is *phobos*, which is defined as "fear, terror; reverence, respect, honor."[11] When used of the fear of God, it means:

In a moral sense, reverence, respect, honor; shown to persons; to God or Christ, in the sense of a deep and reverential awareness of accountability to God or Christ.[12]

As seen in these definitions, the fear of God is not a fear of being punished by Him. Some Christians think that the Lord is just waiting for them to mess up so that He can judge them. This fear is similar to the way a child may fear an abusive parent. That kind of fear-based relationship is unhealthy. In abusive situations, the child is afraid of his parent's reaction. He is living in a fear of punishment for his actions. But the Bible says, "There is no fear in love. But perfect love drives out fear, because fear has to do with punishment. The one who fears is not made perfect in love."[13] You can deeply respect God—and understand your accountability to Him as a Father—without fearing He is going to fly off the handle because of something you did. This deep, reverential fear is to be in the hearts of believers at all times.

REVERENCING GOD

In Exodus 3, Jehovah first appeared to Moses in the form of a burning bush. At one point in the conversation, Moses asked,

> Suppose I go to the Israelites and say to them, "The God of your fathers has sent me to you," and they ask me, "What is his name?" Then what shall I tell them? (v. 13)

God told Moses to let the Israelites know that YHWH sent him to them. (v. 14) YHWH means "I Am."

There was an interesting practice in the ancient Israelite culture when it came to the name YHWH. The name of the Lord was so revered by the Israelites that they refused to ever say it out loud. In fact, when scribes would meticulously copy the Scriptures, they would not even write the name down on paper. Instead, they would write *Adonai*, which is the word for Lord.[14] That is how holy and revered His name was.

It makes me think about how we treat the name of the Lord in our culture today. Even in the church, you hear the names of God, Jesus and the Holy Spirit used so flippantly. We play games and people say, "Thank you, Jesus!" when they win. We even make silly jokes about spiritual things. We have drifted far from being a people who honor God so much that we would not speak or write down His name.

I am not suggesting God is not into having fun. Nor am I saying we need to be somber and serious in His presence at all times. Some of the most exciting and enjoyable times in my life now are in His presence, but we need to make sure we are keeping reverence for Him in our lives.

HOW TO TEST FOR THE FEAR OF GOD

I found the following information really helpful in examining my own life for evidence of the fear of God. Here is a list of some questions to ask yourself to determine how much you fear Him. Answer the following honestly:

1. Am I diligently searching the Scriptures to know God better?
2. Is there any secret sin (in word, thought or deed) that contaminates and pollutes my heart?
3. Do I harbor any ill will (grudges, bad feelings or unforgiveness) towards anyone that has ever offended me?
4. Do I resent any of the delegated authorities that God has placed over me in my life?
5. Am I angry at God for any of the circumstances in my life that have detoured my plans and expectations?
6. Am I practicing anything that is causing someone else to stumble?
7. Am I addicted to (enslaved by) any hobbies or habits that do not have eternal values attached to them?
8. Are my quiet (prayer) times quality times to pour out my heart to God and then listen to His inner promptings?
9. Is there any human relationship that is interfering with my obedience to God?
10. Does pride keep me from deep repentance when God turns the light on within my soul?
11. Is there any agenda that is more important than God's agenda in my life?
12. Am I broken-hearted over the eternal damnation that awaits unsaved people?
13. Am I transparent and honest in all my business (and financial) dealings with people?
14. Do the things in my house (books, videos, posters, TV, etc.) represent the heart of Jesus?
15. Do I allow my thoughts to wander into forbidden territory through viewing garbage on the television?[15]

Your answers to these questions will give you a clear indicator as to where you are on the fear of the Lord scale. Fearing God will result in lifestyle changes. You cannot grow in the fear of the Lord and stay where you are, especially if you are living a double-life.

THE BLESSINGS OF FEARING THE LORD

There are many Scriptural references to the blessings of fearing God, other than just protection from sin. Several are listed below:

Deuteronomy 5:29- Oh, that their hearts would be inclined to fear me and keep all my commands always, so that it might go well with them and their children forever!

Psalm 25:12-14- Who, then, are those who fear the Lord? He will instruct them in the ways they should choose. They will spend their days in prosperity, and their descendants will inherit the land. The Lord confides in those who fear him; he makes his covenant known to them.

Psalm 31:19- How abundant are the good things that you have stored up for those who fear you, that you bestow in the sight of all, on those who take refuge in you.

Psalm 34:9- Fear the Lord, you his holy people, for those who fear him lack nothing.

Psalm 128:1-2- Blessed are all who fear the Lord, who walk in obedience to him. You will eat the fruit of your labor; blessings and prosperity will be yours.

Psalm 145:19- He fulfills the desires of those who fear him; he hears their cry and saves them.

Proverbs 19:23- The fear of the Lord leads to life: Then one rests content, untouched by trouble.

With all of these promises in view, who would not cry out for more fear of the Lord? The fear of God gives us peace, comfort, joy and so much more! If the Bible tells us godly fear has so many spiritual benefits, we should be people who do whatever it takes to foster it in our lives.

THE FEAR OF MAN VERSUS THE FEAR OF GOD

One of the most potent verses contrasting the fear of man and the fear of the Lord is found in Jeremiah 17:5-8:

Cursed is the one who trusts in man, who draws strength from mere flesh and whose heart turns away from the Lord. That person will be like a bush in the wastelands; they will not see prosperity when it comes. They will dwell in the parched places of the desert, in a salt land where no one lives. But blessed is the one who trusts in the Lord, whose confidence is in him. They will be like a tree planted by the water that sends out its roots by the stream. It does not fear when heat comes; its leaves are always green. It has no worries in a year of drought and never fails to bear fruit.

Jeremiah draws a strong contrast between people who fear the Lord and those who fear man. There is a big difference between the two. You can only be controlled by one at a time. Those who live in the fear of God will not fear men. Those who are controlled by the fear of man will not be living in godly fear.

So the question is, "Which path will you choose?" Hasn't the fear of man had enough control in your life? The most effective way to overcome fear is to face it. If you are afraid of public speaking, studies say you should force yourself to speak in front of a couple people. Then, when you realize it is not as bad as you thought, you can grow in confidence as you overcome it.

In the same way, it is important to face the fear of man head on. Sometimes confession is the biggest obstacle for a hypocrite to face because the fear of people's reactions has them bound. You can either stay in bondage to the fear of man or you can decide once and for all to fear the Lord, and do what He requires. The choice is up to you.

SECTION FOUR

FREEDOM FROM HYPOCRISY

The final chapter will give us a picture of what a life free from Christian hypocrisy can look like. It will define for us what we can expect on the other side of the battle if we are willing to persevere. This abundant life is available to all who choose to take off the mask and surrender fully to the Lord.

Unite:
1. **verb.** to put or bring together so as to make one; combine or join into a whole[1]

*   *   *

James 4:8 (PHP)- Your loyalty is divided: get your hearts made true once more.

Psalm 86:11 (NKJV)- Teach me Your way, O Lord; I will walk in Your truth; unite my heart to fear Your name.

*   *   *

"Make me sincere in religion. A hypocrite has a double heart; let mine be single and entire for God, not divided between him and the world, not straggling from him."

-Matthew Henry[2]

"Our minds are apt to be divided between a variety of objects, like trickling streamlets which waste their force in a hundred runnels; our great desire should be to have all our life-floods poured into one channel and to have that channel directed towards the Lord alone."

-Charles Spurgeon[3]

13

THE UNDIVIDED HEART

WE HAVE SPENT A GREAT DEAL of time in this book talking about the problem. I hope the Lord has brought you into a deeper walk with Him through each chapter. I would be remiss to end the book without telling you the purpose for the process. There is an end goal. As stated many times already, the heart of hypocrisy is a divided life. Because of this, it is God's will for every person to be brought into oneness, wholeness and unity in Him.

In Psalm 86:11, David cries out to the Lord, "Give me an undivided heart, that I may fear your name." The phrase *undivided heart* in Hebrew is *yached lebabi*, which means to "join all the purposes, resolutions, and affections of my heart together."⁴ This is a great prayer for a person to pray who is dealing with areas of hypocrisy in his life.

Having a heart reunited is not something that happens overnight. It is a process that will continue from the moment you are willing to do what it takes to be free and continues until you reach Heaven. The Lord's methods will differ for each individual, but the concepts discussed: repentance, exposure, consecration, humility, mercy and the fear of God will at least establish a framework.

In order to allow the Lord to challenge each reader, it was necessary to save the best for last. Now we come to the main purpose of this journey out of hypocrisy. We have discussed several heavy topics. We have examined our own lives and repented of the things the Lord has brought to our attention. Now we come to the end result He has been trying to accomplish in us all along.

Do you remember the Greek word *anypokritos*? We discussed it in Chapter Two. Literally, it means "inexperienced in the art of acting."[5] This is the Father's desire for all of His children. He is looking for some terrible actors to take the lead roles on the stage of life. He wants Christians who are not good at playing church games. He is trying to find those who are willing to take the religious mask off once and for all *because this is where true freedom is!*

We have talked about the divided heart and the double-minded man. The Lord's desire is for us to be single-minded in our walk with Him. To those of us who have played the part, He is saying, "Just put the mask down. Be who you are, imperfections and all, and let me work with that." Just like we see in Jeremiah's vision of the potter's house, God cannot shape us into the type of pot that He desires when we are not willing to be broken down and rebuilt.[6] If we stiffen our necks and demand our own way, we make it impossible to become what He wants us to be. The Father is seeking those with sincere hearts who are willing to allow Him to do whatever He wants with their lives.

THE UNIFIED LIFE

Finding words to express what a heart transformation feels like is an incredibly difficult task. How can I possibly put into words something that is best understood through experience? Much of this book has been describing what life was like in that slow decline from salvation into total hypocrisy. However, now I want to discuss some of the major differences in my life today. These are all areas that I forfeited by continuing in sin and rebellion. As I walk with the Lord, I am finding myself able to walk in these truths in increasing measure. There is nothing like truly walking with Him. Now that I have tasted how good God is and seen the life He has for me, it is hard to imagine why I tried to run. Nothing compares with His love... absolutely nothing!

Living for Jesus with *all* of one's heart, soul, mind and strength comes packed with benefits. Of course, we do not do it for the blessings, but because we are motivated by love. Yet, His nature is to bless His children. I can attest to the fact that my relationship with Him is much more like what the Bible says it should be now than ever before.

Here are some of the things you can expect from the Lord should you forsake the way of the double-minded, repent and turn to Him. As Acts 3:19 promises, "Repent, then, and turn to God, so that your sins may be wiped out, that times of refreshing may come from the Lord..." God is just waiting for you to turn to Him. If you take the first step, He is there with open arms, ready to restore you completely.

1.) EXPECT LIFE MORE ABUNDANTLY

I used to think that the abundant life Christ promises in John 10:10 was just a theological concept. I did not believe it could actually be a present reality. Because I never really gave Him everything, I kept myself from experiencing what life in Him should be. Now I see that a true life in Christ is more rich, enjoyable and exciting than I could ever have imagined. He really does want us to have more than enough. That is what the word *abundant* means. The NIV reads, "I have come that they may have life, and have it to the full." The phrase *to the full* is the Greek word *perissos* and it means "exceedingly, over and beyond, superabundantly."[7] Jesus did not come only to forgive us of our sins, but to give us more than enough life. Eternal life does not begin when we reach eternity, it starts when we are born again!

This is the life we were designed to live in Christ. It is what He paid for with His own blood. The New Covenant has to mean something much greater than just a bunch of struggling Christians trying to make it to Heaven. The Old Covenant was marked by struggle and human effort. That is why God replaced the Old Covenant with the New. Look at how He describes the New Covenant through the prophet Ezekiel:

> I will give you a new heart and put a new spirit in you; I will remove from you your heart of stone and give you a heart of flesh. And I will put my Spirit in you and move you to follow my decrees and be careful to keep my laws.[8]

Think about that. Under the New Covenant, we now have the Spirit of God living inside of us. Talk about life more abundantly! Before Christ, this was not possible. In the Old Testament, God would occasionally anoint people with His Spirit to accomplish certain tasks; such as anointing the judges for battle.[9] The reality that the Spirit of God could dwell inside of us was unthinkable. As born again believers, we have been given everything we need. When we choose to step out of hypocrisy, come into the light and get right with the Lord, all of the riches in Christ become fully available to us. It truly is an abundant life.

2.) EXPECT TO DISCOVER YOUR TRUE IDENTITY

When I finally took the mask off and repented, I went through a spiritual identity crisis. I had to ask myself, "Now that I am no longer using spirituality to hide behind, who am I?" I began looking to the Scriptures to find out my identity as a son of God. Understanding and learning to walk in my true identity in Christ has been one of the most exciting experiences of my life. In hypocrisy, so much of my identity was caught up in the double-life. I saw myself as worthless, unlovable and hopeless. It was hard for me to believe that God could ever love me, or that He even would.

When I first arrived at Pure Life Ministries, I thought I was too far gone. I believed in my heart that God had turned His back on me. The amazing thing was that He took me back. My Savior rescued me again! He fully restored me and I no longer identify with my sin; I am dead to it. I never have to go back to that miserable life.

The Bible is a book revealing the character of God from cover to cover. The purpose in reading the Scriptures is primarily to get to know the Author of them. But I have found that a secondary purpose the Lord gave us the Scriptures is so that we can find out who He says *we* are. Think about it. God gave us the most amazing gift of eternal life in His Son. He provided this awesome salvation for us. If you were the Lord, would you not want your children to understand what you have given them and for them to enjoy all its benefits?

There are many Scriptures that tell us who we are in Christ. Here are just a few. I encourage you to seek out other passages and begin to believe you really are who the Bible says you are.

- You are the light of the world **(Matthew 5:14)**
- You are a child of God **(John 1:12)**
- You are chosen and appointed by Christ to bear His fruit **(John 15:16)**
- You are a slave of righteousness **(Romans 6:18)**
- You are a new creation **(II Corinthians 5:17)**
- You are a saint **(Philippians 1:1/ Ephesians 1:1)**
- You are righteous and holy **(Ephesians 4:24)**
- You are hidden with Christ in God **(Colossians 3:3)**
- You are chosen of God, holy and dearly loved
  (Colossians 3:12/ I Thessalonians 1:4)
- You are a member of a chosen race, a royal priesthood, a holy nation, a people for God's own possession **(I Peter 2:9-10)**[10]

These verses are just a small sampling of what Scripture says about us because of the death and resurrection of Jesus. You may not feel like your life resembles these traits, but it is time to start believing them in faith. This is what the Lord sees when He looks at you if you are in right relationship with Him. You do not have to live out the identity of a hypocrite another day. If you repent and turn to God, your identity is never tied to your sin, but to what Jesus accomplished at the cross.

3.) EXPECT SPIRITUAL FRUIT

The spiritual fruit that is available to us as believers is a very important subject. This is because spiritual fruit is not only evidence of true faith, but is also a tremendous blessing to us as children of God. I remember studying and teaching from Galatians 5 when I was in hypocrisy. Unfortunately—if I was honest—the fruit of my life looked much more like the list of sinful acts than the spiritual fruit. Paul writes:

> The acts of the sinful nature are obvious: sexual immorality, impurity and debauchery; idolatry and witchcraft; hatred, discord, jealousy, fits of rage, selfish ambition, dissensions, factions and envy; drunkenness, orgies and the like. I warn you, as I did before, that those who live like this will not inherit the kingdom of God. (vv. 19-21)

I got tripped up on this Scripture so many times. I had habitual sin in several of these areas, yet I believed I was still saved. So, I had to try to twist the Scriptures and comfort myself that somehow I had a good relationship with God. What a joy it has been to enter into a life that more closely reflects verses 22-23:

> But the fruit of the Spirit is love, joy, peace, forbearance, kindness, goodness, faithfulness, gentleness and self-control.

In hypocrisy, I did not have a real love for people in my heart; I was always focused on myself. There was absolutely no peace or joy, because fear and guilt made them impossible. I was impatient, unkind, unfaithful and totally lacking self-control. Having been set free from double-living, I am now able to experience all of the fruit. It is so exhilarating to be able to see the Lord moving in ways that I previously prevented Him from doing due to the hypocrisy in my life.

4.) EXPECT ADOPTION

I think the most important concept of the Lord that we could ever grasp as born again believers is that He is God the Father. Until Jesus came, no one could call God 'Father' in the intimate way that He did. God had many names that the Israelites could use to address Him, which are still true to His character. There are a few passages in the Old Testament where the Lord is referred to as the Father of Israel.[11] However, the full revelation of God the Father began with Jesus. Everywhere Jesus went, He was telling people about His relationship with His Father. He said that He obeyed His Father in everything.[12] He told us that He was one with His Father.[13]

You might say, "Well, Jesus was the Son of God, of course He called Him Father." If that is what is going through your mind, you are missing a huge revelation of your identity in Christ. Just look at what the following Scriptures say about us:

Romans 8:15-16- The Spirit you received does not make you slaves, so that you live in fear again; rather, the Spirit you received brought about your adoption to sonship. And by him we cry, "*Abba*, Father." The Spirit himself testifies with our spirit that we are God's children.

Galatians 4:6- Because you are his sons, God sent the Spirit of his Son into our hearts, the Spirit who calls out, "*Abba*, Father."

When we are born again, we enter into the family of God and we too become His sons and daughters. We can call Him Father! The problem is that many have misconceptions of what that means because we all have imperfect earthly fathers. To someone who was abandoned, the word *father* may bring to mind someone who is distant and unloving. God the Father is not like that at all. To someone who has walked through abuse, the word *father* may bring shame, pain and fear. But Father God is not that kind of father either. Even the person with a loving earthly father still cannot understand what it means that God is Father through their earthly examples. The Lord is a Father whose love is unconditional and whose character is flawless. He is a perfect Father, unlike any other. And we have been given the opportunity to be adopted by Him!

5.) EXPECT TO BE DISCIPLINED

Discipline may not sound like a blessing, but the rod of correction is proof of adoption. It is a scary place to be as a Christian if you seem to be able to get away with sin and do not see any consequences. Hebrews 12 tells us that the Lord treats us as sons and daughters when He disciplines us. So, to not be under His discipline could mean that He does not call us His own.

The author of Hebrews expounds on this concept. He references Proverbs 3:11-12, when he writes:

My son, do not make light of the Lord's discipline, and do not lose heart when he rebukes you, because the Lord disciplines the one he loves, and he chastens everyone he accepts as his son. (Hebrews 12:5-6)

This may seem like a strange concept in a fallen world like ours. As human parents, we are often tempted to punish our children out of anger or irritation, but that does not eliminate the truth that good discipline is healthy and necessary. The passage goes on to say:

Endure hardship as discipline; God is treating you as his children. For what children are not disciplined by their father? If you are not disciplined—and everyone undergoes discipline—then you are not legitimate, not true sons and daughters at all. (vv. 7-8)

When I go to the grocery store, sometimes I see someone with a child that is misbehaving. I do not go up to them and discipline them. Why? Because that is not my child. It would be inappropriate to try to discipline a child I have no relationship with. This is what the passage in Hebrews is explaining to us. It proves God the Father has adopted us as sons and daughters when we experience discipline from Him. He will correct us if we sin or if we are straying off course, because He loves us. I do not enjoy disciplining my own children, but I do it because I know they need it. It is out of love for them that I keep them within set boundaries so they can be safe and healthy.

I did not enjoy being disciplined growing up, but when I look back at my life, I am grateful for it. As Hebrews continues:

[Our fathers] disciplined us for a little while as they thought best; but God disciplines us for our good, in order that we may share in his holiness. No discipline seems pleasant at the time, but painful. Later on, however, it produces a harvest of righteousness and peace for those who have been trained by it. (vv. 10-11)

It is not healthy for a parent to let their kids do whatever they please without consequences. They are actually robbing their kids of the opportunity to grow and mature. In the same way, God will discipline us when needed to help us mature in Him. It may not be a benefit that is pleasant at the time, but we should be grateful we have a Father who loves us enough to do it.

6.) EXPECT JOY FROM OBEDIENCE

Many do not understand why obeying the Lord actually brings complete satisfaction to a person. Disobedience is often very tempting. Every temptation that comes our way—no matter what it is—is a temptation to disobey our heavenly Father.

Picture a young boy inside on a rainy day. He asks to go outside and play in the rain, but his father says, "No." Yet, the boy is staring out the window at the mud puddles that seem to be calling out to him. Will he have fun if he runs outside and splashes around in the mud against his father's will? Sure, at least momentarily. But the fun he may experience will piddle in comparison with the hurt of displeasing his father. The consequences will far outweigh the fun. In contrast, the temporary pain of foregoing the pleasure will seem like nothing when he knows in his heart he has pleased his dad.

Then his father says, "Now son, I realize how much you want to go out and get muddy, but it means a lot to me that you are obeying. Why don't we go get some ice cream?" It is just like the Father's heart to bless His children for their obedience.

Sometimes, Christians think of walking in holiness and obedience to God as being trapped in a set of rules. They think that living a holy life would prevent them from enjoying it. In actuality, it is quite the opposite. A life of obedience comes with its own rewards. There are things in my life the Lord has asked me to give up the last couple of years. When He first put His finger on them, my initial reaction was, "Lord, anything but that. I don't think I can live without it. I'll be miserable all the time." Then, as I have obeyed Him and did what He asked, I felt great joy inside. Knowing that I obeyed my heavenly Father was a reward in itself. God wants us to live in the joy of obedience all of the time.

7.) EXPECT AN INHERITANCE

Paul talks about our inheritance as sons and daughters in many areas of Scripture. Here are a couple passages:

Romans 8:17- Now if we are children, then we are heirs—heirs of God and co-heirs with Christ, if indeed we share in his sufferings in order that we may also share in his glory.

Galatians 4:1-7- What I am saying is that as long as an heir is underage, he is no different from a slave, although he owns the whole estate. The heir is subject to guardians and trustees until the time set by his father. So also, when we were underage, we were in slavery under the elemental spiritual forces of the world. But when the set time had fully come, God sent his Son, born of a woman, born under the law, to redeem those under the law, that we might receive adoption to sonship...So you are no longer a slave, but

God's child; and since you are his child, God has made you also an heir.

Paul is explaining here in Galatians that even though a child may be the heir of a fortune, they still have to live under the rules of the household. This is talking about the Old Covenant Law. When Jesus came and died so that we could join God's family, the proper time came for us to receive our inheritance in Christ. We become heirs of all that God has through our relationship with Jesus. We are "heirs of God and co-heirs with Christ." This is an important truth: Everything the Lord has is ours if we are born again. We just need to believe it and walk in it.

One of the obstacles to walking in this reality is that people do not understand what the Bible teaches about their inheritance. It would be like a rich uncle passing away that you never knew you had. He leaves you millions of dollars in a bank account, but no one ever tells you. That inheritance is worthless. However, it would be sheer insanity if you discovered you had millions in a bank account and yet chose to remain in poverty. Yet, many of us as Christians are just like this in the spiritual realm. What I have found from searching the Scriptures is that many in the church have grown comfortable barely tapping into what God has provided for them. We are living way beneath the place that God is calling us to live spiritually.

Let me give you another example in the natural to try to explain what this looks like spiritually. Let us say you lived in a mud hut out in the middle of nowhere with absolutely nothing. You have to fight for scraps and beg for giveaways to survive. Then suddenly someone takes you to a huge mansion with countless rooms and tells you it is yours. They provide everything you need. You have several cars, a jet, and any other mode of transportation you can imagine. You are given a credit card and told, "Anything you need, go and buy it and do not worry about the bill. You have an endless limit. Go and enjoy what has been provided for you."

Now, imagine that you are in that position, yet you still continue to go out and beg for food, even though you can eat the best food money can buy. Imagine yourself walking the streets, even though you have reliable transportation. Imagine yourself sleeping in the back yard when you have a luxurious room to stay in. People would wonder if you had lost your mind.

This is like the Christian who does not live in the inheritance the Lord has provided. Before we are saved, we are dead in our sins and are spiritually bankrupt. We have absolutely nothing, but the Father adopts us and brings us into a spiritually rich place in our lives. Yet, many of us are living without enjoying the benefits that the death and resurrection of Christ have afforded us.

I am not talking about the physical realm. Obviously the Lord takes care of us and provides our needs, but not many Christians will live in luxury the rest of their lives. From a spiritual perspective, this does illustrate what has taken place for us in salvation. I have found it to be true in my own life that, "His divine power has given us everything we need for a godly life through our knowledge of him who called us by his own glory and goodness."[14]

We have been adopted as sons and daughters of the King, yet many of us live as spiritual beggars. Being poor in spirit simply means we are completely dependent on God. We realize there is nothing *in ourselves* that can help us. That does not mean we are to live pathetic, powerless Christian lives. Jesus and His followers displayed lives that were both full of power and completely dependent on the Father.

I encourage all who break free from the grips of hypocrisy to dig into the Word and discover their inheritance in Christ and begin to walk in it.

8.) EXPECT TO BE FULLY ACCEPTED

Perhaps one of the most beautiful pictures of God's love can be found in Luke 15. The story of the prodigal son opens up with the son going to his father and asking for his inheritance. He was ready to break free from his father's rules and wanted to go off and experience life for himself. By taking his inheritance and leaving the country, he was severing ties with his family. Imagine the heartbreak his father must have experienced. Yet, he gives his son what he wants and allows him to leave.

Being away from the watchful eye of his father, the son casts off all restraints. He does everything he had always thought, "If I only had enough money I would…" We hear later in the story that a large portion of his money goes to prostitutes. (v. 30) He wastes all of his inheritance on wild living and ends up broke, working on a pig farm, barely able to survive. This is a place no Jew would ever imagine himself working since pigs are unclean animals according to Jewish Law.[15]

But when he hits rock bottom, he decides to do something about it. He says to himself:

> How many of my father's hired servants have food to spare, and here I am starving to death! I will set out and go back to my father and say to him: Father, I have sinned against heaven and against you. I am no longer worthy to be called your son; make me like one of your hired servants. (vv. 17-19)

At this point in the story, we get a picture of who God truly is. The son is preparing his speech as he walks toward his father's house. The boy's dad sees him and does something that is unheard of in his culture: He runs. Running was something very undignified for men in that time. As one source puts it:

> In the first century…a Middle Eastern man never—never—ran. If he were to run, he would have to hitch up his tunic so he would not trip. If he did this, it would show his bare legs. In that culture, it was humiliating and shameful for a man to show his bare legs.[16]

The father does not care what anyone thinks or about the cultural norms. He sees his son and takes off running. You can imagine the immense joy in his eyes as he embraces his long lost son. The father does not say, "Where is your inheritance?" or "I see you have learned your lesson!" He does not even demand an explanation. Instead, he throws a party.

To anyone reading this book who has hypocrisy in their life, you need to hear that a loving, heavenly Father is crying out to you. He is waiting for you to say in your heart, "I will set out and go back to my Father." When you do, He will run to you and throw a party! Though this book has given many principles to help you along the way, this is the goal: *a united heart in communion with your Father*. You can do everything in this book, but if you miss this, you have missed everything.

WHATEVER IT TAKES

Something powerful happened inside of me during one particular week at Pure Life Ministries. It was after I had been going through an extended breaking-down process. The Lord had allowed me to see all of the ugliness and darkness that was inside of my heart. I saw how my actions had hurt people around me. He showed me that I loved myself more than others and I saw how I had faked Christianity and brought shame to His name.

It brought me to a place where I felt like I just could not take it anymore. It was as if the heaviness would overcome me and I would be crushed under the weight of it. I spent a week without talking to my wife on the phone in order to seek God. I cannot explain to you what happened between the Lord and I that week. It is almost too sacred to talk about. Jesus poured His love out on me in an incredible way.

A song that ministered to me in a deeper way than I can describe is called *Break the Chains* by Misty Edwards. It contains a verse that says, "Whatever it takes, take it away."[17] As I listened to that song, that phrase became a part of my life. I do not know how to explain it but those words became the deepest cry of my heart in desperation to have the Lord and nothing else. It was a dangerous prayer, but I meant it. And I think the Lord is looking for some 'whatever it takes' Christians.

This is a prayer that comes with a warning. If you allow the Lord to make your heart cry out, "Lord, whatever it takes," He will take you up on it. Be prepared to have idols torn out of your life. Be prepared for the trials. Be prepared to go through the valley. But also be prepared for God to lavish His love on you. Be prepared for the Lord to walk through the valley with you hand-in-hand. Be prepared for the Father to throw a celebration when the idols in your heart are toppled over so that He can have more of you. What is standing between you and the unified life? Whatever it is, it is not worth it.

AN ANSWER TO AN IMPORTANT QUESTION

Since the Lord set me free from hypocrisy, I have examined my Christian experience from the beginning to try to understand how I fell away. Everything took place slowly over a period of about eight years. It makes me wonder, "Did I really understand what was happening? Was I consciously pushing the Lord away? Did He ever warn me about backsliding?" Looking back, it all seemed to happen so subtly that I really wondered if I was just ignorant of what was going on inside of me at the time.

Something that helped me answer those questions was a journal entry I found, written shortly after I had finished the one-year Teen Challenge program. I was no longer under the protection of the program. Having been given a little freedom, I decided to compromise in sin 'just a little bit.'

In this journal entry I wrote what I felt like the Lord was speaking to me as a warning. He spoke to me about areas I needed to fix in order to continue to walk in victory. Included in the list were selfishness, spiritual pride, lack of accountability and a lack of discipline in prayer and devotions. I have written about each of these areas in this book.

It was as if the Lord was saying at the very beginning, "These are the areas that are going to trip you up if you do not do something about them now." I understood enough of what the Holy Spirit was telling me to actually put His words onto paper. Yet I did not follow through. I saw it, agreed with it, and continued on my way. The evidence of what was truly in my heart is shown through my story. Never again will I wonder if He had warned me about what was happening.

That causes me to wonder, "What if I had obeyed and completely surrendered? Where would I be today?" I would not be writing this book. Though there is a blessing in being able to share the hope of Christ to the readers, the experiences that have qualified me to write a book about hypocrisy came at a great expense to people I dearly love.

And what about you? Through this book, the Lord may have revealed areas that you need to get in order. Truths in this book have confronted your heart. Your sincerity for Christ has been tested. I beg you not to harden your heart like I did and pay the cost. You are not guaranteed another chance from the Lord. Do not put it off. Many in Hell right now can testify to rejecting the Lord's attempts to get them to repent and the indescribable agony that could have—and should have—been avoided.

It is a guarantee that you will face opposition to embrace what the Lord has laid before you. Satan—the enemy of your soul—and your own will are teaming up to sway your decision. But *you* make the choice. There is no easy solution. No quick prayer to pray. No simple steps to follow. Crawling out of the pit of hypocrisy is messy. It is painful. *But it is more than worth it all.*

I will end the book right here. What more can be said? My prayers have preceded your reading of this book. May the Lord richly bless those who respond to His call, and may He show mercy to those who refuse to.

NOTES

Acknowledgements

1.   Jonah 2:1-10

Opening Quote

1.   A.B. Simpson. as cited online. quote accessed at: http://christian-quotes.ochristian.com/Hypocrisy-Quotes/page-9.shtml.

Prologue

1.   II Corinthians 5:17

Chapter One: Welcome to the Masquerade

1.   *Webster's New World College Dictionary.* 4th ed. (Cleveland, OH: Wiley Publishing, Inc. 2004) p. 884.
2.   David Wilkerson. *World Challenge Pulpit Series.* "Shall We Continue in Sin?" March 20, 2000. accessed online at: http://www.tscpulpitseries.org/english/2000s/ts000320.html.
3.   I Corinthians 5:6
4.   *Strong's Exhaustive Concordance of the Bible.* (Madison, NJ: World Bible Publishers, Inc. 1986) p. 679.
5.   I Samuel 13:14
6.   II Samuel 12:15
7.   Acts 5:1-11
8.   Matthew 23:3
9.   James 1:6-8
10. *Hebrew-Greek Key Word Study Bible.* NIV. "Lexical Aids to the New Testament." (Chattanooga, TN: AMG Publishers, 1996) p. 1609, ref. no. 1500.
11. *Hebrew-Greek Key Word Study Bible.* NIV. "Lexical Aids to the New

Testament." (Chattanooga, TN: AMG Publishers, 1996) pps. 1609-
1610, ref. no. 1500.

12. James 4:4

13. Matthew 6:24

14. Hudson Taylor, as cited in *"Lessons in Discipleship"* by Roger Steer.
OMF International, 1995. p. 34. accessed online at: https://omf.org/
us/about/our-story/quotes.

15. Albert Barnes, as cited in *Standing Firm Through the Great Apostasy*,
by Steve Gallagher. (Dry Ridge, KY: Steve Gallagher, 2008) p. 46.

16. II Corinthians 11:14

17. James 1:17

18. Hebrews 13:8

19. II Corinthians 5:17

20. Mark Hall. "Slow Fade." Lyrics. *The Altar and the Door*. Beach Street/
Reunion, 2007.

Chapter Two: The Heart of the Issue

1. *Oxford American Dictionary and Thesaurus*. (New York, NY: Oxford
University Press, Inc. 2003) p. 677.

2. J. Harries. *The Preacher's Homiletic Commentary*: Matthew. (Grand
Rapids, MI: Baker Book House, 1978) p. 87.

3. Paul Washer. "The Holiness of God." Sermon. 36:05. accessed online at:
http://www.sermonaudio.com/sermoninfo.asp?SID=6190764259.

4. **Hebrew:** *Hebrew-Greek Key Word Study Bible*. NIV. "A Concise
Dictionary of the Hebrew." (Chattanooga, TN: AMG Publishers,
1996) p. 1957, ref. no. 4222.
Greek: *Hebrew-Greek Key Word Study Bible*. NIV. "Lexical Aids to
the New Testament." (Chattanooga, TN: AMG Publishers, 1996)
p. 1637, ref. no. 2840.

5. **Hebrew:** *Hebrew-Greek Key Word Study Bible*. NIV. "Lexical Aids to
the Old Testament." (Chattanooga, TN: AMG Publishers, 1996)
p. 1534, ref. no. 5883.
Greek: *Hebrew-Greek Key Word Study Bible*. NIV. "Lexical Aids to
the New Testament." (Chattanooga, TN: AMG Publishers, 1996)
p. 1688, ref. no. 6034.

6. *Hebrew-Greek Key Word Study Bible*. NIV. "Lexical Aids to the New
Testament." (Chattanooga, TN: AMG Publishers, 1996) p. 1607,
ref. no. 1379.

Strong's Exhaustive Concordance of the Bible. "A Concise Dictionary of the Words in the Greek/ New Testament." (Madison, NJ: World Bible Publishers, Inc. 1986) p. 27, ref. no. 1271.

7. **Hebrew:** *Strong's Exhaustive Concordance of the Bible.* "A Concise Dictionary of the Words in the Hebrew Bible." (Madison, NJ: World Bible Publishers, Inc. 1986) p. 79, ref. no. 3966.
   Greek: *Hebrew-Greek Key Word Study Bible.* NIV. "Lexical Aids to the New Testament." (Chattanooga, TN: AMG Publishers, 1996) p. 1634, ref. no. 2710.

8. *Hebrew-Greek Key Word Study Bible.* NIV. "Lexical Aids to the Old Testament." (Chattanooga, TN: AMG Publishers, 1996) p. 1517, ref. no. 3049.

9. *Hebrew-Greek Key Word Study Bible.* NIV. "Lexical Aids to the Old Testament." (Chattanooga, TN: AMG Publishers, 1996) pps. 1517-1518, ref. no. 3049.

10. *Archaeological Study Bible.* NIV. "Herem, Holy War." (Grand Rapids, MI: The Zondervan Corporation, 2005) p. 419.

11. *Hebrew-Greek Key Word Study Bible.* NIV. "A Concise Dictionary of the Hebrew." (Chattanooga, TN: AMG Publishers, 1996) p. 2017, ref. no. 8533.

12. *Hebrew-Greek Key Word Study Bible.* NIV. "A Concise Dictionary of the Hebrew." (Chattanooga, TN: AMG Publishers, 1996) p. 1985. ref. no. 6189.

13. I Kings 18:21

14. *Hebrew-Greek Key Word Study Bible.* NIV. "Lexical Aids to the Old Testament." (Chattanooga, TN: AMG Publishers, 1996) p. 1558, ref. no. 8969.

15. Charles G. Finney. *How to Experience Revival.* (New Kensington, PA: Whitaker House. 1984) p. 11.

16. John 5:39-40

17. John Bevere. *Extraordinary.* (Colorado Springs, CO: Waterbrook Press, 2009) pps. 30-31.

18. *Hebrew-Greek Key Word Study Bible.* NIV. "A Concise Dictionary of the Hebrew." (Chattanooga, TN: AMG Publishers, 1996) p. 1945, ref. no. 3359.

19. *Hebrew-Greek Key Word Study Bible.* NIV. "Lexical Aids to the New Testament." (Chattanooga, TN: AMG Publishers, 1996) p. 1588, ref. no. 537.

20. Same as previous

21. Jeremiah 32:39
22. Psalm 86:11
23. *Hebrew-Greek Key Word Study Bible*. NIV. "A Concise Dictionary of the Greek." (Chattanooga, TN: AMG Publishers, 1996) p. 2067, ref. no. 1515.
24. *Hebrew-Greek Key Word Study Bible*. NIV. "Lexical Aids to the New Testament." (Chattanooga, TN: AMG Publishers, 1996) p. 1637, ref. no. 2841.
25. II Timothy 3:5

Chapter Three: The Hypocrisy of Israel

1. *Webster's New World College Dictionary*. 4th ed. (Cleveland, OH: Wiley Publishing, Inc. 2004) p. 709
2. Paul Washer. "Practical Holiness." Sermon. 5:05. accessed online at: http://www.sermonaudio.com/sermoninfo.asp?SID=6190764710.
3. Examples are: Exodus 15:24; 16:2; 17:2
4. Exodus 32
5. Numbers 14:26-35
6. *Webster's New World College Dictionary*. 4th ed. (Cleveland, OH: Wiley Publishing, Inc. 2004) p. 1452.
7. Claude Mariottini. "Canaan in Patriarchal Times.- Part 2." accessed online at: http://claudemariottini.com/2006/11/10/canaan-in-patriarchal-times-part-2.
8. *Archaeological Study Bible*. NIV. "Baal and the Fertility Cults." (Grand Rapids, MI: The Zondervan Corporation, 2005) p. 1414.
9. See Psalm 106:34-39; Judges 2:11-13; Hosea 4:14; I Kings 3:3
10. J.R. Miller, as cited in *Meditations in the Revelation*, by Rex Andrews. (Zion, IL: Zion Faith Homes, 1991) p. 199.
11. *New International Bible Dictionary*. (Grand Rapids, MI: The Zondervan Corporation, 1987) p. 461.
12. Herbert M. Wolf. *Interpreting Isaiah*. (Grand Rapids MI: The Zondervan Corporation, 1985) p. 75.
13. Hosea 1:2
14. Examples are: Matthew 9:15; 25:1-13; John 3:28-29; Ephesians 5:25-33; Revelation 19:7
15. Revelation 19:9
16. Exodus 20:5
17. Ezekiel 23:37

18. Ezekiel 20:5

19. Jeremiah 3:14

20. Rex Andrews. *Meditations in the Revelation*. (Zion, IL: Zion Faith Homes, 1991) p. 178.

21. Micah 6:3-4

22. II Kings 21:1-18

23. II Kings 22:15-21

Chapter Four: The Hypocrisy of the Pharisees

1. *Webster's New World College Dictionary*. 4th ed. (Cleveland, OH: Wiley Publishing, Inc. 2004) p. 1079.

2. William Law. *A Serious Call to a Devout and Holy Life*. (Philadelphia, PA: The Westminster Press, 1956) p. 67.

3. *Archaeological Study Bible*. NIV. "Exile and Genocide in the Ancient Near East." (Grand Rapids, MI: The Zondervan Corporation, 2005) p. 1337.

4. *Archaeological Study Bible*. NIV. "The 70 Years of Captivity." (Grand Rapids, MI: The Zondervan Corporation, 2005) p. 1234.

5. *New International Bible Dictionary*. (Grand Rapids, MI: The Zondervan Corporation, 1987) p. 461.

6. I Corinthians 6:19

7. Matthew 5:21-30

8. C. F. Moore, as cited in *New International Bible Dictionary*. (Grand Rapids, MI: The Zondervan Corporation, 1987) p. 778.

9. *New International Bible Dictionary*. (Grand Rapids, MI: The Zondervan Corporation, 1987) p. 779.

10. John 3:1-2

11. Mark 15:43

12. Luke 12:1

13. Nathaniel Hawthorne, as cited in *Living in Victory*, by Steve Gallagher. (Dry Ridge, KY: Steve Gallagher, 2002) p. 26.

14. Examples are: Matthew 9:4; 12:25; Luke 6:8; 11:17

15. Matthew 23:33

16. *Strong's Exhaustive Concordance of the Bible*. "A Concise Dictionary of the Words in the Greek/ New Testament." (Madison, NJ: World Bible Publishers, Inc. 1986) p. 70, ref. no. 3759.

17. Luke 18:11 (NASB)

18. Matthew 7:5

Chapter Five: The Hypocrisy in Today's Church

1. *Webster's New World College Dictionary*. 4th ed. (Cleveland, OH: Wiley Publishing, Inc. 2004) p. 703.
2. Charles G. Finney. *How to Experience Revival*. (New Kensington, PA: Whitaker House. 1984) p. 82.
3. *Webster's Dictionary*. (U.S.A.: Watermill Press, 1991) p. 36.
4. *Webster's New World College Dictionary*. 4th ed. (Cleveland, OH: Wiley Publishing, Inc. 2004) p. 105.
5. II Corinthians 11:3
6. Charles Stanley, as cited in *Systematic Theology*: Volume Three, by Norman Geisler. (Bloomington, MN: Bethany House Publishers, 2004) p. 283.
7. Charles Stanley, as cited in *Enrichment*. Summer 2012: Volume 17, Number 3. "Once Saved Always Saved?" p. 71.
8. Paris Reidhead. "The Possibility of Apostasy." Sermon. 23:24. accessed online at: www.sermonindex.net/modules/mydownloads/viewcat.php?cid=8&min=240&orderby=titleA&show=20.
9. John Higgins & Michael Dusing & Frank Tallman. *An Introduction to Theology: A Classical Pentecostal Perspective*. (Dubuque, IA: Kendall/ Hunt Publishing Company, 1994) pps. 106-107.
10. Norman Geisler, *Systematic Theology*: Volume Three. (Bloomington, MN: Bethany House Publishers, 2004) p. 302.
11. *Life in the Spirit Study Bible*. NIV. "Assurance of Salvation." (Grand Rapids, MI: The Zondervan Corporation, 2003) p. 2016.
12. II Corinthians 13:5
13. John Bevere. *Extraordinary*. (Colorado Springs, CO: Waterbrook Press, 2009) pps. 46-47.
14. David Wilkerson. *World Challenge Pulpit Series*. "Turning the Grace of God Into Lasciviousness." August 27, 2001. accessed online at: https://worldchallenge.org/newsletter/turning-grace-god-lasciviousness.
15. John Bevere. *Extraordinary*. (Colorado Springs, CO: Waterbrook Press, 2009) p. 64.
16. Paul Washer. "10 Indictments Against the Modern Church in America." accessed online at: http://media.sermonaudio.com/mediapdf/102308839520.pdf.
17. Numbers 16:31-35

18. Richard Dawkins, as cited in *Enrichment.* Summer 2012: Volume 17, Number 3. "Is the Old Testament God Evil?" p. 35.

19. Jack Deere, as cited in *Father of Lights*: Deluxe Edition. "Disc 4-Theology." Dir. Darren Wilson. Wanderlust Productions: 2012. DVD.

20. Matthew 21:12-13; Mark 11:15-17; Luke 19:45-46; John 2:13-17

21. I John 4:16

22. Matthew 25:41

23. Romans 3:10-12

24. Genesis 3:1-5

Chapter Six: Pulse Check

1. *Webster's New World College Dictionary.* 4th ed. (Cleveland, OH: Wiley Publishing, Inc. 2004) p. 1599.

2. Charles G. Finney. *How to Experience Revival.* (New Kensington, PA: Whitaker House. 1984) pps. 17-18.

3. *Webster's New World College Dictionary.* 4th ed. (Cleveland, OH: Wiley Publishing, Inc. 2004) p. 1599.

4. Revelation 3:1

5. Genesis 12:1-4

6. Matthew 1:18-24

7. Luke 6:46

8. John 14:15

9. Philippians 2:8

10. Colossians 3:13

11. Luke 6:45

12. Brother Lawrence. *The Practice of the Presence of God.* (Uhrichsville, OH: Barbour Publishing, Inc., 2004) p. 49

13. A. W. Tozer. *The Pursuit of God.* (Camp Hill, PA: Christian Publications, 1993) pps. 47-48.

14. Revelation 2:4

15. Matthew 25:40

16. Exodus 20:5

17. Exodus 40:34

18. I Kings 8:10-13

19. William Law. *A Serious Call to a Devout and Holy Life.* (Philadelphia, PA: The Westminster Press, 1956) p. 31.

20. Leonard Ravenhill. "The Judgment Seat of Christ." Sermon. 1:05:18.

Lindale, TX: 1994. accessed online at: http://www.ravenhill.org/ judgment.htm.

21. A. W. Tozer. *The Pursuit of God.* (Camp Hill, PA: Christian Publications, 1993) p. 20.

22. Martin Luther, as cited online. quote accessed at: http://www. goodreads.com/quotes/35269-i-have-so-much-to-do-that-I-shall-spend.

23. *Strong's Exhaustive Concordance of the Bible.* "A Concise Dictionary of the Words in the Greek/ New Testament." (Madison, NJ: World Bible Publishers, Inc. 1986) p. 74, ref. no. 3927.

24. William Law. *A Serious Call to a Devout and Holy Life.* (Philadelphia, PA: The Westminster Press, 1956) pps. 32-33.

25. I Peter 2:11

26. Romans 6:20

27. Romans 6:2

Chapter Seven: Repentance

1. *Webster's New World College Dictionary.* 4th ed. (Cleveland, OH: Wiley Publishing, Inc. 2004) p. 1215.

2. John Bevere. *Extraordinary.* (Colorado Springs, CO: Waterbrook Press, 2009) p. 80.

3. Marvin Gorman. *The Road to Repentance.* (Branson, MO: Marvin E. Gorman, 1996) p. 56.

4. *Hebrew-Greek Key Word Study Bible.* NIV. "A Concise Dictionary of the Hebrew." (Chattanooga, TN: AMG Publishers, 1996) p. 2020, ref. no. 8740.

5. *Strong's Exhaustive Concordance of the Bible.* "A Concise Dictionary of the Words in the Greek/ New Testament." (Madison, NJ: World Bible Publishers, Inc. 1986) p. 63, ref. no. 3340.

6. *Hebrew-Greek Key Word Study Bible.* NIV. "Lexical Aids to the New Testament." (Chattanooga, TN: AMG Publishers, 1996) p. 1651, ref. no. 3566.

7. Exodus 16:3

8. *Strong's Exhaustive Concordance of the Bible.* "A Concise Dictionary of the Words in the Greek/ New Testament." (Madison, NJ: World Bible Publishers, Inc. 1986) p. 84, ref. no. 4434.

9. Charles G. Finney. *How to Experience Revival.* (New Kensington, PA: Whitaker House. 1984) pps. 101-102.

10. *Strong's Exhaustive Concordance of the Bible.* "A Concise Dictionary of the Words in the Greek/ New Testament." (Madison, NJ: World Bible Publishers, Inc. 1986) p. 60, ref. no. 3077.

11. Matthew 16:23

12. A. W. Tozer. *The Pursuit of God.* (Camp Hill, PA: Christian Publications, 1993) p. 28.

13. Leviticus 20:10

Chapter Eight: Exposure

1. *Webster's New World College Dictionary.* 4th ed. (Cleveland, OH: Wiley Publishing, Inc. 2004) p. 1296.

2. Steve Gallagher. *At the Altar of Sexual Idolatry.* (Dry Ridge, KY: Steve Gallagher, 2007) p. 75.

3. Hebrews 4:13

4. Revelation 2:23

5. I John 1:7

6. Roy Hession. *The Calvary Road.* (Fort Washington, PA: CLC Publications, 1990) p. 40.

Chapter Nine: Consecration

1. *Webster's New World College Dictionary.* 4th ed. (Cleveland, OH: Wiley Publishing, Inc. 2004) p. 310.

2. Watchman Nee. *Love not the World.* (Fort Washington, PA: Christian Literature Crusade, 1974) p. 16.

3. Andrew Bonar, as cited in *Intoxicated with Babylon*, by Steve Gallagher. (Dry Ridge, KY: Steve Gallagher, 2006) p. 17.

4. "Compromise." *Oxford Univeristy Press*, 2016. accessed online at http://www.oxforddictionaries.com/us/definition/american_ english/compromise.

5. Steve Gallagher. "When Satan's Power Reigns Supreme." Sermon. 25:34. accessed online at: http://www.eternalweight.com/audio-2/ babylon-in-the-church.

6. William Law. *A Serious Call to a Devout and Holy Life.* (Philadelphia, PA: The Westminster Press, 1956) p. 22.

7. John Bevere. *Extraordinary.* (Colorado Springs, CO: Waterbrook Press, 2009) p. 47.

8. *Webster's New World College Dictionary.* 4th ed. (Cleveland, OH: Wiley Publishing, Inc. 2004) p. 310.

9. *Webster's New World College Dictionary.* 4th ed. (Cleveland, OH: Wiley Publishing, Inc. 2004) p. 818.

10. Ephesians 2:2

11. II Corinthians 6:16

12. Jackie Pullinger. "Chasing the Dragon- 1 of 2." Sermon. 7:52. accessed online at: http://www.sermonindex.net/modules/mydownloads/ viewcat.php?cid=117.

13. David Wilkerson. *The Cross and the Switchblade.* (U.S.A: Pyramid Publications, 1963) pps. 11-12.

Chapter Ten: Humility

1. *Webster's New World College Dictionary.* 4th ed. (Cleveland, OH: Wiley Publishing, Inc. 2004) p. 695.

2. Thomas A Kempis. *The Imitation of Christ.* (New York, NY: Penguin Putman Inc. 1952) p. 29.

3. Steve Gallagher. *Irresistible to God.* (Dry Ridge, KY: Steve Gallagher, 2003) p. 19.

4. Stuart Scott. "Manifestations of Pride." taken from *The Exemplary Husband.* accessed online at: http://www.evergreenbloomington. com/uploads/Manifestations_of_Pride_by_Stuart_Scott.pdf.

5. Brother Jerome, as cited in *Irresistible to God* by Steve Gallagher. (Dry Ridge, KY: Steve Gallagher, 2003) p. 16.

6. Matthew 6:1-2

7. Matthew 6:5

8. Matthew 6:16

9. Bill Johnson, taken from *Face to Face With God: Get Ready for a Life-Changing Encounter with God* by Bill Johnson. accessed online at: http://pentecostalpostitnotes.blogspot.com/2008/08/bill-johnson-on-perfect-theology.html.

10. *Hebrew-Greek Key Word Study Bible.* NIV. "Lexical Aids to the New Testament." (Chattanooga, TN: AMG Publishers, 1996) p. 1677, ref. no. 5424.

11. *The NIV Study Bible.* 10th Anniversary Edition. (Grand Rapids, MI: The Zondervan Corporation, 1995) p. 1807.

12. Greg Boyd, as cited in *Do What Jesus Did* by Robby Dawkins (Bloomington, MN: Chosen Books, 2013) p. 56.

13. Genesis 1:3,6,9,14,20,24

14. Luke 13:30

15. Matthew 20:26-28

16. Matthew 17:2

Chapter Eleven: Mercy

1. *Webster's New World College Dictionary.* 4th ed. (Cleveland, OH: Wiley Publishing, Inc. 2004) p. 901.

2. Rex B. Andrews. *What the Bible Teaches About Mercy.* (Zion, IL: Zion Faith Homes, 1985) p. 2.

3. *Hebrew-Greek Key Word Study Bible.* NIV. "Lexical Aids to the Old Testament." (Chattanooga, TN: AMG Publishers, 1996) p. 1516, ref. no. 2876.

4. Rex B. Andrews. *What the Bible Teaches About Mercy.* (Zion, IL: Zion Faith Homes, 1985) p. 2.

5. Rex B. Andrews, "The Mercy Prayer." adapted by online source at: https://desiremercy.wordpress.com/tag/rex-andrews.

6. Matthew 10:8

7. Isaiah 64:6

8. Luke 9:24

9. Matthew 19:30

10. Misty Edwards. "Servant of All." Lyrics. *Relentless.* Oasis House, 2007.

11. Steve Gallagher. *Irresistible to God.* (Dry Ridge, KY: Steve Gallagher, 2003) p. 108.

12. Philippians 2:4

13. Matthew 18:3

14. Steve Gallagher. *Living in Victory.* (Dry Ridge, KY: Steve Gallagher, 2002) p. 58.

Chapter Twelve: The Fear of God

1. *Webster's New World College Dictionary.* 4th ed. (Cleveland, OH: Wiley Publishing, Inc. 2004) p. 518.

2. Matthew Henry. *Matthew Henry's Commentary In One Volume.*

(Grand Rapids, MI: Zondervan Publishing House, 1961) p. 555.

3. John Witherspoon, as cited online. quote accessed at: http://izquotes.com/quote/379540.

4. I Samuel 17:4

5. Edward T. Welch. *When People are Big and God is Small.* (Phillipsburg, NJ: Edward T. Welch, 1997) p. 23.

6. John 15:18

7. Unknown Author. "Fear of the Lord: The Command and Reward of the Fear of God." Article.

8. Exodus 20:20

9. *Hebrew-Greek Key Word Study Bible.* NIV. "Lexical Aids to the Old Testament." (Chattanooga, TN: AMG Publishers, 1996) p. 1521, ref. no. 3707.

10. *Hebrew-Greek Key Word Study Bible.* NIV. "Lexical Aids to the Old Testament." (Chattanooga, TN: AMG Publishers, 1996) p. 1521, ref. no. 3707.

11. *Hebrew-Greek Key Word Study Bible.* NIV. "Lexical Aids to the New Testament." (Chattanooga, TN: AMG Publishers, 1996) p. 1684, ref. no. 5832.

12. *Hebrew-Greek Key Word Study Bible.* NIV. "Lexical Aids to the New Testament." (Chattanooga, TN: AMG Publishers, 1996) p. 1684, ref. no. 5832.

13. I John 4:18

14. *Archaeological Study Bible.* NIV. "YHWH: The Name of God in the Old Testament." (Grand Rapids, MI: The Zondervan Corporation, 2005) p. 89.

15. Unknown Author. "Fear of the Lord: The Command and Reward of the Fear of God." Article.

Chapter Thirteen: The Undivided Heart

1. *Webster's New World College Dictionary.* 4th ed. (Cleveland, OH: Wiley Publishing, Inc. 2004) p. 1562.

2. Matthew Henry. *Matthew Henry's Commentary In One Volume.* (Grand Rapids, MI: Zondervan Publishing House, 1961) p. 671.

3. Charles Spurgeon. *The Treasury of David:* Volume II. "Psalm 86." (Mclean, VA: Macdonald Publishing Company, 1988) p. 467.

4. Adam Clarke. *Adam Clarke's Commentary on the Holy Bible.*

(Kansas City, MO: Beacon Hill Press, 1967) p. 508.

5. *Hebrew-Greek Key Word Study Bible*. NIV. "Lexical Aids to the New Testament." (Chattanooga, TN: AMG Publishers, 1996) p. 1588, ref. no. 537.

6. Jeremiah 18:1-12

7. *Hebrew-Greek Key Word Study Bible*. NIV. "Lexical Aids to the New Testament." (Chattanooga, TN: AMG Publishers, 1996) p. 1662, ref. no. 4356.

8. Ezekiel 36:26-27

9. Examples are: Judges 3:10; 11:29; 14:19

10. Adapted from *Victory Over the Darkness* by Neil T. Anderson. (Ventura, CA: Neil T. Anderson, 2000) pps. 51-53.

11. Examples are: Jeremiah 31:9; Isaiah 63:16

12. John 5:19

13. John 10:30

14. II Peter 1:3

15. Deuteronomy 14:8

16. Matt Williams. "The Prodigal Son's Father Should not Have Run." accessed online at: http://magazine.biola.edu/article/10-summer/the-prodigal-sons-father-shouldnt-have-run.

17. Misty Edwards. "Break the Chains." Lyrics. *Relentless-Unplugged*. Forerunner Music, 2007.

ABOUT THE AUTHOR

Dustin Renz is the founder of Make Way Ministries. He holds a Bachelor of Science in Church Ministries from Southeastern University in Lakeland, Florida. He is also the Associate Pastor for a church in Kettering, Ohio and a contributing writer and speaker for Pure Life Ministries in Dry Ridge, Kentucky. He and his wife, Brittany, have two wonderful daughters and they currently reside in Xenia, Ohio.

MAKE WAY MINISTRIES

If the truths contained in this book have impacted your life, consider purchasing a copy for others. Many who need to hear its timely message will not obtain this writing unless someone shares it with them. To purchase more copies, please visit our online store at www.makewayministries.com.

Make Way Ministries was established with the purpose of inspiring the Body of Christ to awaken, mature and arise to its responsibility in these last days. We accomplish this through speaking engagements and resources. For more information about booking an event or to find resources, please visit us at www.makewayministries.com or email us at: contact@makewayministries.com

Follow us on Facebook and Twitter!

www.facebook.com/MakeWayMinistries
www.twitter.com/MakeWayMin